TO SERVE WITH HONOR

DOING THE RIGHT THING IN GOVERNMENT

TERRY NEWELL

Loftlands Press

Crozet Virginia USA

TO SERVE WITH HONOR
Doing the Right Thing in Government
Terry Newell

Published by Loftlands Press
ISBN-13: 978-06923854-3-2
(Also available for Kindle)

Cover photo: Simfalex/Shutterstock
Cover design & page layout: Lighthouse24

For My Father

Born of the sun, they travelled a short while toward the sun
And left the vivid air signed with their honour.
—Stephen Spender, "The Truly Great"

TABLE OF CONTENTS

LIST OF BOXES

LIST OF FIGURES

LIST OF TABLES

ABOUT THE AUTHOR

Terry Newell is the director of his own firm, *Leadership for a Responsible Society*. His work focuses on values-based leadership, character, ethics, and decision making. He is an adjunct faculty member at the Federal Executive Institute, a residential executive education center for the federal government in Charlottesville, Virginia, and at the University of Virginia.

A former Air Force officer, Terry also served previously as Director of the Horace Mann Learning Center, the training arm of the U.S. Department of Education and as Dean of Faculty at the Federal Executive Institute. In the latter capacity, he was responsible for the Institute's four-week, interagency *Leadership for a Democratic Society* program.

Terry's publications have addressed such issues as values and ethics in leadership, organizational change, human resource development, the future and its implications for leadership, and the impact of diversity on organizations and leaders. He also writes a blog on the *Huffington Post*.

Previous Books
The Trusted Leader: Building the Relationships That Make Government Work
Statesmanship, Character, and Leadership in America
Reflections on America

INTRODUCTION

S hortly after Hurricane Katrina hit New Orleans on August 29, 2005, the Federal Emergency Management Agency (FEMA) ordered almost $2.7 billion of trailers for more than 300,000 people whose homes were destroyed by the monster storm. The agency's procurement request, which consisted of just 25 lines of specifications, made little mention of safety issues. That may be understandable, given the pressure to help victims and the criticism for lack of preparedness raining down on FEMA.

What happened next was not understandable. By early 2006, FEMA's own field workers were sending back reports of health problems experienced by those living in the trailers. The culprit was suspected to be formaldehyde, a chemical in resins and glues used in constructing everything from flooring to wall panels and cabinets in the trailers. By March 2006, early testing by FEMA had revealed formaldehyde levels 75 times the recommended safety limit. FEMA's response, characterized later by House Oversight and Government Reform Committee Chair Henry Waxman as "premeditated ignorance," was to stop testing. On June 16, 2006, according to a FEMA staffer, agency lawyers "advised that we do not do testing, which would imply FEMA's ownership of the issue." On June 27, a man in Slidell, Louisiana was found dead in his trailer after complaining of the fumes. FEMA lawyers rejected both an investigation and independent testing of the trailers out of a concern that this "could seriously undermine the Agency's position" in any future lawsuits.

The lawsuits came. In 2012, a federal judge approved a $42.6 million settlement of a class-action brought against trailer manufacturers on behalf of more than 55,000 residents of four states. If that sounds like FEMA escaped, it did not. While its own Inspector General wrote a scathing report and

Congress castigated FEMA for a "sickening" response to Katrina victims, Paul Stewart, a former Army officer who lived in one of the trailers with his wife, captured a more long lasting impact of the damage FEMA did: "We have lost a great deal through our dealings with FEMA," he said, "not the least of which is our faith in government."[1]

FEMA's actions reflect a lack of both competence and character. The result was to damage the most essential resource for government effectiveness – the trust of citizens. The lack of competence – poor preparation, inadequate specs for the trailers, lack of oversight of manufacturers – can and hopefully has been corrected. These are technical tasks that can be addressed thru policy, procedures, and training. The failure of character – valuing organizational self-protection over citizen safety, ignoring the long-term consequences of present actions, inability to think and empathize from the vantage point of those the agency was sworn to serve - are not so easily corrected. These are moral tasks that require good people in an ethical environment. FEMA did not break any laws. But what they did is not what they should have done. In the end, they probably knew it. The purpose of this book is to help public servants know it sooner and do the right thing.

To be realistic, no matter how much public servants succeed in doing the right thing, they will still face a citizenry that is skeptical, quick to criticize, and distrustful. Much of the distrust of government today arises from nearly forty years of politicians, the media, interest groups and others claiming that, as President Reagan so famously said in his first inaugural address, "government is not the solution to our problem; government is the problem."[2] Some of the distrust emerges from our very origins as a nation - it's in our political DNA. The Declaration of Independence is a clarion call to be skeptical of centralized authority.

The hill that public servants have to climb is not only with citizens but in their own agencies. When given the sentence "my organization's leaders maintain high standards of honesty and integrity," one of every four federal employees say they disagree. The same percentage say they are just not sure.[3] When asked about the ethical culture in their organizations in a 2007 survey by the Ethics Resource Center, where culture was defined as consisting of ethical leadership, supervisor reinforcement, peer commitment, and embedded ethical values, nearly half said it was "weak or weak leaning."[4] When asked if their organization "puts the public interest first," only 60 percent agreed.[5]

But the picture is not as bleak as it might seem. While only 13 percent of Americans said, in 2014, that they could "trust the government in Washington to do the right thing 'most of the time or just about always'," that figure was 73 percent in 1958.[6] While the percentage of Americans who rated the ethical standards of top officials of the Obama Administration in 2013 as "excellent or good" was 50 percent, that percentage was 67 percent for the Reagan Administration at the end of his first term.[7] In short, we can get better because we have been better. This book is designed to help public servants do that too.

Government Ethics is Not an Oxymoron

The scandal surrounding the Internal Revenue Service (IRS) in 2013, in which it was accused of targeting conservative groups seeking tax-exempt designation, certainly gave support to those who distrust government. It did not help when Lois Lerner, Director of the Exempt Organizations Unit of the IRS in Washington, DC told a House committee that "I have not done anything wrong. I have not broken any laws. I have not violated any IRS rules and regulations" and then took the Fifth Amendment, refusing to testify.[8] Nor has it helped that a large set of her emails were deleted. But it might help to recall a different time in the history of the IRS.

Donald Alexander was sworn in as IRS Commissioner in May 1973. The very next day, he learned about an internal unit that had been searching the tax returns of 3,000 "notorious" groups and 8,000 individuals. He dissolved the unit, saying years later his reason was that political views "extremist or otherwise, are irrelevant to taxation." He refused to audit people on President Nixon's "enemies list," and he insisted – despite Nixon's anger - in proceeding with an audit of the president when his name came up through a random process. Nixon tried to fire Alexander more than once, but the feisty – and honest - commissioner outlasted him, retiring in 1977.[9]

Government ethics, Alexander's story demonstrates, is not an oxymoron. It is possible to earn the trust of the American people through doing the right thing. It is even possible to earn the trust of Congress. General George C. Marshall stands as testimony to that. Marshall was a virtual unknown when he came to Washington, DC in 1938 to work in the Army's War Plans Division. Even President Roosevelt knew little about him, but that changed quickly. Within a year, he selected Marshall over 33 more senior generals to be the next Army Chief of Staff, in part because of the latter's penchant for disagreement with him when Marshall thought it necessary. Marshall was the point man for the White House in testifying before Congress, where isolationism still ruled the day. Thus, as the nation was pulled inexorably toward global war, Marshall had to convince the Hill to help the nation prepare. The reputation he earned for honesty and forthrightness proved essential to getting funds for the military buildup and keeping the military draft in place. As Speaker of the House, Sam Rayburn, said of Marshall: "When General Marshall takes the witness stand to testify . . . We know we are in the presence of a man who is telling the truth about the problem he is discussing. He would tell the truth even if it hurt his cause."

Skills are Not Enough

As Warren Buffet put it, "Somebody once said that in looking for people to hire, you look for three qualities: integrity, intelligence, and energy. And if they don't have the first, the other two will kill you."[10] Most of those who work for government, especially at the upper levels, are very intelligent. Many not only have strong technical skills but the ability to lead, if we define that as gaining followers and using power and influence to accomplish organizational purposes. Despite the public perception, they often work long hours in dedication to their tasks. They suffer no lack of energy. But if they lack character, look for trouble. Alexander and Marshall had it. Key people in FEMA in 2005 and in the IRS in 2013 did not.

Character has been needed since the founding of the public service, even though you won't usually find it on lists of leadership competencies. When Alexander Hamilton, our first Secretary of the Treasury, created the Revenue Marine (the forerunner to the U.S. Coast Guard), he gave its commanding officers important advice in his first letter to them, on June 4, 1791:

> "They will always keep in mind that their countrymen are freemen, and, as such, are impatient of everything that bears the least mark of a domineering spirit. They will, therefore, refrain, with the most guarded circumspection, from whatever has the semblance of haughtiness, rudeness, or insult. . . . The foregoing observations are not dictated by any doubt of the prudence of any of those to whom they are addressed. These have been selected with so careful attention to character, as to afford the strongest assurance, that their conduct will be that of good officers and good citizens. But, in an affair so delicate and important, it has been judged most advisable to listen to the suggestions of caution rather than of confidence, and to put all concerned on their guard against those sallies with which even good and prudent men are occasionally subject. "[11]

The Coast Guard's attention to character remains, two and a quarter centuries later. It was credited with saving more than 33,000 lives in the aftermath of Hurricane Katrina and played a pivotal role in evacuating downtown Manhattan on 9/11. As Admiral James Loy, former Commandant of the Coast Guard, put it in describing their leadership approach: "The model starts with an unequivocal commitment to character and values. Words like honor, respect, trust and courage become the mandated norms on which the leadership culture is built."[12]

Plan of the Book and the SERVE Model

For the past ten years, I have had the privilege of working on ethical issues that face senior, federal, career civil servants who come to programs at the Federal Executive Institute, a residential leadership education center in Charlottesville, Virginia. I began that work with intensive interviews of nearly two dozen senior executives, in which they shared ethics issues they faced and how they addressed them (or were not able to do so). Those interviews led to the design of instructional materials and a course which has been delivered to more than 200 senior leaders.

Senior government executives are dedicated to their jobs, their agencies, the public purpose for which they work, and to doing right by the American people. They all face ethical dilemmas that go beyond concerns about conflicts of interest and financial disclosure. There are rules on those things, and government workers either know the rules or can find an ethics official who does. But how do you balance the public's right to know about the construction of nuclear power plants against the agency's requirement to keep information out of the hands of potential terrorists? The rules don't provide enough help for that. How do you assure money is spent wisely when Congress has earmarked funds for a project and the local people running it know they will get the money almost no matter what they do? There is no regulation that offers a simple answer. How do you maintain your objectivity when inspecting local plants if you live in the community and know that problems you find could hurt the profits that sustain that community and the people who are your friends? How do you deal with an abusive boss whose leadership style is harming your own employees?[13]

For such difficult issues, career civil servants face two problems. First, as 90 percent of practitioners noted in a survey conducted by the American Society for Public Administration (ASPA), ethics laws don't make government ethical. Laws may give guidance and establish penalties – but they don't make decisions. Second, civil servants are constrained by the lack of mechanisms in their agencies to surface and deal with ethical dilemmas and the fact that sometimes senior officials do not welcome them doing so. The same ASPA survey bears this out. In 2006, 50.8 percent said that their organizations "have no consistent approach" to addressing ethical concerns, and another 21.7 percent said they their organizations had only "a reactive, legalistic, blame/punishment approach." Only 21.7 percent said that their organizations "have a proactive, human development, problem-solving approach that focuses on encouraging ethical behavior and deterring unethical behavior." A third (35 percent) reported that supervisors are pressured to compromise personal standards.[14]

This book is designed to help address these issues as well. The approach is organized around an acronym that speaks to public servants: SERVE.

The SERVE Model

SPOT THE ETHICS ISSUE

EXAMINE THE ETHICAL DILEMMA

RECOGNIZE AND REALIGN THE ORGANIZATION'S CULTURE

VOICE YOUR DECISION

ESTABLISH JUSTICE

To illustrate the approach, consider the case of Kwame, a program analyst with the Department of Health and Human Services. He joined the agency after completing his master's degree in public health. After a few years, he rose to become a senior analyst and is now a team leader for a group focused on addressing a future pandemic, such as one caused by a new strain of the H1N1 virus. His team recently compiled data on the potential economic and sociological impact of a pandemic as well as strategies to mitigate it. Asked by his boss to attend a briefing, where the team's data would be shared with a higher level official, Kwame is excited about seeing the team's work put to use. Yet, three minutes into the briefing, before most of his report has even been shared, the higher level official cuts the meeting short, announcing he does not agree with the team's data and recommendations, pronouncing both "faulty," with no explanation. Kwame's boss says nothing; nor does anyone else in the room. It is no secret that this higher level official prefers a particular direction that is not supported by the team's work.

What should Kwame do? In trying to answer this question, he first needs to *Spot the Ethics Issue.* Is he responsible for doing anything other than preparing the data for his boss? Is he just a technical specialist, or does he have a moral responsibility in this situation? If there is an ethics issue, how does he define it? In short, is this just a disagreement over a technical matter, or is this an ethical dilemma? If it is an ethical dilemma, is he responsible for addressing it alone? If others have some responsibility, who are they?

If he believes there is an ethics issue, he needs to *Examine the Ethical Dilemma*. This entails finding what values are in conflict, for an ethical dilemma always involves a conflict in values. For example, is the conflict between truth, as reflected in the team's data, and the pressure to be loyal to his boss and the chain of command? Or is something else going on? With an understanding of what values are in conflict, Kwame must also figure out how to frame options for proceeding. It would be easy – but not always right - to just conclude that he needs to "blow the whistle," but he knows that this may ruin his career and may not even work. He needs to make sure he creates more than just an either-or choice. With options identified, he must assess their strengths and potential pitfalls. Before he chooses, he has to navigate the minefield of making a decision – a minefield strewn with potential mental errors and biases.

Since Kwame is embedded in an organization, he also needs to *Recognize and Realign the Organization's Culture,* to the extent he is able. Understanding how the organization's structure, norms, processes, and incentives impact ethical action is key to finding support for doing the right thing. For example, how could he express his disagreement about what happened in the briefing? The culture, at least as represented by the higher level boss, does not value dissent. What can he do in this atmosphere? While he cannot change the culture by himself, being ignorant of it will either restrain his options or lead him into a decision that flies in the face of powerful norms in the place where he works – or both.

Once clear on how to proceed, Kwame needs to *Voice His Decision*. This recognizes that there are two key parts to acting ethically: deciding what to do and doing it. Knowing what to do is useless unless he has a way to put that decision into words and actions. This will probably entail leading up – trying to change the behavior of those above him. To do that, he will also have to anticipate what concerns may be expressed about his desired course of action and what rationalizations for not addressing the ethical dilemma exist and how he can confront them. This may also require moral courage in speaking truth to power.

Finally, Kwame also has to consider what it means to *Establish Justice*. In most private sector organizations, this last step would not exist. But as a public servant, he has sworn an oath to the Constitution. Its Preamble says that "We, the People" must "establish Justice." Those words seemed steeped in history and quaint to Kwame, at least when he read them in high school, but now he has to decide what "justice" really means. Is justice even involved in this situation? What if ignoring what he and his team believes are essential steps costs lives in a future pandemic? Would that be unjust? If higher level management truly ignores what he feels is essential data and recommendations, is there anything he is obligated by his oath to do? Is the "public interest" just a fuzzy slogan, or does he need to find a way to honor it if it is not being served?

Naturally, he will not be doing SERVE in lockstep. He may shift back and forth among various steps as he gathers information, talks to others, tests the waters, and moves ahead.

How to Use This Book

Each section of the book explores an element of the SERVE model, using questions that public servants need to ask. Extensive use is made of case studies, models, and action steps. Appendices contain supplemental material, including Web sites, an annotated bibliography, and cases for use in continuing to learn about handling ethical issues.

The concluding chapter raises a final question: how can we restore honor to public service? All the steps, checklists and rules designed to help analyze and act in ethical situations depend on public servants who have the character and concern for honor essential to turn a technical specialist into a promoter of democracy. Without these, working in government may be a job but it will never be a calling. But even when they act honorably, public servants are often confronted with a skeptical and scornful citizenry. This is as unhealthy for our republican government as it is for its public servants. Honor, unfortunately, seems a concept deemed more appropriate to the founders, like George Washington, or to those in the military. Honor seems to have little meaning for lower level civil servants working away on technical tasks in small cubicles in massive government buildings. It seems neither an expectation of - nor a recognition that emerges from - citizens. This needs to change.

Terry Newell
Crozet, Virginia

SPOT THE ETHICS ISSUE

EXAMINE THE ETHICAL DILEMMA

RECOGNIZE AND REALIGN THE ORGANIZATION'S CULTURE

VOICE YOUR DECISION

ESTABLISH JUSTICE

—1—
Are You an Ethics Agent?

—2—
Is There an Ethics Issue and
Are You Responsible for Addressing It?

–1–

ARE YOU AN ETHICS AGENT?

"A constitution is a standard, a pillar, and a bond when it is understood, approved, and beloved. But without this intelligence and attachment, it might as well be a kite or balloon flying in the air." — John Adams

In 2010, Jeff Neely, public buildings commissioner for the San Francisco region of the General Services Administration (GSA), approved and led an $823,000 conference for 300 GSA employees in Las Vegas. The conference included a commemorative coin set, a mind reader, a comedian and a clown. Neely's wife, Deborah, though not a government employee, handled party arrangements and directed event planners. In February 2011, the couple took a 17-day government trip to Hawaii, Guam, and the Mariana Islands, in part to celebrate her birthday. Neely has since left GSA, and the scandal forced the resignation of GSA Administrator Martha Johnson, though she was not directly involved. Dan Tangherlini, who replaced Johnson, commented on GSA's web site that: "Those responsible violated rules of common sense, the spirit of public service and the trust taxpayers have placed in all of us."[15]

In January 2004, Sergeant Joe Darby, an Army reservist assigned to office duty in Abu Ghraib prison in Iraq, was handed a couple CDs by a friend and prison guard, Charles Graner. Darby had wanted to send some photos of his buddies home and knew Graner was a camera buff. On the CD's, Darby found disturbing – and now infamous – photos of Iraqi prisoners being abused by guards. Not wanting to be seen as a "rat" by his fellow soldiers but nonetheless believing that, as he later put it, "I've always had a moral sense of right and wrong," Darby copied the photos to a disc, added an anonymous letter, and took both to the Criminal Investigations Division (CID). "This was left in my office. I was told to give it to the CID," he said. Within an hour, the investigator called Darby, told him he would keep his name confidential, and got him to confess that he knew where the photos came from. Darby slept with a gun under his pillow for months, and his life was not made any easier when Secretary of Defense Donald Rumsfeld revealed his name in a Congressional hearing.[16]

Jeff Neely never understood that public office is a public trust. Joe Darby did. Jeff Neely did not appreciate his ethical obligations or even realize he had them. Joe Darby knew what the Army values of duty, honor, selfless service, integrity, and courage required him to do. Acting ethically, which is essential to restore honor to public service, requires an acknowledgement that your job in government requires it.

Do You Have a Role as an Ethics Agent?

If you work for government, you have ethical obligations. Though the same might be said for anybody in any role, public or private, public servants are a special class of "anybody." There are at least four reasons why public servants must accept ethical responsibility, beyond what they'd need to do if they worked for Microsoft or McDonald's.

Reason #1: It's the Law

There are multiple laws setting out the ethical obligations of civil servants. The *Compilation of Federal Ethics Laws*[17] is 109 pages long and covers topics such as conflict of interest, financial disclosure, procurement, gifts, travel, nepotism, post-employment restrictions, and political activities. Some of these laws emerged early in our history (such as the need to prevent abuses that occurred in Civil War procurement), but the great bulk have been enacted since the rapid expansion of federal organizations, responsibilities, and employment beginning in the 1930s with the New Deal legislation of the Great Depression.

Most of these laws speak directly to *individual* ethical responsibilities, but there are others that govern how the federal government operates from an *organizational* perspective. Especially notable is the Administrative Procedures Act (APA). Recognizing that the expansion of government operations put not only administrative but also legislative (rule making) and judicial (administrative hearings) functions into the hands of civil servants, President Franklin Roosevelt said that this "threatens to develop a fourth branch of government for which there is no sanction in the Constitution." The APA thus governs *how* government agencies (and the people in them) must go about their work to ensure citizen input and appropriate oversight.

The APA promises citizens they will have: (a) an open decision making process with a chance for input to rule-making; (b) access to public records; (c) a way to appeal government decisions; (d) a way to hold government officials accountable by penalizing behavior inimical to the public interest; (e) documentation of decision making to establish a publicly accessible record of decisions made, input considered, and who was involved; (f) protection of individual privacy; (g) a way to hold contractors accountable by requiring them to be bound by the same requirements as government workers; and (h) higher level review to ensure actions taken are or can be reviewed by those outside the decision making process. Each of these features of the APA establishes ethical obligations for government organizations and those who work in them.

Reason #2: You Took an Oath of Office

On your first day at work, public servants take an Oath of Office, prescribed by Article 6 of the U.S. Constitution. This step may seem rather insignificant, sandwiched as it often is between signing a form to select health insurance and meeting new co-workers. That is unfortunate, because an oath is defined as "a solemn appeal to a deity, or to some revered person or thing, to witness one's determination to speak the truth, to keep a promise."[18]

The Oath of Office has a long and important history. The very first act passed by Congress under the Constitution, on June 1, 1789, was to prescribe the manner and content of that oath. Very significantly, and simply, that oath said: *"I, A.B., do solemnly swear or affirm (as the case may be) that I will support the Constitution of the United States."* The wording has gotten longer over the years, but the core element remains. The Founders did not want the oath to be taken to support the president (many oaths then and some now are taken to a king/queen or head of state). Nor did it want public servants to think their primary loyalty was to their organization or their boss.

Clearly, then, you cannot honor that oath unless you understand what the Constitution requires of you – and can judge when an action you might contemplate or be asked to take is or is not "supporting" the Constitution.

Consider the case in Box 1.1. What would you do?

Box 1.1
Testing Your Oath of Office

You led a research project to determine the frequency with which commercial airline pilots have near-collisions, runway interference or other safety problems. The survey was anonymous, and pilots reported a far greater incidence of these problems than the airlines or the FAA have previously reported. Your boss – and her boss – will not release the data for fear it would scare the flying public and thus hurt the aviation industry. What, if anything, will you do?

Clearly, your loyalty to your boss and your organization is being tested. But is that your greatest loyalty? Does your oath to the Constitution require you to engage your management on this issue? What if you push your boss to release the data and she refuses? What if a staff member in Congress learns of the study and asks you to provide the data? What would you do then?

Reason #3: Deference to Authority is No Substitute for Thinking

You were not hired because of your skill at ethical reasoning. You may even feel that confronting work-related ethical issues is the job of higher level leaders. As they say, "that's why they pay them the big bucks." But as the case suggests, deferring to authority is a dangerous default position.

We rightly detest Adolph Eichmann, the infamous Nazi SS officer who played a major role in sending millions to their deaths in gas chambers. One of the reasons he was so despicable appears in notes for a memoir he never wrote (he was executed after being captured in Argentina and tried in Jerusalem). In those notes, he said: "Now that I look back, I realize that a life predicated on being obedient and taking orders is a very comfortable life indeed. Living in such a way reduces to a minimum one's own need to think."[19]

The United States government is not immune from such unthinking deference to superiors. Dr. John Cutler of the U.S. Public Health Service and his staff, from 1946-1948, proved the point. The team led a study in Guatemala – because it would never have been approved in the United States - to test the efficacy of antibiotics in treating syphilis. The subjects were soldiers, prostitutes, mental patients and prisoners, and their informed consent was not sought. They were either deliberately infected or, in some cases, prostitutes with the disease were paid to have sex with prisoners. Dr. Thomas Parran, Jr., U.S. Surgeon General at the time, withheld information from Guatemalan officials about details of the study. Clearly, the chain of command all the way up to the Surgeon General did not find anyone willing to say "no." In October 2010, the U.S. formally apologized.[20]

Institutions, by their nature, value rules and procedures and foster norms of obedience and conformity. While this may be necessary to some extent, as well as inevitable, it should never replace the need for ethical mindedness.

Reason #4: Like It or Not, You are Immersed in Politics

In 1883, after years under the "spoils system," in which people could be hired for government jobs by the winning political party as a reward for their loyalty, Congress enacted, and President Chester Arthur signed into law, the Pendleton Act. Passage was no doubt aided by the fact that Arthur succeeded to office when President Garfield was assassinated by a disgruntled office seeker. The new law required that applicants for federal jobs take a competitive examination and be hired on their merits. It also stated that they could not be fired for political reasons. In short, it tried to separate politics from the civil service.

Subsequent reformers expanded the notion that "neutral competence" was the role of civil servants and that it was possible to separate "politics" from "administration" in government. As Woodrow Wilson framed it, when still a professor at Bryn Mawr College:

> "... administration lies outside the proper sphere of politics. Administrative questions are not political questions. Although politics sets the tasks for administration, it should not be suffered to manipulate its offices..."[21]

In short, politicians make decisions; civil servants implement them. The merit system, and the notion that civil servants must be separated from politics, are still the prevailing philosophy of governmental administration. That philosophy has much to commend it, particularly in making sure that civil servants do not engage in partisan politics. But it has led to a dangerous confusion. The "politics – administration" dichotomy acts as if civil servants can be vaccinated against politics, as if a "wall of separation" exists between the political and the administrative.

This idealized separation breaks down in the real world. For example, Congress often passes laws that are global in their intent but vague on how that intent is to be carried out. That forces civil servants to grapple with exactly what to do to achieve the intent of the law (and what not to do). It forces them to decide who has access to what, in terms of rights and resources. It also sets them up for having to defend themselves and their agencies in front of the same Congressional committees that wrote the law that put them smack in the middle of those political questions.

As another example, what does a civil servant do if a bill or a law will have a deleterious effect on large segments of the public? Do they just keep their mouths shut, or should they feel an obligation to engage in trying not just to administer the law but to promote benevolent democracy as well? As yet another example, civil servants, especially at the upper levels, interact with politicians on a regular basis. In some cases, these are political appointees in their agencies. In other cases, they may be members of Congress or hill staffers. In even more cases, they may be engaged with lobbyists and a host of others with political agendas who visit or seek them out in meetings or conferences. Many of these interactions raise ethical issues. Consider the issue in Box 1.2.

Put simply, almost any issue you face has – or can have – political aspects. When that happens, ethical issues will often come up. To do your job, you have to recognize and deal with them.

Box 1.2
Politics or Administration: What's Your Job?

A senior manager from a professional association approaches you at a conference to suggest that proposed regulations soon to be published by your office will, if not crafted properly, have an adverse effect on the ability of her member firms (mostly large businesses) to compete in the global marketplace. She mentions, seemingly in passing, that she is a good friend of the chair of the House Appropriations Committee that handles your agency's budget and that she knows he shares a similar concern. You listen to her concerns but of course make no commitments. You remind her of the public comment process the association can use to formally register any concerns once the proposed rules are published. After she leaves, on her way to see your boss and others in your organization, you have an uneasy feeling. Was what she did appropriate? Did you handle it properly? What about those thousands of small business owners that could also be impacted by the regulations but lack the resources to either form an association or come to Washington, DC to register their concerns?

What is Your Role as an Ethical Agent?

Accepting that public servants have a role to play as ethical agents does not clarify what that role is. It would be simple – and comforting – to define that role as following the law, adhering to the Oath, and staying out of politics. It's not that simple.

Ethics laws and regulations constitute a large catalogue of "thou shall nots." Yet, as John Rohr, one of the most eminent public administration theorists, observed, most of these situations don't come up very often in the life of a public servant.[22] How many times in a career will a contractor try to bribe an official or a relative ask for a job? If we consider ethical issues as an iceberg, what law and regulation proscribe constitute a small part of what appears above the water line. The great mass of ethical dilemmas lie submerged, lurking beneath everyday awareness but ready to confront public servants just the same.

As importantly, ethics laws and rules most often clarify what one *can* or *cannot do*. A public servant, for example, cannot accept a gift of value from a contractor. The rules make that clear. But, as political scientist Louis Gawthrop so well reminds us, ethics rules do not tell us what we *should* do, in situations where they offer no clear guidance.[23] What does a supervisor do when an employee, who may not be that great a performer, applies for another job and the prospective supervisor calls for a reference? Providing a great reference may enable one to finally get rid of the mediocre performer. On the other hand, giving a poor reference may irreparably harm that employee's life – and the lives of those who count on him. But there is no law or rule to help figure out just how to handle this in a way that is honest and fair.

The proliferation of laws and regulations on ethics may actually make acting ethically harder. They can do this in two ways. First, they telegraph – and annual Congressionally-mandated ethics training reinforces this – that acting ethically is a matter of following the law and the rules. The danger: if a proposed action does not violate a law or rule, it can be perceived as being ethical. There is no ethics rule that says "do not ignore a member of the public who contacts you to ask a question." But doing so repeatedly would nonetheless be an ethical lapse. In the days of legal segregation, barring black Americans from many public places was legal. But it was never ethical.

Second, the mass of rules may discourage good people from even working for government – and they may discourage people already in government from staying. Both would weaken ethical government. Working for government, especially at the upper and most visible levels, means opening one's actions (and often one's private life) to constant criticism. As Bayliss Manning, who chaired President Kennedy's Advisory Panel on Ethics and Conflict of Interest in Government put it, "in an orgy of virtue we seem to lose our grip on decency."[24]

If the mass of laws and regulations still leave public servants with a lack of clarity on what to do in many situations, so does the Constitution, to which they took an oath. It does not contain any of the following words: public administration, civil servant, government employee, or ethics. Article II, which established the Executive Branch, is principally concerned with the president, how he is elected, and his responsibilities. So while ethically bound by the Constitution, public servants won't find much in it that speaks directly about how to be faithful to that pledge.

Finally, as we have observed, public servants can't just "stay out of politics." Even if they can fend off partisan politics, political issues are by their nature inherent in doing government work.

If the question - what *is* my role as an ethical agent? – is not easy to answer, that does not mean it has no answer. The American Society of Public Administration (ASPA), for one, offers a very helpful way to think about the ethical role of a public servant. Its Code of Ethics consists of eight principles and 37 practices that constitute "a statement of the aspirations and high expectations of public servants."[25] The principles are shown in Box 1.3. The full set of principles and practices are in Appendix A.

Box 1.3
The ASPA Code of Ethics - Principles

The American Society for Public Administration (ASPA) advances the science, art, and practice of public administration. The Society affirms its responsibility to develop the spirit of *responsible* professionalism within its membership and to increase awareness and commitment to ethical principles and standards among all those who work in public service in all sectors. To this end, we, the members of the Society, commit ourselves to uphold the following principles:

1. Advance the Public Interest. Promote the interests of the public and put service to the public above service to oneself.

2. Uphold the Constitution and the Law. Respect and support government constitutions and laws, while seeking to improve laws and policies to promote the public good.

3. Promote democratic participation. Inform the public and encourage active engagement in governance. Be open, transparent and responsive, and respect and assist all persons in their dealings with public organizations.

4. Strengthen social equity. Treat all persons with fairness, justice, and equality and respect individual differences, rights, and freedoms. Promote affirmative action and other initiatives to reduce unfairness, injustice, and inequality in society.

5. Fully Inform and Advise. Provide accurate, honest, comprehensive, and timely information and advice to elected and appointed officials and governing board members, and to staff members in your organization.

6. Demonstrate personal integrity. Adhere to the highest standards of conduct to inspire public confidence and trust in public service.

7. Promote Ethical Organizations: Strive to attain the highest standards of ethics, stewardship, and public service in organizations that serve the public.

8. Advance Professional Excellence: Strengthen personal capabilities to act competently and ethically and encourage the professional development of others.

Just scanning the principles suggests that the ethical role of public servants falls in three distinct but interconnected domains: (a) public, (b) organization, and (c) individual. We can roughly describe the domains as follows. In the public realm, "advancing the public interest" takes primacy (Principle 1) and also involves "promote democratic participation" (Principle 3) and "strengthen social equity" (Principle 4). In the organizational realm we find "uphold the Constitution and the law" (Principle 2), "fully inform and advise" (Principle 5), and "promote ethical organizations" (Principle 7). Finally, in the individual realm are "demonstrate personal integrity" (Principle 6) and "advance professional excellence" (Principle 8).

While the ASPA Code does not address "roles" in explicit language, several emerge from a review of the practices provided for each principle. Chief among these would seem to be the following:

- *Upholder of Values*: The public servant is obligated to support and strengthen core values on which our republican government depends. Some of these values apply to how to deal with citizens, some on how to work with colleagues, and many on how to work in both realms. The list of values is long. In regard to the public, it includes compassion, benevolence, optimism, equality, fairness, representativeness, responsiveness, equal treatment, due process, openness, transparency, impartiality, effectiveness, and efficiency. Inside the organization, the Code notes the importance of impartiality, ethical integrity, efficient use of resources, open expression of views, encouragement of dissent, merit principles, excellence, competence, professionalism, avoiding conflicts of interest, objectivity, and promoting representativeness in the work force. In all actions, the Code expects public servants to treat others with integrity, courage, truthfulness, courtesy, respect, dedication to high standards, respect for confidential information, and the conduct of official acts without partisanship or favoritism.

- *Advocate for Ethical Action*: Public servants make decisions, and those decisions should be ethical ones. The organization should have, and employees should adhere to, a code of ethics. Public servants are not only responsible for acting ethically but for speaking up when they spot unethical behavior and for seeking "external sources or agencies for review and action" if the organization does not address the issue that was raised. The Code is quite clear on the responsibility to dissent, to make recommendation even when they may not be "popular or preferred by superiors or colleagues." Public servants must also "resist political, organizational, and personal pressures to compromise ethical integrity."

- *Competent Practitioner*: Accepting a public position means acknowledging the responsibility to act competently in performing work. In short, poor performance is unethical. Public servants have an ethical responsibility to learn as well, to "keep up-to-date on emerging issues, practices, and potential problems," and to use their competence to "develop proposals for sound laws and policies."

- *Educator*: Public servants have a dual responsibility as educators. On the one hand, they must educate and engage the public so that it may participate in the process of governing. This requires being proactive, providing information to members of the public and involving them "in the development, implementation, and assessment of policies and programs, and seek[ing] to empower citizens in the democratic process." On the other hand, it means developing the current and future public workforce. According to the Code, public servants must "allocate time and resources to the professional development of students, interns, beginning professionals, and other colleagues" and "provide support and encouragement to others to upgrade competence."

- *Advocate for Social Justice*: Echoing the Constitution's promise to "establish Justice," the Code recognizes that not everyone has the same access to power and a voice when government makes decisions. As a result, it emphasizes the need to: "empower citizens . . . including special assistance to those who lack resources or influence." It requires the provision of services "tempered by recognition of differences." It also states that public servants should "oppose all forms of discrimination and harassment and promote affirmative action" as well as "other efforts to reduce disparities in outcomes and increase the inclusion of underrepresented groups." Within the government organization, it not only expects public servants to "support merit principles" but to "increase the representativeness of the public workforce" and to work for "the full inclusion of persons with diverse characteristics."

The Public Servant and Future Generations

In ancient Athens, young men who were about to be accorded the privilege of citizenship and enter military service took an oath. It had some aspects of our modern oath, but it had one element our oath does not make explicit: "My native land I will not leave a diminished heritage but greater and better than when I received it."[26]

We have discussed ethics in terms of how to behave when faced with a specific challenge. But there is a timeless dimension to current ethics challenges as well. Each challenge has an impact on what happens downstream. If the FEMA official who first heard the report of toxic fumes ordered a halt to trailer shipments and demanded testing of the air quality, then illness and death might well have been avoided – as well as damage to trust in government. The actions of public servants also set a precedent, for good or ill. What they do establishes a positive example for others or fosters a slippery slope that encourages future unethical behavior.

As ethical agents, public servants might well remember the Athenian oath as well as their own (Box 1.4). Public servants are included in "We, the People."

> ### Box 1.4
> ### Preamble to the Constitution of the United States
>
> We the People of the United States, in Order to form a more perfect Union, establish Justice, insure domestic Tranquility, provide for the common defence, promote the general Welfare, and secure the Blessings of Liberty to ourselves and our Posterity, do ordain and establish this Constitution for the United States of America.

To serve current and future generations, those in government must acknowledge their role as ethical agents. But there is more. They must know how to identify and make decisions about ethical issues.

–2–

IS THERE AN ETHICS ISSUE AND ARE YOU RESPONSIBLE FOR ADDRESSING IT?

"It's often the little things that you let go and somehow they chip away at your integrity. It's not about taking the government pen home . . . It's much more complicated than that. Part of it is making yourself sensitive to things."
— a Government Executive

On August 3, 2002, the *Washington Post* reported that over two million active documents filed by foreigners in the U.S. legally were in a warehouse outside Kansas City, Missouri, collecting dust. Among these were roughly 200,000 change-of-address forms. Since failure to file a change-of-address form is a deportable offense, it is possible that some people here legally and who were no threat to the country, were deported in the aftermath of the 9/11 attacks because their forms had never been processed. "It exposes one of the INS's [Immigration and Naturalization Service] dirty secrets," said Lucas Guttentag, director of the American Civil Liberties Union's immigration rights project."[27]

Was this an ethics issue or just a regrettable problem due to failure to process the forms? The question matters, because if you accept your role as an ethical agent, you need to be able to decide when you face an ethics issue. If you don't see the ethics issue, you may see no reason to act (or push others to do so). You may also miss the fact that ethics issues have a way of coming back to hurt your organization and you, such as by appearing as articles in the *Washington Post*. An ethics issue will not always come with "Ethics Alert" stamped on it.

Indeed, if you think about the ethical iceberg discussed earlier you can see (Figure 2.1) that many ethics issues are not immediately obvious. They are often hidden in a sea of other issues that are purely technical or managerial. Like the government executive quoted above, you have to be sensitive to ethics issues that lurk below the surface.

Figure 2.1
The Ethical Iceberg

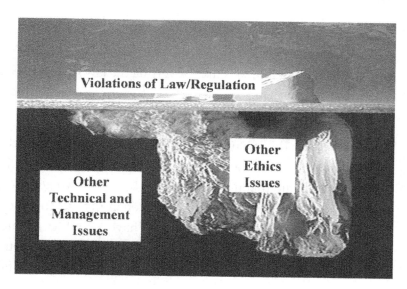

Consider the events shown in Box 2.1. Are any of these ethics issues?

Box 2.1
Technical, Management or Ethics Issue?

For each item below, check the box if you think it involves an ethics issue.

Ethiics Issue?

1. You are asked to complete an evaluation of a proposal for a grant from your office's major new program. ☐
2. You give a low performance appraisal to an employee who has performed well for you before. ☐
3. A peer in your office calls in sick (she has done this often) and you suspect she is just taking the day off to have a long weekend. ☐
4. You cancel a planned hire because the person you want to select is ranked lower than a person with Veteran's Preference. ☐
5. A new piece of software designed for your organization has flaws, so you withhold payment to the contractor. ☐
6. In a staff meeting, your boss ignores an objection to a new set of guidelines you got from top management about how to assemble this year's budget submission. ☐
7. The IT office has issued new requirements to ensure the security of off-the-shelf software applications used in agency offices. ☐
8. Your boss just cancelled your trip to oversee the work of a contractor, citing budget cutbacks. ☐

Clearly, something seems ethically amiss in items 3 and 4. If a person lies about their health to take a day off, they are abusing the government's sick leave policy. When someone refuses to hire a veteran who qualifies for a job, they are subverting the law intended to honor the service of those in uniform. The other items seem, on the surface, to represent technical tasks or concerns (items 1, 5, 7) or management issues (items 2, 6, 8).

Admittedly, you don't have much information about these other items, so you may feel tentative in saying that ethics is not involved. That's good. Let's take item 1. Suppose you pick up the proposal to evaluate it and find that it was submitted by a firm owned by someone you shared an office with in a previous job. You were friends then, often going out together for a drink after work, though you have since lost touch. You feel that you have a conflict of interest – you cannot assure yourself of objectivity in reviewing the proposal (and even if you think you could be objective, a neutral observer might question that). Thus, a seemingly technical issue now takes on ethical dimensions.

Or take item 8. The contractor is at a pivotal point in its work, and the inability to observe and meet with key contractor staff first-hand means that you will have to take their word on a number of matters that require onsite inspection. There does not seem to be a way to compensate for your lack of personal presence. The release of significant public funds to continue the project depends on your progress report. Thus, a seemingly managerial decision now takes on ethical dimensions.

These examples (and our iceberg analogy) highlight two common problems in confronting ethics issues. First, you have to decide if there actually *is* an ethics issue. Second, you have to decide what kind of ethics issue it is. Without a way to answer these questions, it's hard to act as an ethical agent.

Is There an Ethics Issue?

The simplest test to use is to ask a question: is there a conflict among moral values? If the answer is "yes," you face an ethics issue. This is clear in cases 3 and 4, and it became clearer in cases 1 and 8 when we added more context. In the case of your former colleague (case 1), you face a conflict between your loyalty to an old friend and your obligation to be objective. In the case of your cancelled trip (case 8), you face a conflict between your need to protect the public's investment and your agency's concern to be a careful steward of limited resources (and your loyalty to your boss).

In the movie, *The Dish*, an Australian crew, inside a building on whose roof is perched a radio telescope, is asked by NASA to raise the "dish" so that it can receive television transmission signals from the first-ever moon walk by astronauts Neil Armstrong and Buzz Aldrin. Winds, gusting up to thirty knots, are pushing the dish towards the limit of its ability to be raised without collapsing. Cliff, the team's leader, must decide what to do.

At first, Cliff approaches this as a technical matter. He gets input from his team on whether the dish can hold up in the wind and decides to watch the wind speed and see if it dies down. But he soon feels pressure from NASA. He is told that the main dish, at NASA's Goldstone facility, has gone down so his is the only one available. He gets pressure from his boss, and from the Prime Minister who is visiting the small town where the radio telescope is located to celebrate (and no doubt bask in the glory of) the town's accomplishment.

The wind speed increases, gusting to fifty knots. At that speed, raising the dish could well cause it to fall and injure or kill everyone inside. The technical matter has now morphed into a clash of moral values. Cliff must balance loyalty to his superiors against his responsibility for the safety of his team. He must balance the town's short-term desire for a place in history against the long-term effects of a deadly accident, not just on his staff but on the town itself. He must balance the world's desire to see this epic event against these other concerns, and he realizes as well that his responsibility to be cautious is being tested against his ability to demonstrate leadership courage.

Inside every technical or managerial issue is the *possibility* of an ethics issue. One danger is that we will see only the technical or managerial issue. The INS knew they had a management problem - a huge backlog of forms to process. They may not have seen that they also had an ethics issue, a clash of values (e.g. the commitment to due process for legally admitted immigrants vs. efficiency (the importance of getting other work tasks done first)). Cliff knew he had a technical issue. He only discovered the ethics issue as the situation deteriorated. (Indeed, had he spotted it earlier, he might have had more time to deal with it, and deal with it better than he ultimately did.)[28]

A second danger is that we may misunderstand (or miss entirely) the ethics issue because we cannot see what moral values are at stake. To prevent this, it helps first to differentiate moral values from all other values and second, to know what kind of value clashes might be present.

A moral value is a value viewed as a right thing to do or be (and its absence as to some degree wrong). Honesty is a moral value. Effectiveness is also a moral value for those in government. Moral values are not just preferences. The fact that I like chocolate may mean that I value it, but that preference is not a moral value.

As Figure 2.2 suggests, there are at least six sets of values that might come into play. Clashes can occur within a set as well as between sets.

Figure 2.2
Value Sets That Can Pose Ethical Issues

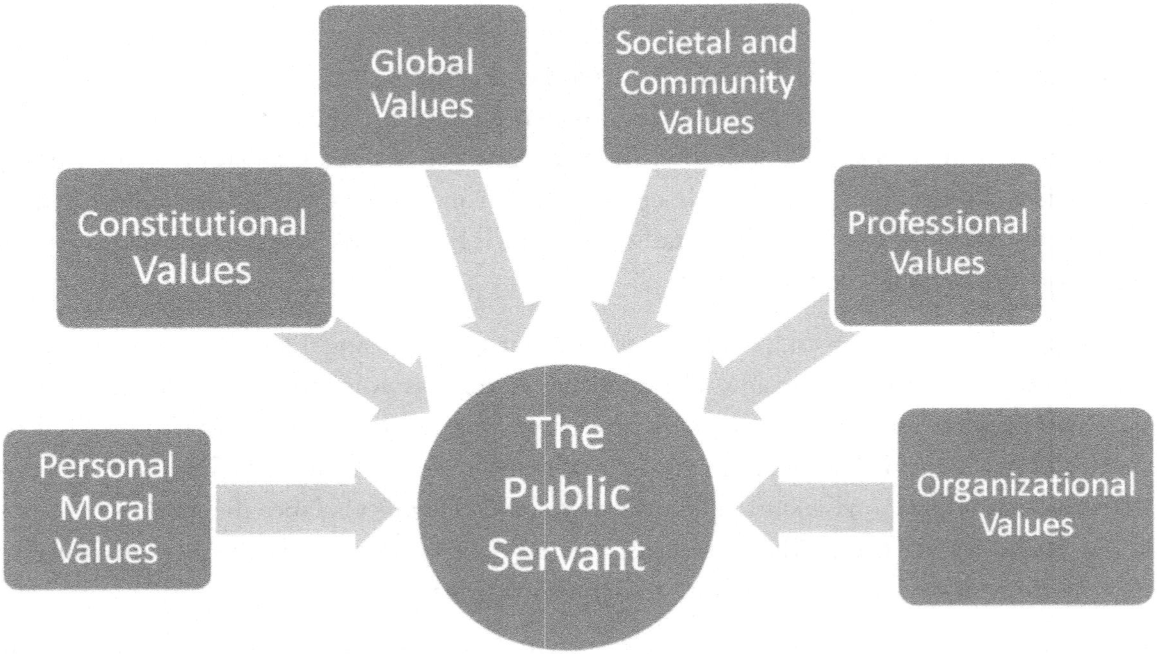

To explore the situation Cliff faced in *The Dish* a bit more, consider at least the following values in play in his situation and how they might come into conflict:

- Personal Moral Values: safety, fairness, empathy, courage, personal responsibility

- Constitutional Values: accomplishing public purposes, fidelity to elected officials

- Organizational Values: loyalty, following chain of command, goal achievement

- Professional Values: engineering expertise, reputation for excellence

- Societal/Community Values: achievement, recognition, love of country

- Global Values: reverence for life, compassion, love of historic achievement, building a global community through a shared experience

In the American context (since *The Dish* was set in Australia), consider just the following three abbreviated sets of values and how they can conflict in the issues public servants address in their daily work:

Constitutional Values	Organizational Values	Personal Values
Representative government	Efficiency	Achievement
Due process	Effectiveness	Honesty
Separation of powers	Chain of command	Fairness
Equality	Timeliness	Compassion
Responsiveness	Collaboration	Responsibility
Subordination of military to civilian authority	Creativity	Freedom
	Stewardship of resources	Loyalty

You could easily pick one from each column (or any two from one column) and see how these could come into conflict. How to *resolve* such conflicts is the question we take up in the next chapter. For now, it is important only to note that the potential for such conflict is endemic to public life. Such conflict may be obvious or subtle - in more daily activities than you suspect.

What Kind of Ethics Issue Is It?

Knowing you have an ethics issue to deal with is the first hurdle. What kind of ethics issue confronts you is the second. Not all ethics issues take you down the same path when you seek a resolution.

Rushworth Kidder, an ethicist and founder of the Institute for Global Ethics, differentiated between two kinds of ethics issues. In his book, *How Good People Make Tough Choices*, Kidder contrasted "moral temptations" with "ethical dilemmas" (see Box 2.2).[29] Both involve a conflict in values. But "moral temptations" involve a conflict between right and wrong, while "ethical dilemmas" involve a conflict between two or more "rights."

In case 4 above, the supervisor who cancelled a job hire because he would have had to select a veteran succumbed to a moral temptation. Law and regulation directed him to hire the veteran. He did the wrong thing. In Cliff's case, he was confronted with an ethical dilemma. There were a multitude of choices he could make – and none of them would have violated law or regulation. For example, he could have chosen to raise the dish because of his professional value of achieving the mission he was assigned. That would have subordinated the value of safety for his crew. Or he could have done just the opposite, choosing safety over mission. Yet a third choice might have been to tell NASA that he needed more time – even though that would have put safety over loyalty to his bosses, who wanted no delays or problems to mar the day (or their reputations). All of these choices were "right" in the sense that they all adhered to one or more moral values.

Box 2.2
Two Kinds of Ethics Issues

Moral Temptation	**Ethical Dilemma**
Right vs. wrong	Right vs. right
Governed by law or regulation	Governed by conscience
One right answer	Two or more right answers
A conflict between moral and immoral values	A conflict between moral values

Source: Kidder (1995)

This does not mean, of course, that all of Cliff's choices were equally appropriate. The task of ethical decision making, which we address later, involves *how* you choose among competing "right vs. right" choices. The algorithm in Figure 2.3 can be used to help you decide if you have an ethics issue and if that issue is a fairly simple choice between right and wrong or a more complex choice among two or more moral "rights."

Figure 2.3
Identifying Ethics Issues

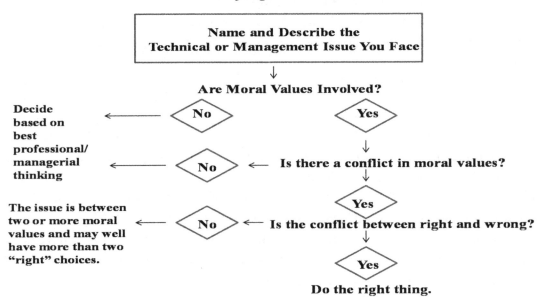

Are You Responsible for Addressing the Ethics Issue?

Just because there is an ethics issue, however, does not mean it is your responsibility to address it. Even if you have some responsibility, it does not necessarily follow that you are the only one responsible. This is not said to give you an easy out. It is said because deciding exactly who has responsibility to address an ethics issue is one key to addressing it effectively.

The first question to ask is thus: is this ethics issue covered by one of the roles I have to fulfill as an ethical agent? In Chapter 1, drawing on the ASPA Code of Ethics, we suggested several such roles.

Consider the case in Box 2.3. What should Pat do?

Box 2.3
The Case of Caustic Greg

Pat and Sarah are peers, each of whom is a Branch Chief in the same Division of the Department of Commerce. Sarah has an employee, Greg, who is a fifty-something, long-time worker who has a reputation for offending and angering those he works with. Lately, however, Greg has "shared the wealth" of his anger with two of Pat's staff, who he's working with on a six-month joint project that began last week. Both of Pat's employees complained to Pat when Greg shouted at and insulted them in their first meeting on the project. Pat talked with Sarah. It was clear from that conversation that Sarah does not want to do anything about this. "That's just the way he is," she told Pat. Pat seems stymied, not wanting to hurt the good relationship he has with Sarah but not wanting to just back off either.

It's clear that Pat feels some responsibility for addressing this problem. The role demand that he be a competent practitioner means that he cannot just ignore the problem because doing so may mean the joint project fails. His loyalty to his staff and concern with project effectiveness are just two values that call for action. That's the reason he talked with Sarah about the situation. Yet Sarah refused to do anything, so Pat is now faced with a choice. He can drop the whole thing, tell his staff to just "deal with it," and move on. That might preserve his harmonious relationship with Sarah, but it would undermine his own leadership. Word would go out that he won't confront tough issues and fight for his own employees.

Faced with this ethical dilemma, Pat wonders: "what should I do?" Posed that way, the question may block him from resolving the dilemma. If Pat defines the problem as one for which he alone has responsibility, he may stay stuck. After all, there are others who share responsibility: (a) Sarah, who has put up with a dysfunctional employee for too long (and whose own staff no doubt continues to suffer as a result); (b) the Division Director, under whom this joint project falls and who will ultimately be held accountable by higher management if it fails; and (c) Greg himself, whose behavior is damaging not just this project but the entire work environment in the Division. Even further, there is an Employee Relations office in the department with staff trained to help supervisors deal with such employees. There are also counselors available who could work with Greg on his behavior.

Pat's best chance is to identify who else is responsible and craft an approach which gets them to share that responsibility (for example, he might ask Sarah to come with him to meet with people in Employee Relations). He may fail. Others may refuse to help or act without success. But Pat will at least know that he acted ethically to the full extent to which he was capable.

Faced with an ethics issue, a productive approach is thus always to ask: who is responsible for resolving this? Figure 2.4 offers a simple way to think about that question.

Figure 2.4
Zones of Ethical Responsibility

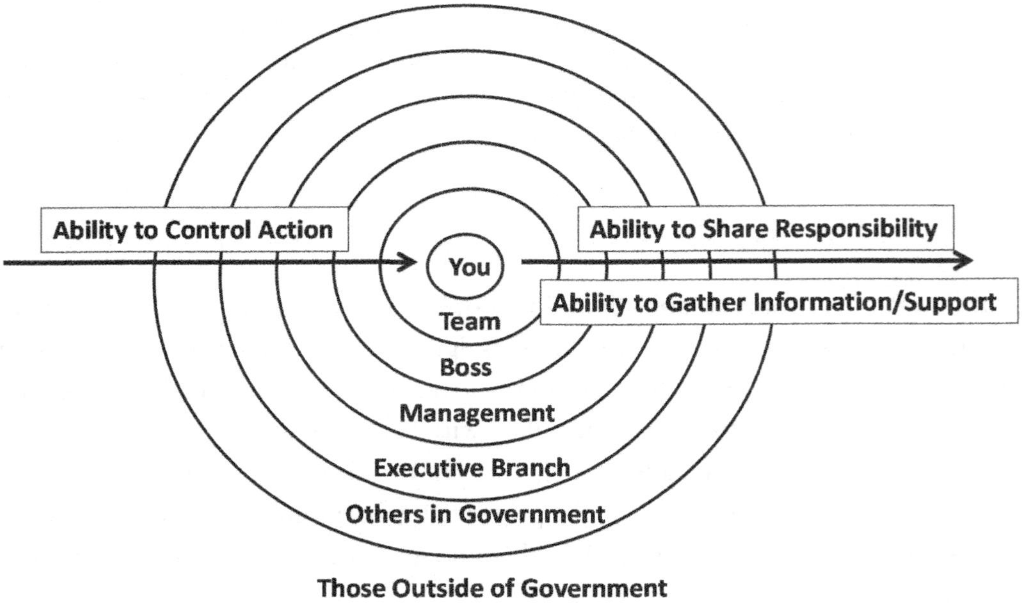

As the Zones of Ethical Responsibility suggests, the closer the action is to you organizationally, the more you can control it. This is one reason many try to resolve ethical dilemmas on their own. Other reasons, of course, are that they feel they *are* the only one responsible or that asking for help means admitting some weakness or surfacing an issue that others may wish they had left alone.

On the other hand, the more you engage others, the more you can gather information that may shed more light on the problem and thus open up more options. Also, the more you share the responsibility, the more you remind others that they also have an ethical and organizational responsibility to address it - and the more support for doing so you can often generate.

Are You a Delegate or Trustee?

The decision about who is responsible for addressing an ethics issue involves another consideration – one that asks you to think about your Constitutional oath.

As a thought experiment, consider yourself as working within the Department of Energy for a president who campaigned on a pledge to reduce greenhouse gases. To keep his campaign promise, he asked the department to draft legislation that would raise the federal gasoline tax by a substantial amount (this discouraging the use of gasoline) and use the increased tax revenue to create incentives for the production of electric vehicles and charging stations across the country. You have been asked to draft a bill, for review by top management and the Office of Management and Budget, on its way to the president. In setting about your task, you realize that nothing in the guidance you have been given speaks to the impact of such a tax on lower income Americans who have to drive to work and who probably cannot even afford an electric vehicle.

Would you raise this concern with your boss?

Let's say you do raise the issue, and your boss responds that this is not your concern. She tells you to just draft the legislation using the guidance you have been given. "If they want to worry about the impact on poor people, that's up to them," she says. "It's not for us to be inserting our personal views into this."

Would you accept this response or try to get your concern addressed some other way?

How you answer these two questions depends not only on whether you decide the issue addresses one of the ethical roles you have to play (e.g. advocate for social justice) but on *whether and how* you play that role. In the literature of public administration, two opposing role definitions are the public servant as "trustee" or as "delegate."[30] If you would raise the concern with your boss, and even bump it up the chain of command later, you are acting as a "trustee." You see your role as being concerned about the welfare of the citizens of the nation, especially (in this case) those who may be harmed by a law's unintended consequences. The Constitution's Preamble speaks of justice and the general welfare, and a highly regressive tax seems to work against both.

When your boss replied that "it's up to them," she was responding as a "delegate." That is, she probably believed that elected officials get to make this call, not you, since only they are directly accountable to the voters. After them, appointed officials like the Secretary of Energy get delegated authority to make such decisions. You are way down the delegation line. You have delegated authority as well, but, in her view, it comes from all those above you and thus your job is to respond to legal orders and not take on more responsibility than you have been delegated.

The question of ethical responsibility thus may require you to decide where you fall on the trustee-delegate continuum. There are ethical dangers at both extremes. If you see yourself only and always as a delegate, you can avoid responsibility when you ought to accept it. Adolph Eichmann, the Nazi official who helped implement Hitler's "Final Solution," took this position.

If you over-identify with the trustee extreme, you can take on responsibility that exceeds any reasonable claim that you have in your role as a public servant. Leaks of classified information are often justified by the leaker claiming that he was only looking out for the public's interest. While in some cases we may find sympathy with that claim, in many cases there is no evidence that the person sought redress for his concerns within government first. Adopting the trustee role without due regard for the limits inherent in your Oath of Office means the public servant may practice civil disobedience, which undermines not only the boss but republican government.

Assuming you have identified an ethics issue, accepted that it falls within your role as a public servant, and identified who else may also be responsible for addressing the issue, the next step is to examine the issue in detail and craft an ethical decision.

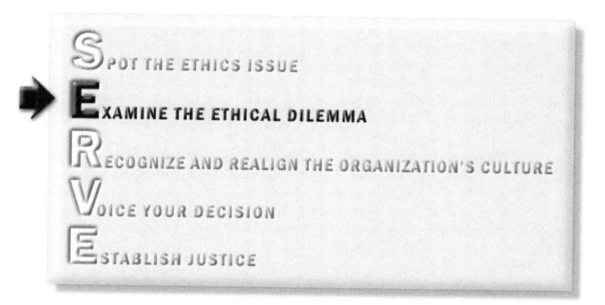

SPOT THE ETHICS ISSUE

➡ **E**XAMINE THE ETHICAL DILEMMA

RECOGNIZE AND REALIGN THE ORGANIZATION'S CULTURE

VOICE YOUR DECISION

ESTABLISH JUSTICE

—3—
What are the Value Conflicts and Facts, and What Options Do I Have?

—4—
Why is Decision Making So Tough?

—5—
What is the Best Decision?

–3–

WHAT ARE THE VALUE CONFLICTS AND FACTS, AND WHAT OPTIONS DO I HAVE?

"If possible, don't react immediately. Go back and think about it, about repercussions."
— a Government Executive

On January 15, 2003, Navy General Counsel Alberto Mora sent an unsigned, draft memo to his boss, Pentagon General Counsel William Haynes. Mora's draft, which he said he would sign later that day – making it official and on the record – described the interrogation techniques he learned were being used on detainees at Guantanamo Bay in Cuba as "at a minimum cruel and unusual treatment, and, at worst, torture." The strong phrasing referred to both the prohibition of such treatment in the Constitution and the Geneva Conventions. Mora had learned of these techniques the previous December 17th from the head of the Navy's Criminal Investigative Service, and he had spent the last month verifying what he had been told, speaking with peers and confronting Gordon England, Secretary of the Navy. He had even met with Haynes and tried to convince him that the policy being followed and the memos used to support it could lead to criminal prosecution of many of those involved, including very high level officials. Haynes was not swayed. Since no one chose to act, Mora did.

Mora was no "dove" or "bleeding heart." His parents were both refugees from communist rule. He had admired President Reagan and had served in the first Bush Administration before being asked to serve under President George W. Bush. He supported the war on terror. But, as he later told a reporter, "I was appalled by the whole thing. It was clearly abusive and it was clearly contrary to everything we were ever taught about American values."[31]

Mora recognized he confronted an ethical dilemma that tested his Oath of Office. Yet he did not react impetuously or without careful vetting of facts and consideration of options. He did not resign,

35

nor did he call the *Washington Post* and "blow the whistle." He chose to be what Harvard Business School professor Joseph Badaracco, Jr., calls a "quiet hero."[32]

Quiet heroes leverage rather than leave their official positions. If you value public service and want to preserve your career along with your moral values, you need a solid understanding of how to examine and think through an ethical dilemma. If you can do that, you can also do a better job of serving the public and your organization – in both of whose interests resolving an ethical dilemma resides.

Identify Value Conflicts and Facts

In addressing the issue that troubled him, Alberto Mora not only had to confront his own values, he had to consider a wide range of stakeholders and their values. Some of those clearly conflicted with his own. He also had to make sure he got his facts right, because challenging your boss will surely lead to disaster if you don't stand on solid factual ground.

Since most of us may never face such weighty ethical dilemmas, let's explore a more typical one. Read the case in Box 3.1 and consider four questions: (1) what's the ethics issue?; (2) who has a stake in this issue and what values matter to them; (3) is there a clash of values and, if so, what is it?; and (4) what are the facts of the case? Late, we'll explore what options Bill, the supervisor in this case, has in proceeding. (An entire set of questions – an ethics decision making model – appears in Appendix B. The approach here is based on that model.)

Box 3.1
What Rating Do I Give?

"The Director has her reasons, I know," Bill Jamerson told himself, "but this still rubs me the wrong way." Bill was facing the second annual appraisal of his employees since the office director, his second level boss, had declared she would no longer tolerate so many high ratings. The bureau had switched to a numbered rating system two years ago. Your score could be anywhere from 0 to 500 (the highest), and a score of 300 was supposed to be average or "Fully Successful."

Just before ratings were due last year, the Director declared a policy that final ratings would be spread out – not everyone was "outstanding." She set a score of 400 for each unit's expected average, knowing that most people were somewhat better than "fully successful."

But that meant if you wanted to rate a few people at 450 or above, for example, you had to rate others lower than 400. That was the tough part. While she did not declare a specific ratings distribution, it was understood that your ratings might be sent back if they did not fit expectations. In short, everyone knew that a "bell curve" distribution of ratings was expected, even though Bill's boss recoiled at that term when someone used it.

This had caused no end of problems, and it would probably cause more this year. What upset Bill was that the official policy said you rated employees against their performance standards, not each other. And he knew he could not give the ratings he felt his employees deserved if he had to adhere to her policy. "How can I do what she wants," he grumbled, "when the expected distribution forces me to compare one employee to another?"

This was not a minor issue. Ratings had consequences. You couldn't get a bonus unless you rated above 450. Promotions were also dependent on your rating. "It's true," Jamerson reminded himself, "that an average rating would still get you the normal cost-of-living raise, but that was not much money and little consolation to those who had knocked themselves out in a tough and busy year."

"What does this do to teamwork?" he thought. Last year, he had had some success talking to his immediate boss and getting leeway to give ratings slightly above the expected average for one of his two teams, but that was unlikely to fly this year. Some of his peers complained and said it was their turn to get that extra leeway in rating their employees.

Bill was supposed to submit his proposed ratings to his boss in a few days. He was not supposed to tell his employees about the bell curve approach, though he suspected they had figured it out. He was concerned about a complaint from one person, who was unhappy last year and said just yesterday, "I sure hope my rating comes up this year; I've got a baby on the way." He could empathize – he had a growing family too and wanted to advance in his own career. Most irritating, he knew that the other offices in the bureau did not follow this policy. Their second level boss did not feel any need to rate on a curve, so their employees were probably rated higher than his.

Jamerson' s mood was grim. The director believed her policy was the best way to manage the office. "How can you stimulate people to perform better if they always get high ratings," she said. "Further," he remembered her saying once that "I have to manage my relationships with the Secretary and those outside the agency. Congress and the American people just don't buy that everyone is outstanding."

First, it's important to identify the ethics issue (to make sure there is one!). Bill is torn between his desire to rate his employees according to their performance and management's desire to spread the ratings out to achieve a desired average. This is a "right vs. right" dilemma. There is no law that proscribes the "wrong" thing to do. Both major sides in the case have a point, and there is more than one "right" way to approach this.

Next, Bill has to think about who has a stake in this besides himself. As soon as he realizes why the situation is troubling him, other stakeholders come into view: his employees, his boss, and the director. To push a little further, other managers in the office and their employees are also stakeholders, since the policy he wants to challenge affects them. The employee union also has a stake and could become active on the issue. Even further, the director's concern about how ratings are viewed outside her organization means that higher level officials also have a stake. A "breach" in the attempt to rein in ratings could open the "floodgates" in other parts of the agency. Even the Department's Secretary could be impacted if, in the worst case, a disgruntled employee takes his concern online, to the press or to an outside advocacy group.

Each stakeholder has a set of values that matter. Sometimes the values will be similar to the values of others, but they will not always be interpreted the same way or equally ranked in importance. Box 3.2 shows some of the values at work here, in terms of how the stakeholders may rank them.

Box 3.2
Values in the Bill Jamerson Case

Bill Jamerson	Bill's Employees	The Director	The Secretary
Truthfulness	Fairness	Effectiveness	Effectiveness
Loyalty	Compassion	Credibility	Efficiency
Career Advancement	Rewards	Efficiency	Service
Effectiveness	Loyalty	Loyalty	Freedom of Action

Bill wants to give truthful ratings, based on what the facts warrant. He also wants to be loyal to his employees and bosses and values his career advancement, which could be in jeopardy if he doesn't handle this well. He does value effectiveness, but it's not his primary concern now.

Bill's employees want him to be fair – to rate them on their performance not other concerns. They also want him to be compassionate, to understand their needs as human beings with careers and families. They value the rewards that depend on the rating they get, and they want Bill to be loyal to them.

The director's primary concerns are with the effectiveness of the overall organization and her credibility with her superiors. She values efficiency, including a well-designed and smartly run ratings process, and she expects the people who report to her to be loyal. Note that loyalty matters to several stakeholders, but they think of it in different ways and rank it differently.

The Secretary, who is several steps removed from this immediate dilemma, wants an effective and efficient department. Anything less will be seen as his failure. He values serving his superiors, which may include loyalty but also includes not having distracting issues like this one. He values his freedom of action, which could be compromised if this issue escalates and takes his time and attention away from other priorities.

Clearly, there are value conflicts in this case. Bill's desire to be truthful conflicts with his desire to be loyal to his bosses. Bill's employees expect fairness, which may conflict with the higher value placed on effectiveness and efficiency by superiors. Bill values loyalty to his staff, but this seems to conflict with the director's demand for loyalty to her.[33]

Note also that Bill, if he is honest, has concerns for his own career advancement (and that this value may come into conflict with both truthfulness and loyalty to staff). There is nothing wrong with this. One of Badaracco's eight tactics for quiet leaders is "trust mixed motives" (see Box 3.3). Badarraco argues that our motives (and the values underlying them) are rarely singular in nature. If we act like they are, we hurt our ability to think creatively about solutions to an ethical dilemma. Note also the first tactic – "don't kid yourself." Your first thoughts about an ethical dilemma rarely surface everything you need to know and think about. This also connects with "buy a little time," because it takes time to think through an ethical dilemma, as we are seeing with Bill Jamerson.

Box 3.3
Eight Tactics for Quiet Leaders

- Don't Kid Yourself
- Trust Mixed Motives
- Buy a Little Time
- Invest Wisely
- Drill Down
- Bend the Rules
- Nudge, Test, and Escalate Gradually
- Craft a Compromise

Source: Badaracco (2002)

There is yet another way to think about the value conflicts in an ethics case. Kidder suggests that there are four "global" value conflicts. Any ethical dilemma is likely to involve one or more of these:[34]

- Truth vs. Loyalty
- Justice vs. Mercy
- Short-Term vs. Long-Term
- Individual vs. Community

Bill's concern for truth, as we have seen, clearly conflicts with the demands on him to be loyal. The short-term need to please his bosses seems to conflict with the long-term need to maintain effective working relationships in his team. The need for individual employees to get the rating they deserve seems to conflict with the director's concern to pay attention to the demands and expectations of the broader public and political community.

Clearly, a lot of values are in play in this case. Bill's goal ought to be to find a solution which honors as many of them as possible, though at some point he may have to make a final ranking among them to decide what to do. But that point has not arrived. For now, he just needs to understand what values and value conflicts are "alive" in the dilemma. He also needs to get his facts straight. That can be more difficult than it seems.

Consider the list in Box 3.4 and decide which statements are facts in this case.

Box 3.4
Fact or Assumption?

Which of the following statements are facts in this case?

1. The director will no longer tolerate too many high ratings.
2. The distribution of ratings for Bill's unit must be a bell curve.
3. Ratings will be sent back if they do not meet the overall average of 400 for the unit.
4. An employee cannot get a promotion without a high rating.
5. Bill cannot ignore the director's policy.
6. Not all other offices in the bureau follow the policy that Bill's director has established.
7. Bill's peers will not allow him to rate his workers in violation of the director's policy.
8. If everyone gets a high rating, there is no incentive to improve.
9. It's up to Bill to resolve this ethical dilemma.
10. The numerical rating system is the approach that must be used.

On first examination, these would all seem to be facts in the case. Yet, for Bill, with the exception of number 6, all are assumptions. They may flow logically from the case, but that does not make them facts. For example, Bill had success last year in escaping the harsh limits of the "400 average" rule, so items 1, 2, 3, and 5 are assumptions. While a high rating helps get a promotion, it does not follow that promotions are impossible without such a rating, so number 4 is also an assumption. While Bill's peers were not happy that his unit got more high ratings last year, that does not guarantee that they will (or can) stop him from awarding high ratings again this year, so number 7 is also an assumption. Number 8 may be a fact for the director, but, for Bill, it is an assumption that could be challenged. Number 9 would seem to be a fact but is also an assumption. Bill does need to address this dilemma, but it's not his dilemma alone. At least his boss and the director must face this dilemma, because all three of them will suffer consequences from not handling it well. Finally, number 10 is also an assumption – at least in considering the long term. While Bill may not be able to change the system by himself or this year, nothing demands that the numerical rating system must prevail for all time to come, especially if it is causing such problems.

This parsing of assumption vs. fact may seem a minor point. After all, Bill is weighed down with these issues, whether they are facts or assumptions. But an assumption can be tested and challenged, while a fact cannot. Among Badaracco's eight tactics, four of them rely on this. If you "drill down," you can uncover facts and distinguish them from assumptions. An assumption suggests the possibility for you to "bend the rules," "nudge, test, and escalate gradually," and "craft a compromise." In short, assumptions open up options.

Identify Options

Ideally, Bill would like to resolve this dilemma in a way that allows him to do right by his employees and also meet the legitimate concerns of his superiors. He also, in Badaracco's terms, needs to "invest political capital wisely." He can't be seen as "going to the mat" on every issue that matters to him.

There are two extremes he needs to avoid. The first is to rate his employees exactly how he wishes irrespective of the consequences. The second is to follow the director's guidance and ignore in some cases the higher rating an employee deserves. To do the first could jeopardize his career as well as his ability to get the resources and support he needs from higher levels in the future. To do the second would violate his most important values – truthfulness and loyalty to his staff – and could destroy the trust of the team in his leadership. He seems caught between the proverbial rock and a hard place.

Bill needs to avoid the most common fault in decision making - viewing the decision in "either-or" terms. In a study of 169 major business decisions, management researchers found that 71 percent of them were posed as having only two choices. That is, they were "either we do this or we do that."[35] What Bill needs is more options. By its nature, the initial definition of an ethical issue as a "dilemma" leads to the assumption that there are only two choices. Bill needs what Kidder calls at least one "trilemma" option.

Said another way, Bill has to reframe the ethical issue. He needs what DePaul University ethicist Patricia Werhane calls "moral imagination." "As Werhane puts it, "[M]ost managers and their institutions do not lack moral principles. Rather, they sometimes have a narrow perspective on their situation."[36]

There are at least four tools Bill can use to generate options. These are: (1) assumption testing, (2) moral empathy, (3) the ethical triangle, and (4) conversational inquiry.

Assumption Testing

If some of the supposed "facts" of the case are actually assumptions, then mentally testing them may suggest options for resolving the ethical dilemma. For example, since the director did tolerate higher ratings than desired last year (countering assumption 1), perhaps there is leeway to submit ratings that exceed the "400" average again this year. Since some people who got high ratings last year deserve them again this year, such ratings do not necessarily destroy the incentive to improve (countering assumption 8). Bill might use this as evidence in conversations with his boss and the director.

Moral Empathy

Moral empathy is the ability to see an ethical dilemma from others' vantage points. As Werhane suggests, it takes more work to see how others may look at it, but that work can pay off. Look at the questions in Box 3.5.

These questions suggest options. Consider these examples:

- Perhaps Bill's boss and the director do not even see an ethical dilemma. That suggests he might talk with them about the issue he sees and the potential dangers to them in pursuing the course they have asked him to follow.

- Seeing the values that matter to the director, Bill might think about ways to frame the issue in terms of how it will promote the effectiveness of the entire organization by avoiding a huge morale issue and tying up time in dealing with potential employee or union grievances or EEO complaints.

- What Bill considers assumptions in the case may be what the director thinks are facts. She thinks that a pattern of high ratings is just not acceptable outside the agency. Bill may have to consider a way to diplomatically show that this is an assumption, not a fact. Sometimes ethical conflicts are just over values, but they can also be due to different views on what the facts are.

- Bill might also ask his boss and his peers what other options they see to address the issue. He could well get ideas he never thought about.

Box 3.5
Moral Empathy

As You See It	**As Others See It**
What is the ethical dilemma?	What is the ethical dilemma?
What's at stake for you?	What's at stake for them?
What values are primary for you?	What values are primary for them?
What are the facts? assumptions?	What are the facts? assumptions?
What options do you see?	What options might they see?
What are the dangers for you of acting as directed?	What are the dangers for them of acting as directed?
How can your core values be satisfied?	How can their core values be satisfied?

The Ethical Triangle

The ethical triangle (Figure 3.1) is a simple yet powerful model devised by Arizona State University political scientist James Svara.[37] Each point of the triangle poses a question, and each question can generate options. For example, the "principles" point asks: "what principles are at stake and what actions follow from these principles?" The "consequences" point asks: "what is the greatest good for the greatest number?" The "virtues" point asks "what would a person of good character and integrity do?"

Since each point looks at the ethics issue differently, posing all three questions makes sure you don't overlook something. According to Svara, that gets you closer to the center triangle, leading to a better resolution of the ethics issue because you have considered it more comprehensively. Note also that there is a danger in thinking about an ethics issue from only one point of view. If you take only the "virtue" point, you might answer its core question as "I must be courageous. I can't be bought off by other considerations." While temporarily comforting (we all like to think we will not compromise our core values), in Bill's case that firm stand closes off thinking about options and may hurt employees, the organization, and Bill himself.[38]

Figure 3.1
The Ethical Triangle

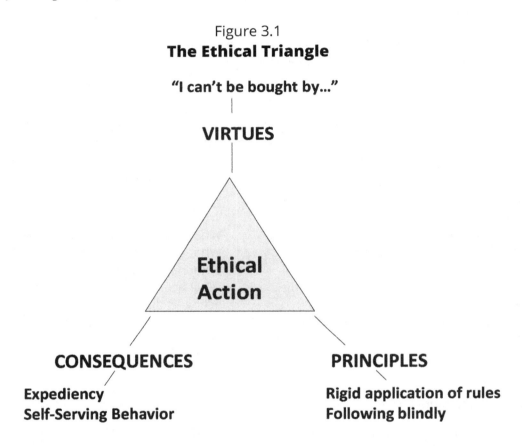

From James Svara, "The Ethical Triangle: Synthesizing the Bases of Administrative Ethics," in *Public Integrity Annual*, ed. James S. Bowman (Lexington, KY: Council of State Governments, 1997). © 1997 by M.E. Sharpe, Inc. Used by permission.

Note also that the ethical triangle can help Bill diagnose how other stakeholders see the issue. The director, for example, is clearly concerned about consequences, what she defines as the greatest good for the greatest number. Bill might consider helping her see that there are some broader principles at stake, such as the need to maintain employee morale for long-term effectiveness. It will not be to the greater good of the organization or the public if the ratings process produces internal turmoil, damaging mission effectiveness.

Conversational Inquiry

The previous approaches can be used alone. It is better to engage others (especially other stakeholders) in shared inquiry - a process that opens up thinking. It is not the same as "discussion." Discussion can easily devolve into arguing. People advocate their point of view, trying to prove they are right. But as we know with ethical dilemmas, there can be many "right" ways to proceed. As Figure 3.2 shows, when a group uses inquiry, they talk to discover not persuade. They search for alternatives. They invite criticism and dissent, and they aim for collective ownership. That is exactly the atmosphere needed to resolve an ethical dilemma. This is not to demean the importance of advocacy. At some point, organizations need people to argue for a particular course of action. But with ethical dilemmas, it is usually best not to do that too soon.

A simple way to see if you are in advocacy mode is to ask yourself, while someone else is talking: "Am I listening or am I formulating an argument to counter what I am hearing?" If it's the latter, you are in advocacy mode.

What would happen if Bill went to his boss in advocacy mode? His boss might shut down, argue back, and each of them would be locked in a contest of wills. However, if Bill approached his boss in inquiry (and his boss agreed to such a conversation) they could explore many of the values and options we have discussed – and might well find other options too.

Figure 3.2
Two Modes of Exploring an Issue

Inquiry vs. Advocacy

Inquiry	Advocacy
• Collaborative problem solving	• A contest of wills
• Talk to discover	• Talk to persuade
• Remain open to alternatives	• Defend your position
• Invite criticism	• Downplay criticism
• Cultivate dissent	• Discourage dissent
• Aim for collective ownership	• Aim to win

If Bill has done his ethical thinking well, by this point he has a clear understanding of the values at work, the true facts of the situation, and he has multiple options to consider. A short list of at least some of them is in Box 3.6. Note that the first two options are where Bill started, but he has been able to add many others.

Box 3.6
Options to Address "What Rating Do I Give?"

1. Rate each employee according to performance, ignoring the requirement to reach an average score of 400 across the unit.
2. Prepare the ratings to achieve the average score of 400.
3. Meet with the boss to share the dangers of adhering to a "bell curve" and explore a strategy for proceeding.
4. Meet with other supervisors to explore how they see the issue and what options may exist for collective action to resolve it.
5. Gather data to persuade the director that: (a) high ratings do not dampen the incentive to improve and (b) a forced rating distribution could create even bigger problems for her and those above her.
6. Identify ways to provide recognition - to employees who have performed well – that are not contingent on a specific rating.
7. Show the director why this is an ethical issue and seek her commitment to find a resolution that meets her values too.
8. Push back gently by submitting draft ratings that are somewhat above the "400" average.
9. Identify why other units in the agency are not bound by the "bell curve" policy and use that information to identify ways to approach the boss and the director.
10. Demonstrate why organizational effectiveness may actually decrease if lower ratings are forced into the overall distribution.
11. Explore whether other rating systems might be better to propose, if not this year then for the future (e.g. "pass-fail").

Ready to Decide?

All that seems to remain is for Bill to make a decision. But things are not always as they seem. Before Bill can choose one (or more) of these options, he needs to be aware that there may be subtle biases and errors in his thinking about the ethical dilemma and the people involved. The brain, as it turns out, is not a purely logical processing machine.

–4–
WHY IS DECISION MAKING SO TOUGH?

"The heart has its reasons of which reason knows nothing."   — Blaise Pascal

In a 1970s experiment, researchers tested whether a stranger who dropped papers outside a phone booth in a shopping mall would get help from a person coming out of the phone booth. This seems like a simple ethical decision: do I delay where I am going next so I can help a stranger? In the control condition, with the facts as you just read them, only one person in 25 stopped to help the stranger (4 percent). Yet, when the researchers made sure that the person in the phone booth first found change in the phone's coin return slot, 6 out of 7 helped the stranger (86 percent).[39] Can ethical thinking be shifted by something so subtle?

We like to think that reason governs our ethical decisions. We can name stakeholders, identify value conflicts, generate options, and pick the best one. Nearly 250 years ago, Benjamin Franklin penned a decision making approach that is still strikingly familiar:

> *"My way is to divide half a sheet of paper by a line into two columns; writing over the one Pro and over the other Con. Then during three or four days' consideration, I put down under the different heads short hints of the different motives, that at different times occur to me, for or against the measure. When I have thus got them altogether in one view, I endeavor to estimate their respective weights; and where I find two, one on each side, that seem equal, I strike them both out. If I judge some two reasons con equal to some three reasons pro, I strike out five; and thus proceeding, I find where the balance lies; . . . I come to a determination accordingly."[40]*

As the phone booth study suggests, however, we are not logical automatons. Even in Franklin's scheme, the weighting has inherent subjectivity. Our emotions demand attention. We think, but we also feel. That, as it turns out, is a very good thing. Yet it means we need to understand how our

47

brains work if we are to avoid serious mistakes. Considering the case of Bill Jamerson in the last chapter, he needs to make sure, in reaching his decision, that he does not fall victim to these mistakes.

Mistake#1: Failing to Integrate Reason and Emotion

Consider the following now-classic experiment, and decide what you would do.

A trolley is speeding down the tracks towards a Y-shaped junction. On one side of the Y are five workers, laying on the track to repair it. They have ear plugs on to muffle the surrounding noise. On the other side of the Y is one worker, also laying on the track and wearing ear plugs. You see that the trolley will take the fork in the Y towards the five workers. It will kill them because they cannot hear it coming. You cannot warn them because they cannot hear you. You spot a lever next to you and realize that if you pull it, the trolley will divert to the side of the Y that has only one worker. It will kill him. Would you pull the lever, knowing that this will kill one worker but save the lives of five others? Answer before reading further.

Now consider yourself in a similar situation, with a trolley again speeding down a track. This time, you are standing on a footbridge over the track. There is no Y in the track; it is a single straight track. There are five workers laying on it, wearing ear plugs. You cannot warn them. Now you notice that a very heavy (350 pound) man is standing in front of you on the footbridge. You realize that if you push him from behind, using all your weight, he will fall on the track, the trolley with hit and kill him, but he will thus top the train before it hits the five workers. You are not big enough, so you cannot jump off the footbridge instead. Would you push the man onto the track? Once again, answer before reading further.

Most people, presented with the first situation, decide to pull the lever, saving five lives. Most people, presented with the second situation, do not push the man onto the track. From a logical standpoint, this makes no sense. In both cases, you can save five lives at the expense of one life. The utilitarian point of view (greatest good for the greatest number) should make this an easy choice in both cases.

How can we explain this? Researchers can observe the brains of subjects in this kind of experiment using functional Magnetic Resonance Imaging (fMRI), a method that shows the parts of the brain firing (using energy) when engaged in decision making. When subjects work on the trolley dilemma, researchers find that two centers of the brain – the amygdale (an older part of the brain in evolutionary terms and one concerned with emotions) and the ventromedial prefrontal cortex (which integrates emotions into thinking) - fire more with the *push* option. In short, our emotions take control as we find the thought of pushing the man abhorrent. They also note that the dorsolateral prefrontal cortex (one of the most recently evolved parts of the brain and associated with higher-level, cognitive thinking) fires only for those who overcome the emotional reaction to pushing and decide, from a utilitarian standpoint, that this is in fact the best thing to do.

Harvard University researcher Joshua Greene explains these findings.[41] Most people have a harder time with the *push* scenario because it is very personal. This is a good thing. If all of our thinking was strictly utilitarian, we could make some very bad ethical choices, such as abandoning our elderly parents. After all, there is probably little that they can do for us near the end of their lives (especially if they have no inheritance to pass on).[42]

It also takes longer in the footbridge (*push*) scenario for people to decide what to do because their emotions are fighting with their reasoning and that slows them down.[43] For some, they agonize and conclude that they just cannot push the man. For those who do decide to push him, they have had to overcome that emotional response by applying reason to justify their impending action.

Greene says that we have a "dual-process" brain. We have an "automatic mode" that is driven by our emotions and we have a "manual mode" that is designed for the application of reason. Reason may confirm or over-ride the emotional response but, to make the best decisions, we have to call upon both. (There is a danger, of course, which we will explore later. In some cases, we use reason to convince ourselves that our emotional reaction is OK even if it is not. This is what we call "rationalization.")

There are several implications from such findings for public servants who face ethical dilemmas:

- Don't kid yourself that you can make purely logical decisions on ethics issues.
- Probe for your emotions when you face a dilemma. They exist and are trying to tell you something. They may suggest that the course of action you are about to take is really not the best response.
- When your emotions are engaged, give yourself some time to apply reason to your thinking. But watch out for rationalizations.

Mistake #2: Basing Ethical Actions on Beliefs Not Facts

People who can integrate reason and emotion will make better ethical decisions. Unfortunately, when our emotions are involved, we often don't even know how they are impacting our decision making.

This can happen in very subtle ways. The result is that we may actually *think* we are acting based on the facts in a situation when we are really basing our decision on beliefs, shaped as they are by all kinds of things other than facts.

Harvard business professor Chris Argyris captured this problem in a concept he called the Ladder of Inference (Figure 4.1).[44] According to Argyris, we assume that we act based on data we observe in the world, anchoring our actions on hard, objective evidence. But, being human, we can't possibly attend to all the data in a situation. We selectively attend to some data not others, driven by everything from limited time to perceptual difficulties to our emotions. Using the data we have selected, we place meaning on the situation. We are meaning-making beings and can do no other. Thus, for example, one person selecting a particular set of climate data decides that it supports the concept of global warming while another, attending to a different set of data, sees just warmer temperatures in some areas and cooler temperatures in others. As we ascend the Ladder of Inference, we next make assumptions based on the meanings we have assigned (e.g. climate change is due to human activity or temperature changes are just due to natural variation.) Those assumptions lead to conclusions (e.g. we need a carbon tax or we need to stay out of international climate talks), which often become strongly held beliefs, and then we take action based on those beliefs.

The implications of the Ladder of Inference can lead us ethically astray. Once we start to ascend its rungs, we may become so anchored in the meanings, assumptions, conclusions, and beliefs that emerge that some ethical actions become impossible to consider and others gain such emotional commitment that we cannot see that they are based on selected data - a partial snapshot of the context in which the ethical dilemma is embedded - and a host of emotion-filled meanings, assumptions, conclusions and beliefs.

The Ladder of Inference can be helpful, however, if we use it to probe our thinking:

- What data am I seeing and what data might I be ignoring or missing? How can I involve others, who may see things I miss and thus enrich my picture of the situation?

- Where am I on the Ladder of Inference? How might my understanding of the "facts" of the ethical situation be affected by my assumptions, conclusions, and beliefs?

- Where do my assumptions come from? How might I act if I made a different set of assumptions?

- Since we usually go up the Ladder of Inference in our thinking, how might my ethical thinking be affected if I went down one rung or more? For example, how might my beliefs about an ethical situation be leading me to selectively attend to certain data and not others? How might my conclusions be locking me into certain assumptions?

Figure 4.1
The Ladder of Inference

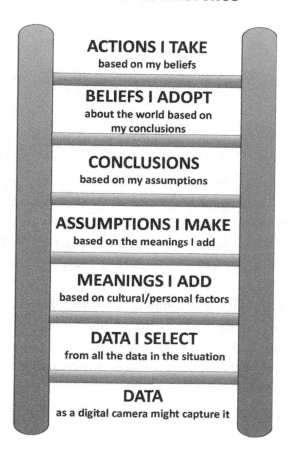

ACTIONS I TAKE
based on my beliefs

BELIEFS I ADOPT
about the world based on
my conclusions

CONCLUSIONS
based on my assumptions

ASSUMPTIONS I MAKE
based on the meanings I add

MEANINGS I ADD
based on cultural/personal factors

DATA I SELECT
from all the data in the situation

DATA
as a digital camera might capture it

Mistake #3: Allowing Status Threats to Overwhelm Good Thinking

Another way that emotions get engaged in organizational life is through our concern with status. In the popular movie, *A Few Good Men*, actor Jack Nicholson plays Col. Nathan Jessep, the Marine Corps Commandant at Guantanamo Naval Base, Cuba. In an early scene, Jessep confronts what to do about a letter written by Pfc. William Santiago to Jessep's superiors in Washington, DC, requesting a transfer off the base. Santiago has had trouble doing hard physical drills (we later learn he has a serious medical condition) and in fact had already written several such letters. In this latest one, he offered to provide evidence of a fence-line shooting incident that might embarrass Jessep were it known in headquarters. In the scene, Jessep is meeting with his second in command, Col. Matthew Markinson, and Jessep's aide, Lt. Jonathan Kendrick. Here is dialogue from that scene:

Col Jessep: What is going on in Bravo Company?

Col. Markinson: Can we discuss it in private?

Lt. Kendrick: I can handle this situation, sir.

Markinson: Don't interrupt, I'm your superior!

Jessep: And I'm yours, Matthew. What are we going to do about this?

Markinson: He should be transferred [off the base] at once.

Jessep: He's that bad?

Markinson: If word of this letter gets out, he'll get his ass whipped.

Jessep: Transfer Santiago? You're right. Yes, that's the thing to do. Wait! I've got a better idea. Let's transfer the whole squad... No, let's transfer the whole division off the base. Jon, go and tell the boys to pack their bags.

Tom! [his adjutant] Get me the President. We're surrendering our position in Cuba... Wait a minute, Tom. Maybe we should consider this for a second... Dismissed, Tom.

Maybe it's our responsibility to train Santiago. Maybe we have a responsibility to this country to see that those protecting it are trained professionals. I think I read that somewhere once. And I'm thinking, Colonel, that your idea of transferring Santiago, while expeditious and painless, might not be quite the American way.

Santiago stays where he is. We're going to train the lad. Jon, you're in charge.

What Jon is then directed to do is to administer a "Code Red" to Santiago – an administrative punishment (that the Marine Corps had previously prohibited) meant to shape him up. Meted out by two other Marines, the Code Red consists of entering Santiago's room in the middle of the night, gagging him, and tying him up. Because of his underlying medical condition, Santiago dies as a result.

We might wonder why Jessep gets so angry about a lowly private, why he abandons reason to make such a poor ethical decision. In short, Jessep feels threatened - by Santiago's presumed challenge to his authority in writing the letters and by being what Jessep considers a "substandard Marine." Jessep also gets angry at Markinson for intervening with Kendrick. Both acts are a threat to Jessep's status (amply fed by his ego). Research shows that when status is threatened, the same areas of the brain fire as when we are in physical pain.[45] In short, status threats hurt. You can spot this not only when superiors feel threatened by their direct reports but when anyone feels that their expertise, credibility, or position in a group is challenged. Most of us have a strong need for feeling that we are at or near the top in any social ranking.[46]

Since status usually matters to people in organizations, there are several implications for ethical behavior:

- Raise the perceived status of those in an ethical conversation. A feeling of enhanced status actually releases chemicals in the brain that promote clear thinking. For example, when the group first meets to confront the ethical dilemma, begin by speaking about each member of the group, their skills and their importance in the decision making task.
- Have a "second chance" meeting to revisit an initial decision - so that emotions (including concerns about status) can cool down.
- If you are the leader, minimize status differences in the process of reaching an ethical decision. For example, sometimes you may need to stay out of the process at least some of the time, while the issue is being discussed and options explored. This creates a more level playing field. During the Cuban Missile Crisis, President Kennedy stayed out of most meetings so participants could speak freely without worrying about his reactions and what this meant about their status in the group.

Mistake #4: Coming to an Ethical Decision When Mentally Taxed and Tired

The brain is an energy sponge. Only two percent of the body's weight, it consumes about 25 percent of all the glucose in our system.[47] In doing all the work of dealing with reason and emotion in ethical situations, the brain uses even more energy than normal.[48]

For example, deciding whether to grant parole (or changes in parole conditions) to a felon is an ethical decision that requires carefully weighing the needs and conflicting values of various stakeholders. A study of the parole decisions of ten Israeli judges in 1,112 cases over a ten-month period produced the graph in Figure 4.2. The dashed vertical lines represent breaks that the judges took during the day. What do the data suggest?

Time of Day

Since the cases were randomly spread across both the judges and the time of day, the most plausible explanation is that something extraneous to the cases must be causing the spikes (favorable decisions for the prisoner) and dips (unfavorable decisions). In fact, a prisoner is more likely to get a favorable ruling at the start of the day and after the judge has taken a refreshment break. The study authors speculate that these results may be "consistent with previous research demonstrating the effects of a short rest, positive mood, and glucose on mental resource replenishment."[49] In short, after working hard, the brain gets tired. A gain of energy (from more glucose) and a more positive mood (from rest and food) may well lead to ethical decisions that are less biased. At any rate, a prisoner's chance for parole should not depend on the time of day the judge picks up his case.

Figure 4.2

Proportion of Rulings in Favor of Parole

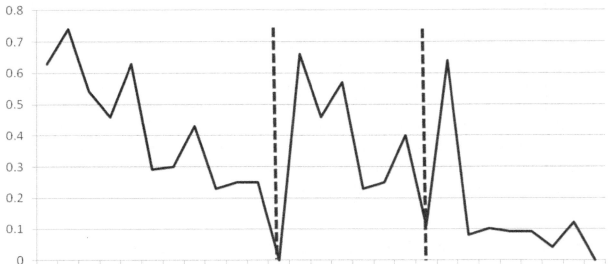

But it's not just low energy that poses a problem for the ethical brain. Too many demands at the same time can cause problems too. David Rock, a professor who specializes in integrating brain science with leadership, notes that the prefrontal cortex of the brain – the part just behind the forehead – is where conscious thought works to make decisions. Rock likens the brain to a stage in a play. All kinds of inputs (the actors) want to be on the stage, and the job of the director (the prefrontal cortex) is to control the process to produce the best performance.

Managing energy demands, as we have seen, is one such task of the director. Another is to manage how much information floods the stage at a time. Research suggests that we can only hold four to seven discrete bits of information in short-term memory, where we have to work with it. Thus, too much information at once can degrade decision making. Related to this is the problem of multi-tasking. We think we can juggle a lot of mental balls at the same time, but the reality is less comforting. For example, one experiment, as Rock reports, "had volunteers rapidly pressing one of two foot pedals to represent when a high or low tone sounded. This exercise took a lot of attention. When researchers added one more physical task, such as putting a washer on a screw, people could still do it but experienced a 20 percent decrease in performance. Yet when they added a simple mental task to the foot-pedal exercise, such as adding up just two single-digit numbers, (a simple 5 + 3 =), performance fell 50 percent."[50] Task interference thus impairs thinking (no matter what your kids may tell you).

There are a number of implications for ethical decision making from these and other studies of the brain's capacities and limits:

- Make tough ethical decisions early in the day when you are rested and more energetic. If you make a decision later in the day or when you feel tired, revisit the decision when your energy has been replenished.
- To decide effectively, guard the level of complexity and amount of information you try to deal with. Use visuals to summarize lots of data; chunk the data into smaller segments; prioritize so you don't tackle everything at once.
- Don't multi-task. You will sacrifice quality for quantity.
- Keep distractions off the decision-making stage. These can be external (e.g. competing tasks, interruptions) or internal (e.g. emotions, thoughts about other parts of your day, events in your personal life). They eat up energy and keep important information away from getting on the stage.
- If you feel overwhelmed, it is a sign that your prefrontal cortex is not at peak efficiency. Stress is a signal that your limbic system (buried deeper in the brain) is taking energy needed by the prefrontal cortex. So, calm the limbic system down through physical exercise or a break. Then, return to the ethical dilemma. This does not mean you ignore what the limbic system (emotions) may be telling you. You just need to adjust the balance between reason and emotion.

Mistake #5: Thinking Too Fast

One way the brain responds to the fact that it has limited energy resources is to take short cuts that use less energy. Answer the following question. Don't spend a lot of time on it. Just jot down the first answer that comes to you:

A bat and a ball cost $1.10. The bat costs one dollar more than the ball. How much does the ball cost?

If you answered 10 cents, you are in good company. You are also wrong. Eighty percent of students at typical colleges agree with you, as did 50 percent of students at Harvard, Princeton and MIT. But if the ball costs 10 cents, then the bat (which costs one dollar more than the ball) would cost $1.10 and the total would be $1.20. The correct answer for the cost of the ball is five cents.

Once you know the answer, it seems obvious. So why do we get it wrong? Daniel Kahneman, a Nobel-prize winning behavioral economist who uses this simple test, suggests that our brains have two ways to think. He calls these thinking fast and thinking slow (see Figure 4.3).[51]

When confronted with most mental challenges, we prefer to think fast (System 1), because that saves energy. In fact, as Kahneman argues, we can't turn off this mechanism because it is so useful from an evolutionary standpoint. If a wild animal came to the front of your cave, you reacted. Those who stopped to think were not around to think much longer. To use a modern example, consider the decisions you make between getting out of bed and going to work. There are dozens. If you had to stop and think, confronting each decision (e.g. what's the best way to take a shower?) as if you had never encountered it before, you'd be mentally exhausted (and no doubt late) by the time you left home. So you fall back on mental routines or heuristics – ways you developed and your brain then encoded - to handle typical situations. Thinking fast is tremendously useful – except when it's not.

In many of the ethical dilemmas we face, the automatic (first) response may not be the best one. For that, you need to think slow (System 2). In fact, you will have to over-ride the problems that thinking fast throws in your way. Consider the case in Box 4.1.

While most might think this inappropriate, it does not seem so to Joe. He thinks of the idea, and then sends out an email to his staff. The downsides don't even occur to him (e.g. some staff may feel compelled to attend or suffer possible consequences; use of government time and space for religious worship). Joe does not, as System 2 would demand, slow himself down, question his model of the world, see if his own biases are leading him astray.

To avoid the problems that can come when inappropriately thinking fast:
- Slow your decision timeframe down. Most ethical decisions do not need to be made "right now." Give yourself time to "think slow."
- Consider if you are under stress, feel pressured, have too much on your plate. These are all signals that you may revert to System 1 thinking when that is not the best thing.
- Test your assumptions – your model of the world. Thomas Jefferson was a lifelong slaveholder. One reason he gave for not freeing his slaves was that they were not intelligent enough to live independently. Yet he refused to educate them, so he had no way of knowing what they were capable of doing. He never challenged his own "mental model."
- Invite others to question your ethical judgment – before you lock yourself in. If Joe had done that, he could have avoided the problems he was sure to create for himself.

Figure 4.3
Two Ways We Think

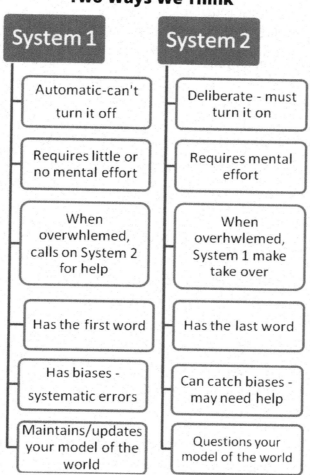

Box 4.1
The Case of "Reverend Joe"

Joe is a very religious man, and he attributes much of his success in government to his faith as well as his hard work. Recently promoted to his first supervisory job, he is anxious to mentor those who report to him. He thinks that short prayer sessions at the beginning of the day would be helpful. He's done this in private but now thinks he should offer his staff the chance to join him – all voluntary of course.

Mistake #6: Avoid Mental Biases and Heuristics

One of the dangers of thinking fast is that it leads us to rely on biases and mental shortcuts that are wrong for the situations we face. That happened to the FBI in an important case.

On May 6, 2004, the FBI arrested Brandon Mayfield as a material witness in the coordinated, May 11th bombings of the commuter train system in Madrid, an attack that killed 191 people and wounded 1,800. Partial fingerprints on a bag containing detonating devices, found by Spanish authorities, had been shared with the FBI. Using an examiner and its computerized fingerprint database, the FBI identified the prints as belonging to Mayfield ("100% verified"). In addition to the initial examiner, two additional examiners also compared the partial prints with Mayfield's and concurred.

Because of its findings, the FBI opened an investigation, including 24-hour surveillance. It then learned that Mayfield was an attorney and a Muslim (he had converted after meeting his wife, an Egyptian national). The FBI also found out that the year before, he had offered legal aid to Jeffrey Leon Battle in a child custody case. Battle was one of the "Portland Seven," convicted of trying to travel to Afghanistan to help the Taliban. But the FBI uncovered no evidence linking Mayfield to the Madrid attacks.

On April 13, Spanish authorities told the FBI that their examination of Mayfield's fingerprints did not yield a match to the partial from the Madrid bombing. The FBI sent an examiner to Madrid on April 21st to justify its conclusion. The Spanish police said they would review their findings again.

In early May, the FBI began receiving media inquiries about a possible American suspect in the Madrid attacks. Concerned that Mayfield's identity might become known, leading him to flee or destroy evidence, they arrested him. He was held for two weeks, with no access to family and limited access to legal counsel. The FBI initially refused to inform either Mayfield or his family why he was being detained or where he was being held.

On May 17, the Court appointed an independent expert to review the FBI's fingerprint identification. Two days later, the expert concurred with the FBI's finding. However, that same day the Spanish National Police informed the FBI that it had positively identified the fingerprint as belonging to an Algerian national named Ouhnane Daoud.

The court released Mayfield to home detention the next day and, on May 24, the FBI laboratory withdrew its identification of Mayfield and he was released from custody. Ensuing lawsuits resulted in a formal apology from the U.S. government and a $2 million settlement.

Assuming that the FBI did not set out to investigate and then arrest an innocent man, what happened? The FBI asked itself the same question. An internal review and an investigation by the Inspector General (IG) of the Department of Justice uncovered the following errors:

- The initial examiner failed to conduct a complete analysis of the partial print before using the computer database to look for a match, leading him to disregard important differences between the partial and Mayfield's prints.

- The power of the database (the system stores millions of prints) and the pressure of the high-profile case were contributing factors.

- The verification by later examiners was "tainted" by knowing what the initial examiner found.

- According to the IG report, "examiners' interpretation of some features [of the latent print] was adjusted or influenced by reasoning backwards from features that were visible in the known prints of Mayfield . . . a process called "circular reasoning."[52]

- When the Spanish National Police (SNP) informed the FBI on April 13 that it had reached a "negativo" (negative) conclusion . . . the FBI Laboratory did not adequately explore the possibility that it had erred . . . before reiterating that they were "absolutely confident" in their earlier identification.

- According to the IG: "the FBI examiners were not aware of Mayfield's religion at the time they concluded Mayfield was the source" [of the latent print]. "However, by the time the SNP issued the April 13 Negativo Report, the Laboratory examiners had become aware of information about Mayfield . . . including the fact that Mayfield had acted as an attorney for a convicted terrorist . . . and was a Muslim."

The mistakes in this case illustrate several dangers that come from mental biases and heuristics that sit as silent traps when we "think fast" in making ethical (and other) decisions. Here are a few of them.[53]

> *Errors of Attention:* We can easily miss or misinterpret important information. We can see things that are not there (biased perception) or miss things that are. In Mayfield's case, the FBI could not see important differences between the partial print from Madrid and Mayfield's prints. It was not looking for these differences, even though they were there from the start.

> *Attribution Error:* We sometimes ascribe facts or characteristics to a person because of his or her demographic, physical, religious or other attributes. When the FBI found out that Mayfield was a Muslim, married to an Egyptian, and had defended a

Taliban supporter, they attributed terrorist tendencies to him, despite lacking evidence to do so.

Confirmation Bias: Once a decision has been made, there is a strong tendency to find confirming evidence for it. After the first examiner concluded there was a match between Mayfield and the latent prints found at the scene so did the other two "independent" examiners and even a court-appointed examiner.

Overconfidence: We can become too confident in our abilities, correctness, data or decisions, leading to the tendency to ignore contrary views. The FBI was "absolutely confident" in their conclusion ("100% verified"). They sent an expert to Madrid to defend it even when the Spanish authorities said that Mayfield's prints were not a match to their suspect. (Notice that a threat to the FBI's status played into this as well.)

Motivated Blindness: Business professor Max Bazerman argues persuasively that we sometimes fail to see what is right in front of us - to notice - because we have a powerful motive to ignore information that might force us to change our minds or act differently.[54] The FBI examiners, and FBI leadership, became so committed to seeing Mayfield as the culprit that they literally could not notice contradictory data.

Sunk Costs: Once we put a lot of effort, resources, and reputation into a decision, we are reluctant to change course. Despite indicators that they were making a mistake, the FBI never gave up on their insistence that Mayfield was guilty – until forced to do so by the arrest of a suspect in Spain.

Anchoring Bias: Sometimes one piece of information serves as an anchor for all future decision making and locks us into a very narrow range of options. Once the FBI concluded that they had a fingerprint match (which was based on a partial not even a full print from the scene), it served to anchor all future decisions.

Can You Ever Make an Error-Free Ethical Decision?

At this point, you may well be wondering if a good ethical decision can ever be made. Given the power of emotions to confound (as well as help) logic, the fact that the brain runs less well when its energy tank is low, and the seeming endless supply of mental errors that are inherent in the way our minds work, how do we ever get it right? Knowing what can go wrong is one part of the answer, because with that knowledge we can spot and adjust for errors. Another part is the importance of engaging others in thinking through an ethical dilemma. They can spot our mistakes (and we theirs) and participate jointly in avoiding others. A final part is to use a good decision making process – one that forces you to ask relevant questions as you reach the point of decision. We encountered some of those questions before – about stakeholders, values, value conflicts, and generating options. But there are still more questions to ask.

WHAT IS THE BEST DECISION?

"Always ask yourself: how would this look in the paper tomorrow morning, even if it looks good now. Would it pass independent judgment? What does your moral compass say?" – interview with a Government Executive

Previously, we left Bill Jamerson pondering his options for dealing with the director's insistence that he rate his employees on a bell curve. He feels that doing so will violate his core values of truthfulness in ratings and loyalty to his staff as well as his employees' core value that they expect him to be fair. He has to keep in mind, of course, that his director has different core values, especially a need for effectiveness and maintaining her credibility with her bosses.

Chastened by the potential pitfalls in decision making that we explored in Chapter 4, Bill knows he has to be careful. He knows he feels very strongly about this, and being objective is not easy when you feel that a part of who you are is being challenged. He feels responsible for protecting his employees. He knows their personal situations. He also knows that his career could be at stake if he does not handle this well. The director, he realizes, is more removed, making it easier for her to call for the forced ratings distribution. Bill also realizes that the director's policy threatens his status, both as a supervisor with control over his own unit and in the eyes of his employees. If he can't "deliver" for them, how can he command their respect to lead? At the same time, he needs to proceed in a way that does not cause the director to feel her status as the leader is threatened; otherwise, she may just dig in her heels.

Bill also knows that he should not (attribution error) cast the director as the proverbial "bad guy" in this situation because she is in top management. If he were in her shoes, he might feel as she does. Just because she has made this policy does not mean she is uncaring. He also knows that, for her, she has put her prestige and management approach on the line for two years on this issue (sunk costs) and will not be dissuaded easily. He can see, as well, that she has staked out a position (the "400" average score) that serves as a key starting point for her (anchoring bias), so this will make any option far from that point hard to sell.

Sensing all this, and knowing that it is late in the day, he decides that he will delay his decision until morning, when he is rested (and his brain has more energy). He also decides that, whatever decision he reaches, he will "sleep on it" - revisit it one day later, just to make sure.

After surfacing and testing assumptions in the case, Bill came up with a set of options to consider. These are reproduced in Box 5.1. His task now is to decide which option(s) to pursue. He needs to keep in mind *his overall goal, which is to do right by his employees and also to meet the legitimate management concerns of his superiors.*

Box 5.1
Options to Address "What Rating Do I Give?"

1. Rate each employee according to performance, ignoring the requirement to reach an average score of 400 across the unit.
2. Prepare the ratings to achieve the average score of 400.
3. Meet with the boss to share the dangers of adhering to a "bell curve" and explore a strategy for proceeding.
4. Meet with other supervisors to explore how they see the issue and what options may exist for collective action to resolve it.
5. Gather data to persuade the director that:
   (a) high ratings do not dampen the incentive to improve and
   (b) a forced rating distribution could create even bigger problems for her and those above her.
6. Identify ways to provide recognition - to employees who have performed well – that are not contingent on a specific rating.
7. Show the director why this is an ethical issue and seek her commitment to find a resolution that meets her values too.
8. Push back gently by submitting draft ratings that are somewhat above the "400" average.
9. Identify why other units in the agency are not bound by the "bell curve" policy and use that information to identify ways to approach the boss and the director.
10. Demonstrate why organizational effectiveness may actually decrease if lower ratings are forced into the overall distribution.
11. Explore whether other rating systems might be better to propose, if not this year then for the future (e.g. "pass-fail").

As he considers these options, Bill will need to ask himself several questions:
1. What core value matters the most for him? For others?
2. What option(s) seem to honor those values?
3. Are potential options:
    a. Legal?
    b. Feasible to implement?
    c. Likely to accomplish the overall goal?
    d. Defensible (should they become public)?
    e. Emotionally satisfying (i.e. people can feel good about them)?
    f. Likely to be still seen as preferable some months or longer down the road?
    g. As disinterested as possible (i.e. he would choose them for someone else if he was not personally involved)?

In his office in the morning, Bill closes the door, silences his cell phone, and even turns off his desktop computer - all to give him undistracted time to think. He fairly easily rules out options 1 and 2 because neither meets his overall goal. He is drawn to option 8, because that's what he did last year and it seemed to work. Yet he's not sure the director will put up with it this time, and some of his peers were upset last year when he got away with it. So, since he would not like them to do this to him, he is reluctant to do it again. Option 9 holds out an intriguing possibility, but he knows it will challenge the director's status since he would have to confront her with it. It would also take a lot of time to implement – time he does not have. Option 11 is also one that, while potentially useful for the future, is not one he can pursue this year.

Bill likes the options that remain, and they suggest a coordinated strategy he can follow. He tentatively decides that he will first express his concerns to his boss by meeting with him (option 3). The meeting is not only necessary to honor his chain of command but because he needs his boss as an ally. Still further, it may uncover options Bill has not considered.

At the same time, Bill decides to meet individually with the other supervisors to see if they share his concern and are willing to work jointly to address the problem (option 4). Since they were upset with him last year when he got higher ratings for his staff, it's a fair bet that they are bothered as well by the director's policy. He also decides he will draft a memo that could be jointly signed (or signed alone if he gets no support from others) and sent to his boss (for transmittal to the director) to: (a) express agreement with the director's overall goal of creating the most effective unit possible, (b) highlight the ethical issue the rating policy presents for first-line supervisors as well as for the director; (c) demonstrate the negative impact on unit effectiveness of a forced rating distribution;

and (d) show that the employees rated high last year performed as well or even better this year (options 3, 4, 5, 7, and 10).

Since Bill is not convinced this strategy will work, he decides to hold two things in abeyance. First, he will draft ratings that come close to the 400 average but exceed it where justified by performance (option 8). He doesn't want to do this, but he knows that if all else fails, he could not live with himself if he did not. Second, he will identify ways to recognize employees, including but not limited to cash incentives, that he can use (option 6). This makes sense as a management strategy regardless of the ratings he can give them. He realizes he should have done this before now.

Bill has made a decision, which he will revisit the next day. But he is not done. He also has to consider how to implement it. Some of the implementation steps are implied, to be sure, in the options themselves. But there are other questions he needs to ask himself (see Box 5.2).[55]

Box 5.2
Implementation Questions

1. PREPARE TO IMPLEMENT:
   a. Who is likely to be injured by your decision?
   b. How might you prevent or mitigate harmful effects?
   c. Who is likely to oppose your decision? How will you deal with their opposition? Consider any of the follow questions that may be relevant:
      i. How can you get them to think about long term as well as short term concerns and benefits?
      ii. How can you get them to consider the broader purpose they seek to serve?
      iii. How can you frame the proposed course of action so that it appears less costly than other options, considering both short and long-term costs of acting or not acting?
      iv. How can you gain allies?
   d. How will you implement and communicate your decision:
      i. With those directly affected?
      ii. With other interested parties?
   e. How can you create a support system for implementation:
      i. For you, especially considering the stress you are under?
      ii. For others affected?
2. IMPLEMENT AND ASSESS:
   a. How will you judge the long-term consequences and the effectiveness of your decision?
   b. When will you revisit the decision to assess its impact on the situation, yourself, and others? How will you do so?

For example, Bill likes to think that his strategy will produce only "winners," but when value conflicts are involved, some may lose (or feel they have lost). So he needs to think about who may be injured and what he can do about it. Clearly, that includes himself. If nothing works and his opposition to the director's policy angers her, his effectiveness and even his future in the organization could be compromised. This is a good time to call on his own support system, especially outside of work, as well as to take care of his health amidst this stress.

It might also be a good time for him to review his career plan and options. While he does not want to lose his job and is not anxious to leave the organization, he is concerned enough about the possibility of both that he should at least mentally ask himself: (a) if he wants to stay in an organization led in this way and (b) what he will do if his boss and/or the director get mad enough that he might be forced to consider other career options. In Joseph Badaracco's terms (see Chapter 3), Bill wants to be a "quiet hero," not one who falls on his sword. But he needs to realize that being so wedded to his job that he can think neither of doing anything else nor of being anywhere else leaves him in a precarious position. He might act unethically just because he has too much to lose.

As yet another strategy, Bill can try to frame the overall issue in terms of broader organizational issues and a long-term time frame. That is, he can try to diffuse some of the conflict by trying to get everyone to step back from the issue of 'what do we rate people this year?' to address 'what is in the organization's long-term interests?' This is where option 11 (moving toward another type of rating system) might make sense. Sometimes we are so mired in the day-to-day that we cannot see the issue from a higher vantage point. It is as if we are stuck in traffic and need to get up in the air above the highway to see another route. A way to do so is captured in the notion of "moral horizons" (Figure 5.1).

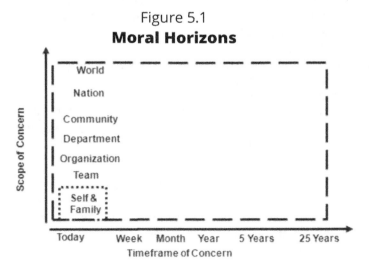

Figure 5.1
Moral Horizons

As the concept of moral horizons suggests, it would be easy – and misleading – for Bill to see the ratings issue as one that involves just him (and because of his career, his family). He knows that it involves his team. But it also involves the whole organization that reports to the director and even the broader department and its effectiveness. It also transcends this year because mishandling the issue now will have an impact on the future, especially if a lot of angry people decide to stay and their anger poisons morale and effectiveness for some time to come.

Clearly, not every ethical dilemma has to be considered in terms of its implications for the world or its impact 25 years in the future. But it is always a good idea to go further up the Scope of Concern and further out the Timeframe of Concern than might be your initial thought. That can open up assumptions, points of view, options, and arguments you may not have considered.

Finally, part of a long-term view is to find a way to judge the consequences of how the ethical dilemma gets resolved. Organizations are prone to "settling" things just so they can move on, but decisions made are often not implemented well and can be remembered in different ways by those with different interests. Also, decisions often produce unintended consequences. So it would be wise for Bill to think about such consequences, how he might deal with them, and how he can follow up with his employees, his boss, and even the director to judge their comfort and satisfaction with how things are progressing.

An especially good tool for thinking about downstream consequences is the Implications Wheel. This technique, devised by futurist Joel Barker, can be used earlier in the decision making process to assess possible and especially unanticipated consequences of taking a particular option. It can also be used here to project what could happen after you act and thus help you think about how you need to prepare for that possibility.[56]

With the Implications Wheel, we place a proposed action for dealing with the ethical dilemma in a circle in the center of the page. Then we ask: what are the potential implications of doing this? Using Barker's technique, we then connect these implications with a single line to the proposed course of action. Then we ask the question again, for each such implication: if this happens, what are the implications? We connect those with a double line, and so on. Using the full technique, we can add weights for the desirability of each implication for a particular audience as well as the likelihood of its occurring. Figure 5.2 shows just a fragment of how this might look.

Notice how even this small start to identifying the implications of an ethical action uncovers possible unanticipated consequences. What if the boss will not even meet with Bill? What does he do then? What if an employee files an EEO complaint – or the union files a grievance?

Figure 5.2
The Implications Wheel

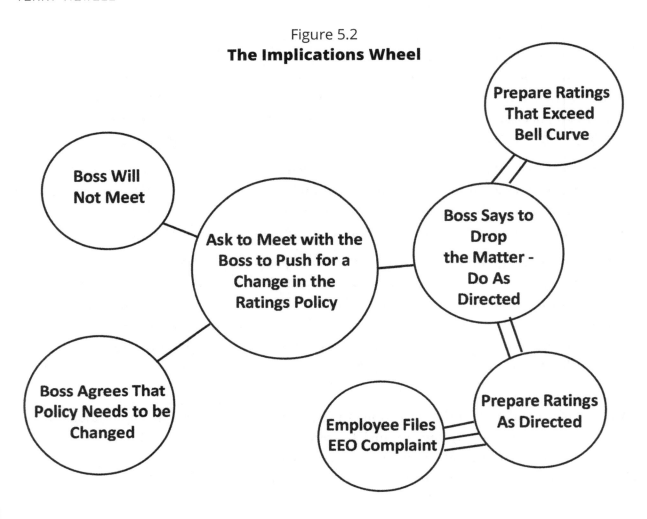

Whether you actually draw an Implications Wheel or not, the potential of thinking this way is helpful. Often, we don't anticipate all of the implications of our actions or think several steps forward in time about the implications of those implications. Constructed individually – or even better with a group – an Implications Wheel can help prevent you from taking imprudent actions and can help prepare you to deal with possible consequences of what you decide to do.

Timing, Temper, Taking It, and the Power of "No"

Public servants who have confronted ethical issues have learned a few other valuable lessons worth remembering when deciding how to act on an ethical dilemma. Here are a few more key points:

- *Timing*: Be careful not to wait too long to tackle an ethics issue. If you do, the situation may deteriorate even further. For example, Bill needs to confront this before other supervisors commit to their ratings. Once they have, his efforts to engage them may be too late and their ratings (especially if they have followed the bell curve) will be a matter of record that constrains his options. On the other hand, he should not act too quickly. He needs some time to "work the issue." As one government executive put it:

   "Sometimes you have to let an ethical issue "ripen." You need to allow others to get concerned about it, bring in others to discuss it, wait for it to percolate up in the organization, or wait for an oversight group to get concerned."

- *Temper:* Stay calm. It's hard to think when you're angry and it's hard to get others to listen. Calmness also has a way of making you more powerful in the situation. As one government leader put it:

   "Calmness can be more effective than anger because you are not rising to another person's level. There are cases where you need to act immediately and with people in the room if something is inappropriate. When you do that, stay calm about it. It has more impact."

- *Taking It:* Living your moral values sometimes comes with a price, and it can be a high price. But that will not always be the case and, even when it is, your career is not necessarily over. In the words of another public servant, sometimes you have to just take the bad that comes from doing the right thing:

   "Put criticism you get in context. You may get criticized for taking an ethical stand, but don't assume that means your career is over. What other messages are you getting about your performance and your reputation? Sometimes doing what is right will not damage your career – realize you can take the consequences of doing the right thing."

- *The Power of "No":* Sometimes you will have to say "no." You will take heat for that, and it may damage your career. But that is not a given. Keep in mind that when you say "no," it will require someone else to say "yes" if they want the (unethical) action to take place. Now the ball will be in their court, and they will have the full weight of the consequences (plus the knowledge that, if they have to defend themselves, people will find out that you advised them against it.) When they have to sign off, instead of getting you to do it, they might just drop the whole thing. Even further, when you say "no," you may get a reputation for being ethically mindful, and that can buttress your leadership credentials – and dissuade people from asking you to compromise your ethics in the future. Again, to hear from a government executive:

> *"Know what your values are and the values of the organization in which you find yourself. If there is a conflict between the two, have the courage to do the right thing because you have to live with you, no matter what. You have to be able to stand up and say 'no can do'."*

A Critical Concern: Organizational Culture

Thus far, we have treated an ethical dilemma as originating with an individual and requiring individual action to resolve it. That is, organizations don't have ethical dilemmas, people do. As ethicist Carol Lewis puts it, "An agency is an abstraction, legal authority, and a set of relationships. It does not really have moral obligations. These are reserved for individuals."[57] Thus, in the end, we cannot avoid those moral obligations or excuse our actions by saying that "the agency did this" or "the organization made me do it". Yet, the organizational culture has a profound impact on ethical behavior in public service. It establishes norms and rules as well as work and decision making processes. It shapes how people think and act. For leaders, it is also something that they create and can change. So, while organizations don't have moral obligations, they certainly have an impact on them. We need to see both how and what that means for public servants.

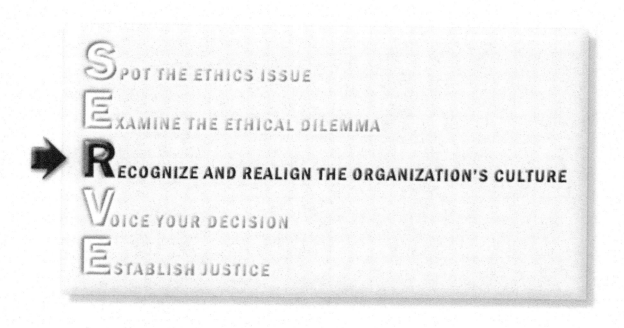

SPOT THE ETHICS ISSUE

EXAMINE THE ETHICAL DILEMMA

➡ **R**ECOGNIZE AND REALIGN THE ORGANIZATION'S CULTURE

VOICE YOUR DECISION

ESTABLISH JUSTICE

—6—
How do organizations foster unethical behavior?

—7—
How can an organization create a positive ethical culture?

—8—
Why do good leaders do bad things?

–6–
HOW DO ORGANIZATIONS FOSTER UNETHICAL BEHAVIOR?

"The ultimate answer to ethical problems in government is honest people in a good ethical environment. No web of statute or regulation, however intricately conceived, can hope to deal with the myriad possible challenges to a man's integrity or his devotion to the public interest."
— President John F, Kennedy, Message to Congress, April 27, 1961

"Chip" Frederick was a corrections officer in Dillwyn, Virginia, before being called up as an Army reservist to serve as the senior enlisted man in Abu Ghraib prison in Iraq in the fall of 2003. A year later, he was sentenced to eight years in prison for sexually and physically abusing prisoners, including carrying out a mock electrocution of a detainee. As recounted by social psychologist and Stanford University professor Philip Zimbardo, who served as an expert witness for the defense, Frederick said "What I did was wrong, and I don't understand why I did it."[58]

Frederick was not the only ethical problem for the U.S. Army. In early 2007, a survey of U.S. soldiers serving there found that one-third would condone torture if it helped gain useful information about insurgents, and two-thirds would not report a comrade for mistreating a civilian or for destroying civilian property unnecessarily. Gen. David Petraeus, then Commanding General, Multi-National Force – Iraq, admonished his troops when the survey results came out, reminding them that "[T]his fight depends on securing the population, which must understand that we - not our enemies - occupy the moral high ground." The *Counterinsurgency Field Manual*, which Petraeus co-authored that same year, contains an entire chapter devoted to "Leadership and Ethics for Counterinsurgency."[59]

It would be comforting to explain away "Chip" Frederick as the proverbial "bad apple." Indeed, that excuse was used by many senior officials at the time. Yet, the survey results make clear that Frederick was not alone. Since the Army did not purposely enlist "bad apples," we must consider that perhaps the Army, as it then operated in Iraq, was a "bad barrel." It took ethically normal men and women and turned some of them into unethical soldiers.

This is not a problem for just the military in wartime. The U.S. Office of Personnel Management routinely surveys the federal civilian workforce on a wide range of aspects of the climate in their organizations. Table 6.1 shares data on a question related to ethics:[60]

Table 6.1
Views on the Integrity and Honesty of Leaders of the Civilian Workforce

"My organization's leaders maintain high standards of honesty and integrity."			
	2011	2013	2014
Strongly Agree	19.8%	17.6%	14.9%
Agree	40.2%	37.7%	34.6%
Neither Agree Nor Disagree	22.1%	22.9%	25.5%
Disagree	9.9%	11.4%	11.9%
Strongly Disagree	8.0%	10.6%	13.1%
Note: Percentages saying "Do Not Know" were 0.3% or less and are not shown.			

There is "good news" and "bad news" in these results. The good news is that half of the workforce agrees that its leaders maintain high standards of honesty and integrity. The bad news is that this percentage has dropped from 60 percent to 49.5 percent in just three years and that now more than one in four are not sure and another one in four disagree. To the extent that leaders establish a climate for ethical behavior in their organizations, these are troubling results.

While we may be prone to conclude that the worsening view of leaders over the three-year period coincided with major budget cutbacks and freezes on federal pay and bonuses in the wake of the 2008 financial collapse, the picture was not much brighter in "better" times, as suggested by data from the Ethics Resource Center (ERC), a not-for-profit in Washington, DC. In 2007, the ERC conducted an ethical climate survey of federal workers. Figure 6.1 displays some of its data.[61]

These findings parallel the OPM results. Over half of federal workers believe the ethical culture in their organizations is strong or leaning that way, yet over 40 percent believe it is weak or weak-leaning. The ERC notes that the ethical climate in an organization is not just a function of top leadership but of whether ethical values are embedded in daily work, whether peers support ethical behavior, and whether supervisors reinforce it as well. In this chapter, we'll see what an ethically weak organizational culture looks like and how it gets that way. In the next chapter, we'll look at organizations and practices that foster "good barrels."

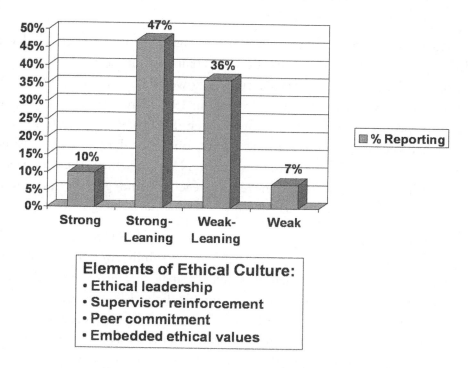

Figure 6.1
Many Federal Agencies Lack a Strong Ethical Culture

The Launch of Challenger: Unethical Behavior That Led to Tragedy

On the morning of January 28, 1986, the space shuttle *Challenger* blew up 73 seconds after launch, killing all seven astronauts, including the first "teacher in space," Christa McAuliffe. The seed for this disaster took root years before. It was fertilized by mostly good people doing some very bad things because of an organizational culture they created.[62]

The story began as the Apollo moon landing program was ending. Looking for its next foray in space, NASA proposed a "Space Transportation System" that would send a "shuttle" into orbit for a variety of missions. Its chief attraction was that the components (the shuttle and the solid rocket motors that lifted it into space) were reusable and could allow frequent flights at reasonable cost.

In November 1973, Morton Thiokol (MTI) was selected to build the solid rocket motors. Though its design was not rated highest, its cost was $100 million lower than competitors. A chief element in

Thiokol's design was that each of the two solid rocket boosters attached to the shuttle's main engine would consist of four stacked sections of solid rocket fuel, separated by "field joints" in which were embedded a primary and secondary O-ring. As the fuel burned in one section, the primary O-ring (a rubber seal, like a vacuum cleaner belt, around the circumference of a booster section) would prevent the hot gasses from escaping, since that could cause a catastrophic explosion. The secondary O-ring was a back-up, in case the primary failed.

The Rogers Commission, established to investigate the disaster, concluded that "the cause of the *Challenger* accident was the failure of the pressure seal in the aft field joint of the right Solid Rocket Motor."[63] Rather than a freak accident, however, potential problems with the O-rings were identified even before the first shuttle flight in 1981. On the second flight, hot gas partially eroded one of the primary O-rings. Yet, the next seven flights were uneventful. In the meantime, President Reagan had declared that the shuttle was "fully operational, ready to provide economical and routine access to space."[64] This put more pressure on NASA to achieve the promised flight schedule of two per month (a rate that would never be reached) and gave it less funding for research and development of what was clearly still an experimental vehicle.

The O-ring hot gas blow-by problem recurred in early 1984, yet the shuttle still flew. This led NASA to proceed on future flights "accepting [the] possibility of some O-ring erosion due to hot gas impingement."[65] In short, what was once a major concern (classified after the first flight as "Criticality-1") was now treated as an acceptable flight risk. After the launch of *Discovery* on January 24, 1985, Thiokol engineer Roger Boisjoly examined the recovered boosters and found black grease on half the circumference of one of the primary O-rings as well as charring on a secondary O-ring. NASA was flirting with disaster. The temperature at launch time had been 53°F, the coldest launch to date.

On July 23, 1985, Richard Cook, a NASA analyst assessing the impact of the seal problem on the agency's budget, warned that "There is little question . . . that flight safety has been and is still being compromised by potential failure of the seals, and . . . failure during launch would certainly be catastrophic."[66] On July 31, Boisjoly sent a memo to Bob Lund, VP of Engineering for MTI, saying that "if we do not take immediate action to dedicate a team to solve the problem . . . then we stand in jeopardy of losing a flight along with all the launch pad facilities."[67] MTI set up a Seal Task Force. By August, MTI had concluded that temperature was a factor, since at colder temperatures the material in the O-ring hardened, making it less pliable and thus harder to fill the space it had to seal. The shuttle continued to fly.

At MTI, the Seal Task Force was making progress at a glacial pace, hamstrung by lack of internal support. A frustrated Bob Ebeling, Task Force Leader, wrote Allan McDonald, MTI's Director of the

Solid Rocket Motor Project, on October 1: "HELP! The seal task force is constantly being delayed by every possible means."[68] A redesign of the boosters was not scheduled until November 1986.

As the January 1986 launch approached, the pressure on MTI and NASA intensified. On January 21, NASA announced that it was seeking a "second source" for the shuttle boosters, a direct challenge to MTI's single source, billion-dollar contract. On the morning of January 27th, the *Challenger* launch was scrubbed for the fourth time, leading ABC's *World News Tonight* to opine that "Once again a flawless liftoff proved too much of a challenge for *Challenger*."[69] President Reagan was scheduled to deliver his State of the Union address the next night, after *Challenger* was in space. On Day 4 of the flight, Christa McAuliffe was to scheduled to teach a lesson. Since that would now be a Friday, further delay would mean she would be teaching on the weekend, when no one was in school.

The projected temperature at launch time was 29 degrees, a full 24 degrees lower than the coldest previous launch. Before *Challenger* could fly, however, approval had to be given at all four ascending levels of the flight readiness review structure, shown in Figure 6.2. MTI would first have to certify that the boosters were a "go" (Level 4). Then, Marshall Space Flight Center (Level 3) would have to give its green light. If it did, the Johnson Space Flight Center in Houston, home of the astronauts, would have to agree. The final "go" for launch then had to come from NASA Headquarters (Level 1).

During the afternoon of January 27th, MTI was asked by Stan Reinartz (Manager, Shuttle Projects Office) and Larry Mulloy (Manager, Solid Rocket Booster Project) at Marshall (Level 3) to assess the impact of the forecast cold weather. MTI VP Bob Lund responded that "it looks to me like 53 degrees is about it. I don't want to fly outside our experience base."[70] Reinartz did not pass this concern on to Level 2; Marshall instead recommended a teleconference with MTI that evening.

The teleconference began at 8:45 pm, with MTI's engineers and management unanimously recommending a launch delay due to the cold weather. Mulloy at Marshall challenged the recommendation. After more than an hour and a half conversation, in which NASA continued to press MTI to defend itself, Joe Kilminster, MTI's VP for the booster program, asked for a five-minute off-line caucus. That conversation lasted a half-hour. At the end of it, MTI management over-ruled its engineers, reversed itself, and went back online to tell NASA it was safe to launch. Roger Boisjoly would later recall that he was so upset that he could not bring himself to watch the launch the next day.

A multi-layered flight readiness review structure, purposely established to ensure safety, failed. Smart individuals who never wanted to risk the lives of the *Challenger* crew did just that. How? There are several ethical landmines they failed to avoid.

Figure 6.2
Flight Readiness Review Structure

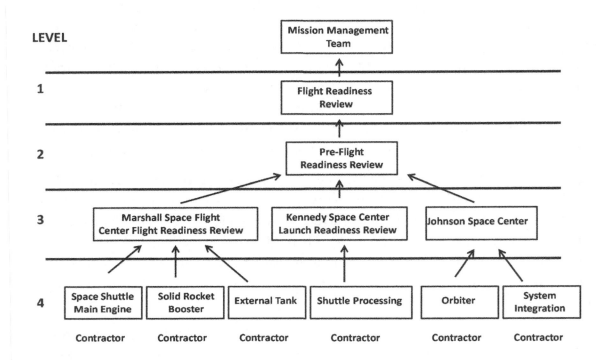

The Subordination of Core Values

Like any organization, NASA was concerned about honoring a number of values in its work. We might easily imagine that, if asked at the start of the shuttle program, the list (for both NASA and MTI) might have looked something like this, in priority order:

Crew Safety

Mission Effectiveness

Efficient Use of Resources/Budget

Loyalty to NASA/Chain of Command

Yet, as the program advanced, it was continually unable to meet an aggressive and promised schedule of two launches a month. Budgets grew tighter once the shuttle was declared "fully operational." As the *Challenger* launch date approached, and was changed four times, the pressure from the media, the White House, and NASA management grew. It appears that the rank order of values inverted over time to something closer to:

Loyalty to NASA/Chain of Command
Efficient Use of Resources/Budget
Mission Effectiveness
Crew Safety

The subordination of crew safety was neither a desired nor even a conscious decision. Concerns about the O-ring's ability to seal had been evident for some time, and MTI had recommended against the launch at the start of the 8:45 pm teleconference. Yet NASA pushed back. MTI management, under pressure, in the words of the Rogers Commission: "reversed its position and recommended the launch of 51-L, at the urging of Marshall and contrary to the views of its engineers in order to accommodate a major customer."[71]

Value conflicts are inherent in organizational life. It is not surprising that NASA and MTI would try to balance conflicting values, but when leaders lose sight of the *priority* in which core values need to be honored, unethical decisions get made. In many organizations, you can hear employees say: "Sure, we have values. They're posted on a chart on the wall, but no one pays attention to them." In this case, it led to the loss of seven lives.

Organizational Norms, Structure and the Normalization of Deviance

The subordination of core values was fostered in part by NASA's very success. It had never lost a shuttle crew, and its Apollo program success – including the recovery of Apollo 13 after a major accident in space – created a norm within the space program that NASA would get the job done no matter what. After the *Columbia* crew was lost in 2003 due to a foam strike on the wing, a Columbia Accident Investigation Board was established. Its report contained a chapter, "History as Cause: Columbia and Challenger," which concluded that very similar mistakes were made in both tragedies:

> *"Despite the constraints the agency was under, prior to both accidents, NASA appeared to be immersed in a culture of invincibility . . . This can-do attitude bolstered administrators' belief in an achievable launch rate, the belief that they had an operational system, and an unwillingness to listen to outside experts."[72]*

Behavioral norms are powerful forces in organizations. They communicate expectations of how to behave as well as what may bring censure. NASA's "can-do" norm operated to its detriment in both shuttle disasters.

NASA did not, of course, just ignore the O-ring problem. The "can-do" norm did not initially overwhelm a significant solid rocket booster flaw. That it did so in time demonstrates the power and subtlety of how organizational norms can chip away at ethical thinking.

As noted, MTI established a Seal Task Force to address the O-ring problem. Yet flights continued. NASA lulled itself into thinking that because an O-ring had not failed that it would not fail. Nobel physicist Richard Feynman, a member of the Rogers Commission, likened this to "a kind of Russian Roulette. [The Shuttle] flies [with O-ring erosion] and nothing happens. Then it is suggested, therefore, that the risk is no longer so high for the next flights. We can lower standards a little bit because we got away with it last time." Sociologist Diane Vaughan termed this the "normalization of deviance."[73]

The normalization of deviance is a danger in any organization. It operates like a "slippery-slope" in which initial ethical transgressions produce no publicly visible damage and so become easier to tolerate. Even this might have been prevented, except for another flaw in NASA's organizational structure. Level 3, set up to prevent a problem at Level 4 from endangering the shuttle, had a conflicting dual mission: protect the crew and launch the shuttle. As the Rogers Commission concluded: "Organizational structures at Kennedy and Marshall have placed safety, reliability and quality assurance offices under the supervision of the very organizations and activities whose efforts they are to check."[74]

The Dangers of Hierarchy

Hierarchy is endemic in large organizations. The larger the organization, the more layers there tend to be. That poses a special challenge: ensuring that those who make decisions have all the information they need. If important information cannot get up or down the hierarchy, unethical action is more likely.

With *Challenger*, the night before the launch, the serious concern about the effect of temperature on the O-rings was communicated within the MTI hierarchy – from engineers to managers at Level 4. Managers communicated that concern to lower-level managers at Level 3, the Marshall Space Flight Center. The concern stopped there. When Jesse Moore at Level 1 gave approval for the launch, he lacked this critical information. Even those at Level 4 who felt that the decision to launch was wrong did not go outside the chain of command to say so.

William Lucas, Marshall's Director illustrates another danger of a rigid hierarchy. As Figure 6.3 shows, Stanley Reinartz reported to Lucas. Unless Reinartz approved the launch, it would have been scrubbed. Lucas told the Rogers Commission that he knew of a concern about 7:00 pm the night before the launch but that, when he saw Reinartz the next morning, he was told the issue had been resolved. When asked if it would have changed his view about the safety of the launch had he known of the unanimous objections raised by the MTI engineers at the evening teleconference, Lucas said that "I'm certain that it would." Lucas thus absolved himself of responsibility. When asked directly if he communicated the O-ring issue to Level 2 (Arnie Aldrich) or Level 1 (Jesse Moore), Lucas replied: "No, sir. That is not the reporting channel. Mr. Reinartz reports directly to Mr. Aldrich."[75]

Yet, it's not quite that simple. An anonymous letter sent to the Marshall Inspector General's Office during the Rogers Commission sheds more light on what took place. Corroborated by other sources, its author maintained that the Flight Readiness Review System was not working:

> "*Rather, it established a political situation within NASA in which no center could come to a review and say that it was 'not ready.' To do so would invite the question, 'If you are not ready, then why are you not doing your job?' . . . Lucas made it known that under no circumstances is the Marshall Center to be the cause for delaying a launch.*" [emphasis in original][76]

Figure 6.3
Level 4 and Level 3 Chain of Command

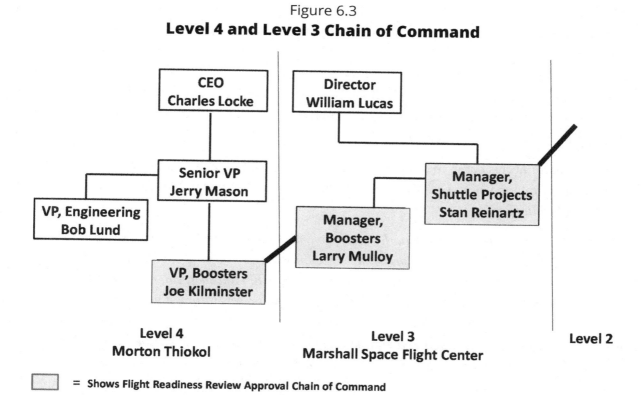

= Shows Flight Readiness Review Approval Chain of Command

In its final report, the Rogers Commission would agree:

> *"The Commission concluded that there was a serious flaw in the decision making process leading up to the launch of flight 51-L. A well structured and managed system emphasizing safety would have flagged the rising doubts about the Solid Rocket Booster joint seal. . . . The Commission is troubled by what appears to be a propensity of management at Marshall to contain potentially serious problems and to attempt to resolve them internally rather than communicate them forward."*[77]

Specialization and the Diffusion of Responsibility

Equally important to hierarchy in large organizations is professional specialization. Without it, accomplishment of complex tasks would be impossible. Ethically, however, the more we divide task accomplishment among different functions and professions, the harder it is to fix responsibility. Anyone can claim "it's their job, not mine" and ethics, especially when tragedy strikes, leads to pointing the finger of fault at someone else.

This can happen in several ways. One disconnect is between managers and professional staff. We've already seen that. Within MTI, engineers and management held different views during the fateful, offline caucus. While all initially recommended delaying the launch, MTI managers changed their position after pressure from NASA. Indeed, as soon as the teleconference caucus began, Jerry Mason, the senior MTI manager present, asked Bob Lund: "[T]o take off his engineering hat and put on his management hat."[78] In about half an hour, the managers voted unanimously to approve the launch (the engineers were not allowed to vote).

A second disconnect is between different technical functions. In the early morning of the launch, the launch pad complex was covered with ice. As management professor Mark Maier recounts in his history of *Challenger*:

> *"The head of the ice team, Charles Stevenson, radioed the Director of Engineering at the Kennedy Space Center to advise him, "'The only choice you've got today is not to go.' The temperature at the joint was measured to be 8°F. However, since the system had not identified any specific launch constraints for joint temperature, it was not reported. A bleary-eyed Larry Mulloy . . . heard Stevenson's remark and thought to himself, 'We aren't going today." . . . Asked why he kept those thoughts to himself, especially in light of his awareness of the earlier Thiokol reservations, Mulloy explained, 'That was out of my territory. I didn't clutter my mind with other people's business.'"*[79]

The ice team did what it was supposed to do, and Larry Mulloy concluded that acting on its findings was not what he was supposed to do. Nor did any launch commit criteria exist for joint temperature (meaning that a launch decision did not formally have to consider temperature). Creating that criterion was presumably someone else's responsibility.

Still a third disconnect was between everyone else and the astronauts (technically part of Level 2). They were never informed of any concerns about the O-rings. Presumably, no one considered that they had any need to know.

A fourth disconnect was inherent in the contracting process. When NASA awarded the contract to MTI, it was not relieved of its ethical obligations to the shuttle and its crew. Yet it distanced itself. When MTI management changed its position on the safety of the launch, it was asked - in an unprecedented step the night before a launch - to put its approval in writing. This allowed Reinartz and Malloy at NASA to distance themselves from responsibility for the fate of *Challenger*.

From a more generic vantage point, research on the brain also alerts us to ethical thinking mistakes that can happen due to specialization. Moral psychologist Joshua Greene argues that moral (ethical) behavior is more likely when the harm we might do is a direct result of an action we take and when we are physically in close proximity to those we would harm. Our brains can more easily handle direct causal chains than the complexity arising from numerous, uncertain (and unintended) side effects of our actions. We can imagine the harm that comes from actions that we take, while it is harder to "see" potential harm from actions we don't take. It is also, he suggests, easier to see the impact on those near to us than those far away. In the case of *Challenger*, those at Levels 4 and 3 could distance themselves from the impact of their teleconference decision making. After all, they were not taking a direct action they *knew* would kill the crew and the crew was distant in both functional, hierarchical, and physical space.[80]

External Pressures Impact Organizational Ethics

The Rogers Commission cast its fault-finding on Levels 4 and 3 and, to a lesser extent, on what it labeled NASA's "Silent Safety Program." Clearly, NASA's top leadership felt what the Commission called "unrelenting pressure to meet the demands of an accelerating flight schedule." They no doubt felt this from the White House, the media, and the Congress (through its control of NASA's budget). Such pressure is the water in which public officials swim, yet we are often not sufficiently aware of how it affects organizational culture and ethics. A task of public service leadership is to contain the impact of such pressures, if it cannot remove them. Instead, in *Challenger*, that pressure was passed down to all levels of the flight readiness decision making structure. Note also that those exerting the external pressure often escape, in the public's mind, any responsibility for an ethical failure due to their distance from it. Public servants need to find ways to share that responsibility and to make sure external sources are aware that ethical failures will be placed, in part, at their doorstep.

The Pressure to Conform Promotes Unethical Behavior

Since there were both individuals and groups that could have stopped the launch, why did everyone go along? Embedded in our discussion thus far are the impacts of the pressure to conform and the demand to obey authority.

Imagine you are sitting in a room with seven other people and are asked to look at the lines in Figure 6.4.

Figure 6.4
A Simple Problem

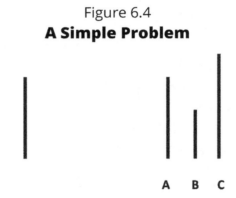

Which of the three lines on the right is the same length as the line on the left?

The clear answer is "A." In an experiment conducted by Solomon Asch in 1951, he put a test subject and seven others (confederates of the experimenter yet not known as such to the test subject) in a room. Ninety-nine percent of the test subjects got it right when they were asked to answer first. Yet, when the confederates in the room choose first, and gave an incorrect answer as they had been directed covertly by Asch to do, a third of test subjects agreed with the incorrect answer. In a series of 12 trails, 75% defied their own senses and went along with the group on at least one trial. When later asked how they could have been so mistaken, most said that they believed the majority must be right. Some admitted that they didn't want to seem inferior to others even though they knew others were wrong.[81] In Asch's case, none of the confederates held any position of power over test subjects. They were peers. When we throw hierarchy into the mix, things get even more troubling.

In a classic series of experiments in 1961 by Yale psychologist Stanley Milgram, a subject - the "teacher" - was asked to help a "learner" (unknown to the teacher but a confederate of Milgram) master word pairs. Before the teaching began, the teacher saw the learner being seated in a separate room and wired to a machine connected to a series of switches on a panel where the teacher sat. When the learner was wrong, the teacher was told by the researcher – who wore a white lab coat signaling his authority - to push a lever that administered an electric shock. The teacher was told that the shocks were designed to improve learning. For each error, the shock voltage increased – in 15-volt increments - all the way to 450 volts. If the teacher showed reluctance to continue because of the moans and then screams of the learner, the researcher uttered a simple sentence, such as "You must complete the experiment." (In reality, the learner was not being shocked but just turned on a tape recording that would play sounds of pain at designated voltage levels.) Every one of 40 subjects "administered" shocks up to at least 300 volts. Sixty-five percent went all the way to 450 volts, even when the learner screamed in pain.[82]

In explaining his results, Milgram said this:

> *"The extreme willingness of adults to go to almost any lengths on the command of an authority constitutes the chief finding of the study and the fact most urgently demanding explanation. Ordinary people, simply doing their jobs, and without any particular hostility on their part, can become agents in a terrible destructive process. Moreover, even when the destructive effects of their work become patently clear, and they are asked to carry out actions incompatible with fundamental standards of morality, relatively few people have the resources needed to resist authority."*[83]

It may be unfair to charge those involved in the *Challenger* launch decision with being cowardly conformists or unfeeling followers of authority, but the pressures to conform and the difficulty in resisting authority were present. George Hardy, a respected engineer at Level 3 had told MTI that he was "appalled" at their recommendation not to fly. Larry Malloy chided MTI saying that, with their views, we "can't launch, we won't be able to launch until April." Under this pressure from authority, MTI asked for their private caucus. When asked by the Rogers Commission, MTI VP Bob Lund explained why he changed his mind when his boss, Jerry Mason, told managers in the caucus to 'take off their engineering hat and put on their management hat:'

> *"We have dealt with Marshall for a long time and have always been in the position of defending our position to make sure that we were ready to fly, and I guess I didn't realize until after that meeting and after several days that we had absolutely changed our position from what we had been before. But that evening I guess I had never had*

those kinds of things come from the people at Marshall. We had to prove to them that we weren't ready, and so we got ourselves in the thought process that we were trying to find some way to prove to them it wouldn't work, and we were unable to do that. We couldn't prove absolutely that that motor wouldn't work."

MTI, under pressure from authority, completely reversed not only its position but its approach to launch decisions, agreeing that instead of proving it was safe to launch, they had to prove it was not safe, when that had never been the case in the history of the shuttle program. And they didn't even seem to realize that they had caved in.

Summary

As *Challenger* demonstrates, unethical behavior in organizations is fostered when any of the following conditions apply:

- Core values are forgotten or subordinated;
- Organizational norms foster a "can-do" attitude that leads people to ignore or downplay ethical considerations in favor of getting the job done;
- Deviance becomes normal since ethical mistakes are made and nothing bad happens, encouraging the unethical behavior to become "business as usual;"
- The organizational structure provides no independent checks on operational decisions that could compromise core values;
- Hierarchy blocks critical information flows so that ethical concerns cannot make it up the chain of command;
- Hierarchy and specialization of function diffuse responsibility for ethical action, weakening each individual's sense of personal responsibility for a decision;
- Ethics is off-loaded to contractors along with technical tasks essential to operations;
- The pressure to conform overtakes independent judgment; and/or
- Those in positions of authority pressure others to obey.

To prevent "bad barrels" requires a proactive series of steps to foster a culture that supports ethical behavior. If you are in a leadership position, that is your responsibility. If you are not, it is your responsibility to be aware of how the organizational culture can impact ethical behavior and to respond in a way that either fosters a positive ethical climate or, at the least, maintains your ethical standards in the face of the pressure to compromise them. As *Challenger* shows, all of this can be difficult. But it can and has been done.

–7–

HOW CAN AN ORGANIZATION CREATE A POSITIVE ETHICAL CULTURE?

"People I know don't get out of bed in the morning and say, 'I think I'll be unethical today!' But organizations can make good people do bad things. . . . Fortunately, organizations can also help people do great things – and to do the right thing."
– Ellen Fox, Chief Ethics in Health Care Officer,
Veterans Health Administration[84]

In 1987, leaders at the Veterans Affairs Medical Center in Lexington, Kentucky made a change in standard hospital practice. When they committed a medical error, they started sitting down with the patient (and in many case the patient's representative) and admitting the mistake – even in cases where the patient would never know a mistake had been made. In addition, they offered, on the spot, to help the patient file a claim. Despite some fears, this ethical policy of honesty and restitution did not lead to skyrocketing malpractice costs. In fact, when data for the period 1990-1996 were analyzed, researchers concluded that liability payments were "comparable to similar facilities." The bottom line was probably better than that, because they also concluded that the policy avoided many of the extensive staff costs that would have been incurred if the errors had resulted in lawsuits and trials.[85]

The practice is now standard in all 153 Veterans Health Administration (VHA) medical centers, embedded in a policy that declares an "unwavering ethical obligation to disclose to patients harmful adverse events" because this "is consistent with VA core values of integrity, commitment, advocacy, respect, and excellence."[86]

Positive Ethical Cultures Improve Organizational Effectiveness

As the VHA example demonstrates, creating a positive ethical culture isn't "nice to do" work that detracts from organizational effectiveness. It's "need to do" work that promotes it.

The National Government Ethics Survey, conducted by the Ethics Resource Center (ERC) in 2007, bears out the payoff from a strong ethical culture (Figure 7.1).[87] Strong ethical cultures lead to significant reductions in such practices as putting one's own interest ahead of the organization, lying to stakeholders and employees, Internet abuse, safety violations, stealing and alteration of financial records, and abusive behavior. Yet, the survey found that only eight percent of employees report a strong ethical culture in their agency.

ERC data from private sector firms also offer a finding that may well be present in government agencies: the stronger the ethical culture, the greater the level of employee engagement.[88] Research by the Merit Systems Protection Board suggests that greater employee engagement is correlated with higher program effectiveness in government and lower levels of sick leave use, EEO complaints, and lost time due to accidents.[89]

Figure 7.1

The Benefits of a Strong Ethical Culture

Indicator of Ethical Behavior	Impact of a Strong Ethical Culture
Pressure to compromise ethical standards	Reduced by 74%
Observed misconduct	Reduced by 50%
Rate of reporting of ethical misconduct	Increased by 40%

Source: National Government Ethics Survey, Ethics Resource Center, 2007, pp. 11-17

Elements of a Positive Ethical Organizational Culture

What constitutes a positive, organizational culture for ethics? The elements shown in Figure 7.2 emerge in research and writing. Ideally, all need to be working and are mutually reinforcing. The following pages explain their importance, list some behaviors that demonstrate their presence and offer examples of best practice.[90]

Leadership by Example

On March 4, 1865, as the Civil War approached an end, Abraham Lincoln took the Oath of Office for his second term as president. In his inaugural address, he pleaded for the nation to come together after the most perilous period in its history. His call for "malice toward none; with charity for all" was an act of exceptional ethical leadership, especially given the desire of so many in the North to extract a heavy price of retribution on the Confederacy. But this was not uncharacteristic of Lincoln. His ability to suppress the human tendency for anger and extend forgiveness instead had been a hallmark of his leadership throughout the war.

Most of those who fought in the ranks of the Union army were farm boys who volunteered or were drafted. They had never experienced the discipline required in a professional fighting force or the terror of warfare. As a result, many failed as soldiers. Due to exhaustion, they would fall asleep on sentry duty. Faced with the horrors of battle they might run from the front lines. Given permission to return home for a short visit, they would overstay their leave. The penalty for such offenses was execution. In most cases, however, before executions were carried out, the order had to be approved by the Secretary of War, Edwin Stanton, and the President.

Figure 7.2
Elements of a Positive Organizational Culture

Stanton would approve the sentences because he felt it essential to maintain the discipline needed for Union victory. Lincoln, however, would look for any reason to use his pardon power under the Constitution or commute the sentence to prison time instead. As Doris Kearns Goodwin describes Lincoln's approach in her book, *Team of Rivals*:

> *"One case involved a private who was sentenced to be shot for desertion though he had later re-enlisted. Lincoln simply proposed, "Let him fight instead of shooting him." Lincoln acknowledged to General John Eaton that some of his officers believed he employed the pardoning power "with so much freedom as to demoralize the army and destroy the discipline." Although "officers only see the force of military discipline," he explained, he tried to comprehend it from the vantage point of individual soldiers – a picket so exhausted that "sleep steals upon him unawares," a family man who overstayed his leave, a young boy "overcome by a physical fear greater than his will." . . . Rather than fearing that he had overused his pardoning power, Lincoln feared he had made too little use of it. He could not bear the sound of gunshot on the days when deserters were executed. Only "where meanness or cruelty were shown" did he exhibit no clemency."*[91]

Lincoln led by example in an area he felt critical to the future of the nation. His example inspired General Ulysses Grant, for example, to offer very reasonable terms to General Robert E. Lee at Appomattox.[92]

Leadership by Example matters because leaders have a powerful impact on the ethical climate in their organizations. Employees look directly to their leaders, especially the immediate supervisor, for signals about whether ethics matters. As public administration professors Terry Cooper and N. Dale Wright point out in their study of exemplary public administrators: "They give confidence in public leadership, they serve as moral guides, and they provide a necessary encouragement for individual moral development."[93]

Those who lead by example:
- Take ethical issues very seriously
- Speak to employees about ethical guidelines
- Discuss ethical dilemmas with employees when the organization or team is facing a tough decision
- Clearly express expectations concerning ethical behavior
- Model ethical behavior in their personal behavior and in the work decisions they make
- Send consistent messages about the importance of behaving ethically

Marie Ragghianti also led by example.[94] In 1974, at age 32, divorced and with three young children, she was offered a job as extradition officer for the State of Tennessee. Within two years, she was called by Bill Thompson, a friend of Governor Ray Blanton, and told that Blanton intended to appoint her as chair of the state's Parole Board. Unbeknownst to Ragghianti, Thompson, Eddie Sisk (her current boss), and Blanton were engaged in selling pardons, including for felons convicted of murder and other serious offenses.

Fairly soon, she discovered that inappropriate pardons were coming before her. Though pressured by Sisk, she refused to approve them. While she did not initially suspect Blanton, she found that he did not support her. Convinced that her responsibility was to the people of Tennessee, she began what would become a multi-year struggle to end the corruption.

She contacted the FBI in 1976, which soon led to threats to fire her by the governor. When she began working with the legislature on a bill to remove control of the Parole Board from the governor's office, retaliation intensified. On August 3, 1977, she was fired. Having retained Fred Thompson (former Watergate prosecutor and future Senator) as her lawyer, she sued for reinstatement.

On July 10, 1978, she won in court, and a bill to reform the Parole Board along the lines she suggested was eventually enacted. On December 15 of the same year, Eddie Sisk and Bill Thompson were indicted. The FBI investigation found that over six hundred pardons and clemencies had been issued by the governor, including 24 for murderers that he signed during his last weeks in office. Though the FBI would continue to struggle to find direct evidence to link Blanton to the scheme, he would eventually be indicted, convicted, and serve three years in prison for taking kickbacks for liquor-store licenses. Marie Ragghianti led by example. Yet, characteristic of many who do so, she would humbly say that: "You don't set out to be a hero. It is more of not being able to live with yourself if you do not do the right thing."

Core Values

When George C. Marshall became Army Chief of Staff on September 1, 1939, the United States had 174,000 men in uniform. They were badly trained, poorly equipped and led by World-War-I-vintage senior officers. One of Marshall's major challenges was to convince the president and Congress that many of these superannuated generals and colonels were not capable of fighting a modern war. President Roosevelt would not take the lead; most of these officers had strong political support. It fell to Marshall. He had two ethical dilemmas to wrestle with. Each involved grappling with core values. First, he recognized that loyalty to officers who had served the nation conflicted with the truth that many of them were not physically or mentally prepared for the approaching world war. He resolved this by setting up what came to be called a "plucking committee" that would review the records and fitness of generals and colonels and recommend removal of those no longer able to lead in wartime. He took intense heat for this, from officers, their families and their friends in Congress.

Second, he set 60 as the mandatory age for retirement to reduce the chance that favoritism would play a role. In doing so, he knew that by the end of 1940 he would himself be 60. He could rationalize himself out of the dilemma – after all, he was the Army Chief of Staff. But he did not. So, he went to FDR and offered his resignation. Two weeks went by with no word from the president. Harry Hopkins, FDR's senior advisor and confidant, told Marshall that "The President just laughs at you. He says no politician ever resigns his job and that's just talk." So Marshall again went to the White House, this time offering a plan to train his successor so he could step down within two to three months. Roosevelt again refused Marshall's offer, though he held on to it in case the political heat was so intense from the "plucking committee" that he had to sacrifice someone. Since FDR was the Commander in Chief, Marshall felt an obligation to continue in his position – adhering to the core value of the subordination of military to civilian authority.

George Marshall lived by – and exemplified – the adherence to core values. In preparing the nation for war, he put country and the Constitution above loyalty to his officers, considerations of personal reputation and his job.

Values guide the actions of individuals and organizations. Employees feel they can act ethically when what work demands of them is consistent with their core moral values. Research suggests that this consistency is often not present. In one study of 615 Americans by International Communications Research, only 44 percent agreed that their own core values were consistent with those of their employer. Thirty percent said this was not always the case. However, only 10 percent felt that core values had little to do with their work.[95] In a survey of 240 federal government executives, "core values" received the lowest rating of eight different aspects of their own organization's ethical climate. Nearly 40 percent (37.3%) disagreed or strongly disagreed that "managers in this organization help employees link their personal core values to the organization's core moral values." A third disagreed or strongly disagreed that "employees in this organization are encouraged to identify their core personal values."[96]

Organizations that wish to foster attention to core values in creating an ethical climate:
- Encourage employees to identify their core values and help them see how they can be realized at work
- Articulate the core values of the organization

- Incorporate core values instruction into employee orientation programs
- Keep the number of organizational core values small; too large a set risks a loss of focus
- Appoint a "champion" for each core value – to measure organizational actions against that value, address potential problems, and recognize good performance
- Tell stories that exemplify the organization at its best, living its core values

After Admiral James Loy left his job as Commandant of the Coast Guard, he was appointed to become the first Administrator of the Transportation Security Administration (TSA). He later recalled one of his early meetings:

> "I remember one of our first off-sites. I asked around the table as to whether or not we had core values at TSA. They said, "Oh, sure," I said, "Well, how many do you have?" They said, "Oh, I think there might be 10 or 11." I said, "Is anybody here able to recite those for me?" Of course, they could not, because they hadn't internalized them. We were at that point about three weeks old as an organization."[97]

Core value exercises that generate a list and post them on the wall are common in organizations. Less common are organizations that keep the list small and work to incorporate core values into every aspect of their work. The Marine Corps, as another positive example, uses stories to transmit core values. Called "sea stories," they are a training staple, and being a good story teller is one expectation of every leader.

Ethics Guidelines

On February 5, 2007, Captain Lisa Nowak, a NASA astronaut who had flown the previous June on the space shuttle *Discovery*, was arrested at Orlando International Airport. Nowak was soon charged with the attempted kidnapping of U.S. Air Force Captain Colleen Shipman. Shipman had become romantically involved with astronaut William Oefelein, with whom Nowak had previously had an affair. According to press reports, Nowak had traveled from Houston and had planned the abduction well in advance.

NASA removed Nowak from the astronaut corps on March 8, 2007 and, on November 10, 2009, she pled guilty to felony burglary of a car and misdemeanor battery. The episode was an embarrassment to NASA and led to several recommendations, one of which called for the development of an astronaut code of conduct. Developed by astronauts, the resulting code "expresses the basic tenets of ethical and professional conduct." While NASA operated without such a code for nearly fifty years, both internal and external pressures argued that it was time to formalize expectations that reflect "a constant commitment to honorable behavior."[98]

Ethical guidelines have been present – and have proliferated - in government especially since the 1960s. Both government-wide, agency-specific, and – as the NASA case demonstrates – even profession-specific codes of ethical behavior exist. Despite such extensive guidance, however, unethical (and sometimes illegal) behavior persists. Clearly, the presence of ethics guidelines no more guarantees ethical behavior than does the presence of traffic laws guarantee accident-free driving. Guidelines help, but they are not enough. Effective implementation, including clear support from leaders, is essential too.

To strengthen the power of ethics guidelines in an organization's culture:
- Use, and support the use of, government-wide ethical codes of conduct in daily operations through publicizing them and having top management model them in daily work
- Identify profession-specific ethical codes that relate to the work of your organization (e.g. public administration, engineers, business managers, psychologists, medical professionals, etc) and work with professional associations and employees to draw attention to and educate people about these codes
- Review ethics guidelines to keep them updated, involving employees in this process
- Conduct new employee orientation and periodic training on the details of the ethics guidelines and the rationale behind them, using hypothetical or real cases to allow employees to practice ethical thinking
- Ensure that contractors adhere to an ethical code of conduct since their unethical behavior impacts public purposes and can pressure government workers to compromise their own standards

It is often hard to gain strong adherence to the value of ethics guidelines. Doing all the steps above can sometimes feel like pushing a boulder up a steep hill. Plus, if the message comes just as a mandate (federal law requires annual ethics training), many downplay its importance. Most people also do not like being told they can't be trusted to be ethical. Further, ethics guidelines are often so detailed that eyes glaze over at the sheer volume and detail of the requirements. And, of course, some employees believe the message is not "lived" by top management.

Yet there are success stories. In the field of engineering, the concept of "technical conscience" is one approach to a profession-specific ethics code. At the Naval Air Systems Command (NAVAIR), for example, those in the research and engineering field subscribe to a set of "technical conscience" principles. They understand that peer pressure can encourage being a team player when sound engineering practice would counsel otherwise. One principle is thus to "understand and believe that we are the last line of defense for the 'technical conscience.'" Another is to "never let emotions or programmatic crises overshadow the technical requirements and our technical judgment."[99]

Still another approach is to point beyond ethics as a set of rules to ethical behavior as a moral commitment on all those who take the oath of office. The U.S. Air Force re-administers the Oath of Office in a public ceremony each time a senior official gets promoted. Some organizations lend weight to the oath through Constitution Day celebrations.[100]

Encouragement of Differences

Between 2012-2014, a number of public failures embarrassed the U.S. Secret Service. These included revelations that some agents hired prostitutes while on assignment in Cartagena and several incidents in which White House security was breached, including one man who made it all the way inside the White House after leaping over a fence. These ultimately led to the replacement of two directors and the appointment of Joseph Clancy, the former head of President Obama's security detail, as acting director. In testimony to the House Judiciary Committee on November 19, 2014, Clancy, who came out of retirement to take the position, made no excuses for the behavior of his agents. But he did express concern that some employees felt it necessary to go to the press to express their worries about their own organization. "I share the concerns expressed by many members of Congress that some employees are more comfortable speaking with people outside the agency than they are with their supervisors. This troubles me and was an integral part of why I agreed to return." Clancy went on to discuss steps he was taking(such as an internal ombudsman) to encourage needed dissent within the Secret Service.[101]

On March 12, 2011, as the result of a massive tsunami, the Fukushima nuclear power plant on the coast of Japan began releasing radioactive materials in what would soon become the largest nuclear incident since the 1986 Chernobyl disaster. Americans were horrified. Attention quickly turned to the question "could that happen here?" The answer is largely up to a small federal agency with a budget equal to about what Social Security pays out in just 12 hours and a staff of only 4,000 people. The Nuclear Regulatory Commission (NRC) usually slips under the radar of daily events. Yet it is charged with the oversight of reactor safety at 104 operating nuclear power plants, many near large urban areas. The NRC's role also includes reactor license issuance and renewal for existing plants, materials safety licensing and oversight, and nuclear waste management.

If this sounds like a job in which there is no margin for error, the NRC would agree. To prevent mistakes, however, requires a work environment in which employees and contractors can speak up without fear of retaliation. Ethical behavior at the NRC means making it easy and safe for people to dissent. The NRC uses thee approaches to do so. It's "Open Door Policy" allows an employee to initiate a meeting with an NRC manager or supervisor, including a Commissioner or the Chairman of the NRC, to discuss any matter of concern. Its "Non-Concurrence Process" allows employees to not concur on any part of a document with which they disagree and document their concerns early in the decision making process, to have their concerns responded to, and to attach those concerns to documents as they move through the approval process. Its "Differing Professional Opinions Program (DPO)" is a formal process that allows employees and contractors to have their differing views on established, mission-related issues considered by the highest level managers in their organization. The process includes independent review by a three-person panel (one member of whom is chosen by the employee). The employee may appeal the decision if he or she still differs with it.

This does not, of course, run as flawlessly as it sounds. Periodic reviews of the DPO program, for example, show that some employees fear retaliation or damage to their careers from using it. Others look to whether DPO submitters are recognized for sticking their necks out. Creating a supportive ethical climate is rarely easy, and perhaps the key message here is that the NRC is both aware of the need and working on it.

The same cannot be said for many other government agencies. As data from the Merit System Protection Board suggests (see Figure 7.3), even in agencies with high levels of employee engagement (i.e. high employee commitment and morale), over half still worry about speaking out on their concerns. In low engagement agencies, the problem is much worse.

Organizations that want to foster dissent in order to encourage ethical behavior:
- Get diverse points of view from various stakeholders, both supporters and opponents, before making a decision
- Ensure that someone leading a decision making meeting speaks last so that others don't try to determine or respond to signals about the leader's point of view
- Encourage employees to say "no" when they believe they are being asked to do something unethical
- Recognize employees who dissent, irrespective of whether the dissent is welcome or ultimately deemed important for action
- Model openness to hearing bad news by sharing their failures as well as what works
- Train employees – and especially managers – on how to spot and counter dangerous and premature agreement

Figure 7.3
Willingness to Dissent

"I can express my point of view to management without fear of negative consequences."

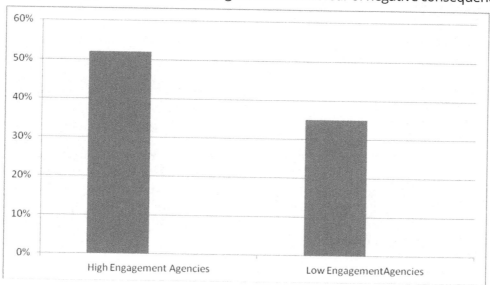

Source: Merit Systems Protection Board

The U.S. Coast Guard has formalized an approach to ensure encouragement of dissent among its small boat crews. It's called a "GAR" review and must be done before a boat leaves port. "GAR" stands for "Green, Amber, Red." Crew members go through a range of questions about the boat and crew's readiness to cast off (each scored on a 1-10 basis (1=lowest)), with each crew member stating his/her score and the reasons. To avoid conformity to the leader's view, crew members speak in reverse order of rank - lowest rank speaks first. If the total score falls in the Amber or Red area, the crew must make adjustments before they leave port.

The Federal Executive Institute in Charlottesville, Virginia, offers a course for senior executives on ethical leadership. Part of that course includes instruction on what we know from social psychology about the dangers of conformity, authority and group-think and how to avoid these problems. The work of Irving Janis on the tendency of groups to suppress dissent – and what can be done to prevent this - is summarized very briefly in Figure 7.4. Janis, drawing on such classic decision making failures as the Bay of Pigs invasion aimed at toppling the Castro regime in Cuba in 1961, argues that the more insular and self-confident groups become, the less open they are to contrary views and the harder it becomes for individuals to dissent.[102] As Figure 7.4 suggests, preventing groupthink requires breaking up the insularity of the group.

Figure 7.4
Groupthink

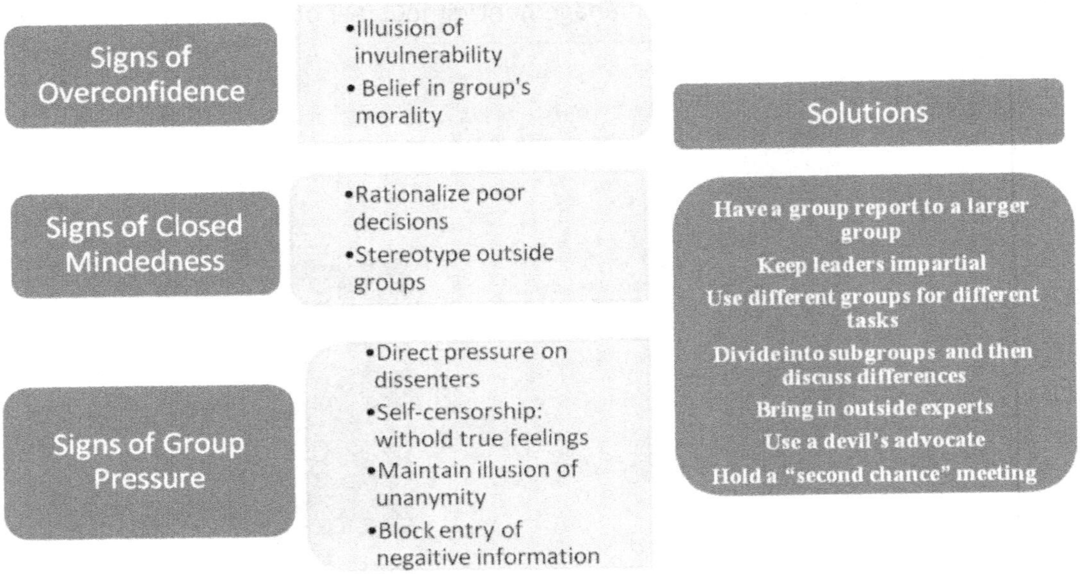

Signs of Overconfidence	• Illuision of invulnerability • Belief in group's morality	
Signs of Closed Mindedness	• Rationalize poor decisions • Stereotype outside groups	**Solutions**
Signs of Group Pressure	• Direct pressure on dissenters • Self-censorship: withold true feelings • Maintain illusion of unanymity • Block entry of negaitive information	Have a group report to a larger group Keep leaders impartial Use different groups for different tasks Divide into subgroups and then discuss differences Bring in outside experts Use a devil's advocate Hold a "second chance" meeting

Box 7.1
Options for Dissent

- Confront the issue directly with the person involved.
- Talk to your supervisor.
- Go over your supervisor's head – talk to your supervisor's supervisor.
- Contact headquarters in your agency
- Create, or arrange for the creation of, documentaries, scientific studies, and scientific papers to describe and analyze the situation that concerns you.
- Neglect policies and directives you disagree with.
- Fail to implement orders you think are unethical.
- Cultivate positive relationships with interest groups.
- Use a National Academy of Sciences review panel or similar independent panel of experts to force scientific attention to the problem
- Forge links with other outside groups; other professionals, nongovernmental organizations, concerned citizens.
- Testify before a legislative body.
- File a complaint with the Office of the Inspector General.

Source: The Ethics of Dissent, *by Rosemary O'Leary*

There are many other approaches to express differences when ethical issues are at stake. In her book, *The Ethics of Dissent*, Syracuse University professor Rosemary O'Leary reviews many ways that public servants have found to do so.[103] Some are shown in Box 7.1. Which to use or encourage others to use in a given situation must be considered carefully. She also discusses approaches, such as publicly blasting the head of your agency or clandestinely plotting opposition, that may work but involve ethical considerations of their own and fall more under the subtitle of her book – "managing guerilla government." Her basic point, however, is that public servants who would act ethically may need to find effective ways to dissent, and that organizations should offer such outlets in order to foster an ethical culture.

Organizational Structure and Processes

Since 2008, IntegratedEthics (the lack of a space between the two words is intended) or "IE" has served as the ethics approach to health care in all of the Veterans Administration's medical centers and regional networks. IE resulted from a multi-year design effort involving a wide range of stakeholders and has been led since its inception by a Harvard-trained physician, Ellen Fox. In 2011, IE won an Innovations in American Government Award from the John F. Kennedy School of Government of Harvard University as well as a Program Excellence and Innovation Award from the U.S. Office of Government Ethics.

IE demonstrates that an organization-wide approach to ethics can incorporate all of the principles we have discussed. IE consciously rejects the notion that ethics can be pigeon-holed into a committee or handled by a few "ethics specialists." Instead, it demands that leaders throughout the Veterans Health Administration (VHA) address "four compass points:" (1) demonstrate that ethics is a priority, (2) communicate clear expectations for ethical practice, (3) practice ethical decision making (including explaining decisions), and (4) support the local ethics program. As shown in Box 7.2, IE is proactive and preventive.

All leaders must take a video course and complete an ethical leadership self-assessment. VHA also provides leaders with a 60-page handbook on ethical leadership. A brief excerpt on the meaning of "demonstrate that ethics is a priority" includes this advice:

"To demonstrate that ethics truly is a priority, leaders must directly and regularly express their support for ethical practices. They should explicitly refer to "ethics," "mission," "values," and "principles." They should use inspiring words like "honorable," "duty bound," "integrity," "fairness," and "truth." Here are some more examples:

> *"I see ethics as a priority."*
> *"If it's the right thing to do, we'll just have to figure out a way to do it."*
> *"Here's a story that illustrates how important ethics can be."*
> *"We have an obligation to do the best we can for our patients."*
> *"Everyone deserves to be treated with respect."*[104]

As the IE approach demonstrations, organizations that want to embed ethics into their structure and work processes:

- Identify the business case for ethical behavior - why it matters to the bottom line of both budget and public purpose
- Engage stakeholders inside and outside the organization in defining where and how to incorporate ethics into the organization's daily operations
- Embed ethics into the job definitions of key people in both line and staff roles
- Ensure that education and training give everyone in the organization the concepts and skills needed to perform their roles as ethical actors
- Embed ethics into how the organization makes decisions, including at the highest levels
- Provide resources sufficient to take ethics from a goal to an operational, daily method of operations

VHA is rare in having such a comprehensive approach. Most government agencies house ethics in part of the Office of General Counsel, unfortunately sending a message that ethics is essentially a matter of legal and regulatory compliance that only experts (lawyers) can fully understand. This approach can also set up the organization for considering ethics only when it has or suspects a problem, rather than creating a preventive and positive approach to ethics as an obligation of everyone who takes the oath of office.

To self-assess where your organization stands, the Organization Ethical Climate Survey, developed as a self-assessment instrument by the Federal Executive Institute, can be useful.[105]

Rewards, Sanctions, and Peer Support

In June 2009, Secretary of State Hillary Clinton was preparing for a trip to Africa, during which she would stop in the Congo to lend focus to concerns about violence against women. A high level official at State suggested that the military provide short-term medical and psychological treatment for victims, and a Major General approved the idea. Yet Diana Putnam, a mid-level U.S. Agency for International Development (USAID) health specialist stationed with the military's Africa Command in Germany, thought it was a bad move.

Box 7.2
IntegratedEthics:
The Approach of the Veterans Health Administration

The Veterans Health Administration (VHA) serves nearly 6 million patients a year in more than 1,500 locations. Discontented with the traditional, "ethics committee" approach – which focused almost solely on specific clinical decisions – VHA wanted to integrate ethics into every aspect of operations in ways where progress could be measured. A physician, Ellen Fox, was appointed VA's Chief Ethics in Health Care Officer, and work on the Integrated Ethics (IE) model began in 1999.

The tagline for IE is "improving ethics quality in health care." Typically, a hospital would worry about whether a procedure was successful. That's the medical side of quality. But Fox insists that there is an ethical side as well, such as whether the patient was fully informed beforehand.

Fox suggests that ethics be looked at like an iceberg. Above the surface are *decisions and actions* – the everyday practices of hospital staff. Just below the surface are *systems and processes*, those things that drive decision making but are not readily visible. Going still deeper are the organization's ethical *environment and culture*, which have a profound impact on everything in the iceberg that lies above.

The IE model has three "core functions" that mirror these iceberg levels:
- Ethics Consultation – targets the quality of decisions and actions
- Preventive Ethics – targets the ethics of system and process
- Ethical Leadership – targets the deepest level of environment and culture

Ethics Consultation - is provided by individual ethics consultants, a consultation team or an ethics committee and focuses on helping patients and staff resolve ethical dilemmas, such as how to handle an end-of-life care issue for a particular patient.

Preventive Ethics – looks at ongoing situations (versus one-time issues or cases) that suggest systemic problems. For example, an ethics consultation might be undertaken when a doctor and patient (or family member) disagrees about whether to do a given procedure. But if this same kind of disagreement comes up frequently, it suggests an underlying system or process issue that must be addressed.

Ethical Leadership – examines the role of managers in creating an ethical environment. The IE approach requires that leaders play four roles: (1) demonstrate ethics is a priority; (2) communicate clear expectations about ethical practice; (3) practice ethical decision making; and (4) support the ethics program in the VHA facility.

Implementing Integrated Ethics at each VHA facility required designating responsible staff and establishing methods, educational materials, and performance expectations. The Facility Director is the Ethical Leadership Coordinator, thus ensuring that ethics receives direct support from the top. Below the Coordinator is an IE Program Officer as well as coordinators for Ethics Consultation and Preventive Ethics.

Source: "IntegratedEthics: An Innovative Program to Improve Ethics Quality in Health Care," by Ellen Fox, *The Innovation Journal: The Public Sector Innovation Journal*, Vol. 15(2), www.ethics.va.gov/IEoverview.pdf

Putnam's reasoning was that nongovernmental organizations (NGOs) were already providing such help and the military lacked the language and cross-cultural skills to be good counselors to the women who were victims. Rather than helping, the military's involvement could actually hurt. She proposed that the military get involved, but in a different way - by building or rehabilitating existing structures that could be used by NGOs or others to provide services. She even found funding to get the job done. Yet those above her were reluctant to take on higher level management, especially senior military leaders, reasoning that doing so could damage their careers.

So Putnam went right to the top, in the form of the head of the Africa Command, Gen. William Ward. After hearing her out, he approved her idea on the spot. In June 2010, Putnam received the William R. Rivkin Award for constructive dissent in a ceremony conducted by the American Foreign Service Association (AFSA), which has sponsored four different creative dissent awards for those in the foreign service for many years.[106] Putnam acted ethically, in the best interests of her clients. Rewarding such behavior is central to creating a culture that fosters ethical action.

Enacting sanctions against those who act unethically is also important. In 2014, the Department of Veterans Affairs was excoriated for lying and covering up the fact that it misreported the amount of time it took veterans to get medical appointments. Congress rushed through legislation to deal with the problem. In signing the Veterans' Access to Care through Choice, Accountability, and Transparency Act of 2014, which gives the agency the power to fire quickly any senior executive who engages in such action, President Obama said that: "If you engage in an unethical practice, if you cover up a problem, you should be fired, period."[107] While there is considerable debate about whether the timelines for appealing a firing decision are fair to the executive (an ethical issue within the broader ethical issue the law is meant to address), the President clearly signaled the importance of using sanctions against unethical behavior among public servants.

Despite these examples, rewards and sanctions are often underutilized tools in government agencies. In a survey of 240 senior career government executives by the Federal Executive Institute, significant percentages found their organization's efforts lacking in these areas, as the data in Table 7.1 shows.

Organizations that want to create a strong ethical culture:
- Use public ceremonies and awards (which do not have to be monetary) to recognize ethical behavior
- Use sanctions to punish those who behave unethically on a regular basis (i.e. a first transgression can sometimes be dealt with through forgiveness, education, and restitution if no laws were violated)

- Nominate employees, who have stuck their necks out to behave ethically, for external recognition (e.g. The Kennedy School of Government's Profiles in Courage Award or the Giraffe Heroes Project)[108]

Table 7.1
Use of Rewards and Sanctions to Foster Ethical Behavior

Question	% Disagree or Strongly Disagree
Employees in this organization receive formal rewards for behaving in an ethical manner (e.g. certificate, monetary award, etc.)	38.3%
Unethical behavior is punished every time it occurs.	35.4%
There is a clear link between ethical behavior and rewards for that behavior in this organization.	30.2%
Rewarding ethical behavior is important to top management.	27.1%

Peer support, which is also what the AFSA does in its awards program, representing as it does the entire foreign service community, also plays a part. As we have seen, groups exert powerful social pressure on their members - for good and ill. Peer support not only recognizes the ethical behavior of an individual but signals that there is a professional community that expects others to do the same.

Ideally, organizations who wish to foster peer support:
- Conduct *group* training in ethical thinking and problem solving so that everyone gets the same message and understands that there is organizational and peer support for doing the right thing
- Practice ethical issue analysis in intact organizational teams, using real cases, current issues, and/or previous cases that represented problems for the organization
- Establish incentives (recognition, awards) for group ethical problem solving as well as for group ethical stands

Finding peer support is not always easy inside an agency, especially when your effort to act ethically is not appreciated by colleagues or superiors. But there are support groups outside that can be called upon. One of these is the American Society for Public Administration (ASPA). This group developed the Code of Ethics that we reviewed in Chapter 1. As of this writing, it is also planning to create an Ethics and Standards Implementation Committee. The purposes of this new group will include, among others, providing advice to members in handling ethics problems and speaking for ASPA in cases involving serious challenges to ethical administration in the public service.

There are also a wide range of organizations, often associated with individual professions that provide members support in tackling ethical issues. There are also centers for ethics, not-for-profits and sometimes associated with universities, that provide ethical readings, cases, and consultation. Appendix C contains a partial list.

Our discussion thus far will not necessarily keep bad people from doing bad things. But an ethically strong organizational culture should keep good people from doing bad things. Unfortunately, even that is not always the case. So we need to ask the question: why do good people, filled with the best of intentions and backed by organizational support, make bad ethical decisions? We'll focus on organizational leaders, for they set the tone for ethical behavior - except when they do not. But our conclusions apply to everyone.

-8-
WHY DO GOOD LEADERS DO BAD THINGS?

"In general, the higher a person goes on the rungs of power and authority, the more wobbly the ethical ladder." – Stephen K. Bailey

On March 8, 2012, David Petraeus was Director of the CIA, having been confirmed the previous July by a 94-0 vote in the U.S. Senate. Petraeus had previously been a four-star General whose assignments included Commander of the International Security Assistance Force, Commander, U.S. Forces-Afghanistan, Commander U.S. Central Command, and Commander, Multi-National Force, Iraq. In the latter post, he was credited with leading the surge and the "Sunni Awakening" that enabled U.S. forces to wind down their involvement in that war. Petraeus, married with two children and at the pinnacle of power, was sometimes compared to such illustrious American military leaders as Generals John J. "Black Jack" Pershing and George C. Marshall.

The very next day, Petraeus resigned, citing as his reason an extramarital affair with writer and Army Reserve officer Paula Broadwell. Broadwell had traveled with Petraeus in writing his biography, begun some time after they first met when he was a speaker and she a student at the Kennedy School of Government at Harvard. Just before he resigned, Petraeus was also informed that the FBI was investigating allegations that Broadwell had sent threatening emails to socialite Jill Kelley, charging her with having an affair with Petraeus. Petraeus had attended events at Kelley's home in Tampa, where she and her husband frequently entertained military officers.

Petraeus was no stranger to the demands of ethical leadership. He even included a chapter titled "Leadership and Ethics for Counterinsurgency" in the *U.S. Army Field Manual*. While we can defend him in part by noting that, according to him, the affair did not begin until late 2011, when he was out of uniform, it is also clear that the general public - and the General, in tendering his resignation - concluded that he was guilty of a serious lapse in ethical judgment and action.

Petreaus is by no means alone, even in recent history. Richard Nixon. overwhelming re-elected to a second term, lost his presidency when he covered up the orchestration and financing of the Watergate break-in. Bill Clinton, re-elected for his own second term, was impeached by the House of Representatives due in large part to his sexual affair with a White House intern.

We are all familiar with bad leaders who do bad things, people who from their earliest days in power seem to lack a moral center. But how do we explain good leaders who do bad things? Because if it can happen to them, it can happen to any of us.

Juvenal, the 2nd century Roman poet, said that "No man ever became wicked all at once." This suggests that something happens in the development of some leaders that puts them on the path to ethical failure. Historian Barbara Tuchman, in her study of leaders who went down a ruinous path, said in her analysis of Pope Alexander VI (1492-1503) that "The most grievous danger for any Pope lies in the fact that encompassed as he is by flatterers, he never hears the truth about his own person and ends by not wishing to hear it."[109] This suggests that leadership success itself can produce ethical failure. Petraeus, Nixon, and Clinton were successful - until they were not. How does that occur, and how can we prevent it?

The Bathsheba Syndrome

Management professors Dean Ludwig and Clinton Longenecker suggest that this problem goes at least as far back as King David. At the height of his power, David saw Bathsheba bathing and desired her. When she became pregnant, he tried to entice her husband, the soldier Uriah, to return from war to re-consummate his marriage and thus hide David's sin. When Uriah insisted on remaining in the field, as he felt honor demanded, David ordered that he be placed in the front lines, where he was killed. David then married Bathsheba, but the child she bore died.

Ludwig and Longenecker use this Biblical tale to name what they call the Bathsheba Syndrome.[110] They argue that the personal and organizational benefits that come with success can set leaders up for ethical failure, as shown in Figure 8.1.

On a personal level, success in leadership yields not only a higher level position in an organization but all the advantages that come with that, such as more pay, awards, greater influence, status, and more powerful networks of influence. In terms of organizational capacity to wield power in the service of getting things done, these personal gains also mean more latitude to act - less direct supervision and more control over the agenda and decision making. These benefits, both personal and organizational, are why many aspire to rise in the leadership hierarchy. In the hands of ethical leaders, these benefits enhance one's ability to achieve organizational goals and serve the public.

Figure 8.1

Possible Outcomes for Successful Leaders

	Positive/Benefit	Negative/Disadvantage
Personal Level	**Privileged Access** Position Recognition Influence Latitude Status Associations Rewards/ Access Perks	**Inflated Belief in Self** Emotionally Expansive Unbalanced Personal Life Inflated Ego Isolation Stress Fear of Failure
Organizational Level	**Control of Resources** No Direct Supervision Ability to Influence Ability to Set Agenda Control Over Decision Making	**Loss of Strategic Focus** Organization on Autopilot Delegation without Supervision Strategic Complacency Neglect of Strategy

Source: Dean Ludwig and Clinton Longenecker, *Journal of Business Ethics*, Vol.12, 1993, p. 270

Yet the benefits of power hold the potential for problems. For some leaders their success sets up personal and organizational traps. In Chapter 4, we visited a scene from the film, *A Few Good Men*, in which Col. Nathan Jessep, played by Jack Nicholson, over-reacts to what he perceives as a threat to his status and orders (through his subordinate, Lt. Kendrick) an administrative punishment - a "Code Red" - that results in the death of Pfc. William Santiago, whom Jessep considered a "substandard" Marine. Santiago, we learn, had a medical condition that Jessep never bothers to learn about. As the film progresses, the two Marines who administered the punishment are on trial for Santiago's murder. Captain Jack Ross (played by Kevin Bacon) is the prosecutor. Their defense lawyer, Lt. Daniel Kaffee (played by Tom Cruise), has only one way to save their lives. He must get Jessep to admit that he ordered the "Code Red."

At first, Jessep maintains his composure on the witness stand. Kaffee becomes increasingly desperate, and in one last encounter finally succeeds. Here is the dialogue from that scene:

Lt. Kaffee: Kendrick ordered a Code Red because that's what you told Lt. Kendrick to do! You cut these guys loose! You doctored the log books! Colonel Jessep, did you order the Code Red?

Judge Randolph: You don't have to answer that.

Col. Jessep: I'll answer that question. . . You want answers?

Kaffee: I want the truth!

Jessep: You can't handle the truth! Son, we live in a world that has walls and those walls have to be guarded by men with guns. Who's gonna do it? You? You, Lt. Weinberg?

I have more responsibility than you can possibly fathom. You weep for Santiago and you curse the Marines. You have that luxury. You have the luxury of not knowing what I know, that Santiago's death, while tragic, probably saved lives. And my existence, while grotesque and incomprehensible to you, saves lives!

You don't want the truth because deep down, in places you don't talk about at parties, you want me on that wall. You need me on that wall!

We use words like honor, code, loyalty. We use these words as the backbone of a life spent defending something. I haven't the time or inclination to explain myself to a man who rises and sleeps under the blanket of the protection I provide and then questions the manner in which I provide it. I would rather you just said thank you and went on your way. Otherwise, I suggest you pick up a weapon and stand a post. Either way, I don't give a damn what you think you are entitled to!

Kaffee: Did you order the Code Red?

Jessep: I did the job . . .

Kaffe: Did you order the Code Red?!

Jessep: You're g-d dam right I did!

Kaffee: Please the court, I suggest the members of the jury be dismissed so we can move to an immediate Article 39A session. The witness has rights.

Judge: Captain Ross?

Kaffee: Jack?

[Ross nods in agreement.]

Judge: The members of the court will retreat to an antechamber until further instructed.

Jessep: What the hell is this? Colonel, what's going on? I did my job. I'd do it again.

Jessep is not a man without strengths and achievements. Indeed, we can only presume that he was given the command of this sensitive Guantanamo Bay post because of a career of significant success. He has a chest full of ribbons to demonstrate that. In terms of what we see in Figure 8.1, he has all of the personal and organizational benefits of high level command. Yet, clearly, he also has demonstrated many of the dangers that success can expose one to:

- He has an inflated ego. He demeans Kaffe and the court. He makes extensive use of "I" language - identifying himself as the sole provider of freedom and forgets that he serves as a delegate of civilian and military authority, not as its sole embodiment.
- He is isolated from rational argument - in the earlier scene he dismissed the suggestion that he just transfer Santiago, making it clear that he did not want to hear dissent.
- He fears failure. Though obviously successful, he cannot stomach the fact that he could not turn Santiago around.
- He has lost strategic focus. A minor problem like Santiago should never have occupied his attention. The whole affair has taken his eyes off the ball that matters - the effective operation of his command.
- He also appears to have an unbalanced personal life. His job is his life so that he cannot step back and adopt the perspective that should have led him to a much more judicious path.

Figure 8.2
The Slippery Slope

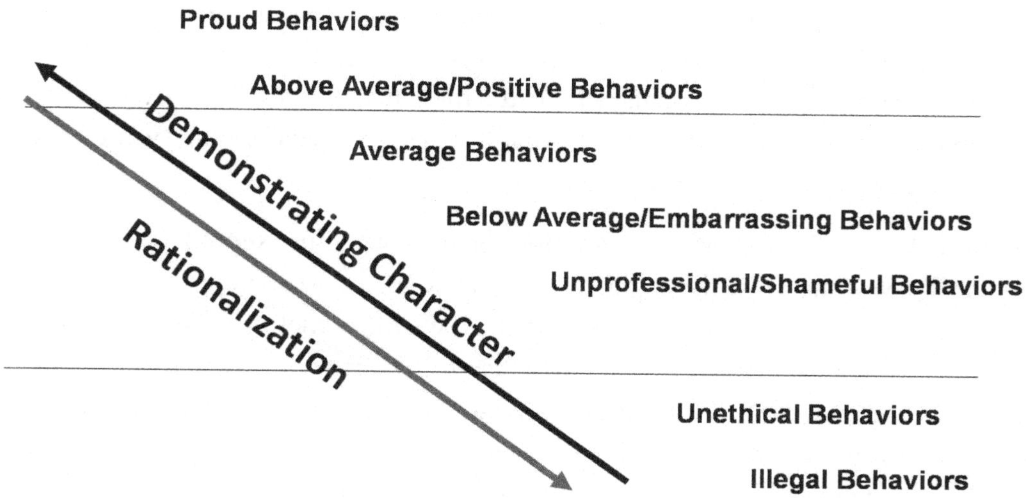

Proud Behaviors

Above Average/Positive Behaviors

Demonstrating Character

Average Behaviors

Below Average/Embarrassing Behaviors

Rationalization

Unprofessional/Shameful Behaviors

Unethical Behaviors

Illegal Behaviors

Source: Dr. Larry Kokkelenberg , Federal Executive Institute (adapted)

The question that begs answering is: how did Jessep get this way? He may have had a big ego much earlier in his life, and that may be part of the explanation. But there has to be more, and that more would seem to be that his very success and its perks set him up for ethical mistakes, as Ludwig and Longenecker suggest. We can think about this as the proverbial slippery slope, as shown in Figure 8.2.

Once a source of pride to himself and the Marines, Jessep gradually got more insulated and there were fewer controls on his discretion. His ego had fewer constraints and no doubt grew in its impact on his actions, so that his behavior became just average, even unprofessional at times (recall the earlier scene where he ignored good advice and ordered the Code Red). He crossed a line from above average to average behavior and then another line to unethical and eventually illegal behavior (the prohibited Code Red). At each step, one can imagine him rationalizing what he did - note his ending statement: "I did my job."

There is another question worth considering: why, at the very end, did Jessep seem so shocked that he was being charged with a crime? Did he not realize what he had done? Rationalization may be part of the answer, but research by business professor Max Bazerman and his colleagues suggests there is more to it.[111] They argue that there are three temporal stages at which our emotions are pitted against our reason as we engage ethical issues. Asked to predict what we would do when confronted with a hypothetical moral temptation or ethical dilemma, our "should" self rules. That is the rational part of us that "knows" we will act ethically - that is what we expect of ourselves and we know others expect of us.

At the moment of decision, however, we can become overwhelmed by stress, strong emotions, and other pressures. We "fool" ourselves by using language euphemisms for what we are doing (e.g. "Code Red" instead of "assault," "enhanced interrogation" instead of "torture"). We become numb to our actions, sometimes because we have repeated them many times. We attribute the cause of our action to something or someone else (i.e. Santiago is "substandard"). Our "want" self takes over, pushing our "should" self to the background.

Then, after the decision is made and our emotions have cooled, our "should" self returns. If we have acted unethically, we must close the cognitive dissonance gap between how we think of ourselves and how we acted. This can take some mental gymnastics. We may redefine what we did so that it is now "ethical," hence Jessep's statement that "I'd do it again." We may only remember positive aspects of what we did. Or we may console ourselves by saying that we're not so bad if we failed to act (an act of omission, such as not disagreeing with an unethical policy decision by our boss) because, after all, we're not the ones who did wrong (the boss's act of commission).

This temporal sequence is shown in Figure 8.3.

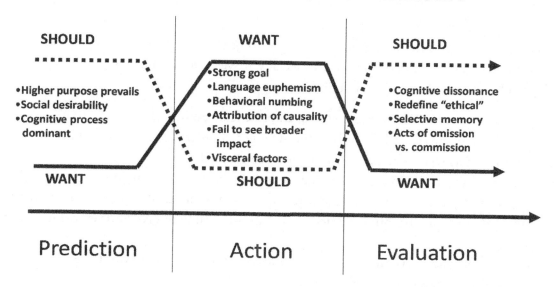

Figure 8.3
Why We Aren't As Ethical As We Think We Are

Source: "Why We Aren't As Ethical As We Think We Are: A Temporal Explanation" – by Tenbrunsel, Diekmann, Wade-Benzoni, and Bazerman, 2007.

Moral Self-Licensing

There is yet another way to think about why good leaders do bad things. Strange as it may seem, the fact that they have done good things, from an ethical standpoint, may make it easier for them to be unethical in future situations. Researchers call this phenomenon "moral self-licensing." In short, doing good gives them a feeling of moral self-worth, kind of like money in the bank, that enables 'withdrawals' in future situations where either their sensitivity or inclination to moral correctness is diminished.

In a summary of the research in this area, Anna Merrit, Daniel Effron and Benoit Monin offer multiple examples of this phenomenon. In one study, participants were asked to write a short story about themselves using morally positive or morally negative trait words given by the researchers. When the experiment ended, each participant was asked if he or she would like to donate to charity part of the payment for the experiment. Those asked to write about themselves using positive words (e.g. fair, kind) donated the least. Those who wrote about themselves using negative words (e.g. selfish, mean) donated the most. The moral licensing effect shows up as well, for example, in simulated hiring decisions, where hiring a minority person in one situation leads some to overlook a highly qualified minority candidate in another scenario.

This phenomenon suggests we can fool ourselves. We can even fool others sometimes. The research suggests that, in certain situation, others may cut us some slack because of our prior moral behavior. But they can also judge us more harshly, especially if we have claimed to be ethical and they see unethical behavior to which we seem blind.[112]

There are many ways to address these ethical traps of leadership:

- Avoid leadership isolation. Ensure that you get other points of view from those above and below you as well as respected peers and even outsiders.
- Minimize the stress of your job. Engage in healthful living (nutrition, exercise, sleep) and use a variety of stress management techniques (e.g. mindfulness training, meditation). If stressed, you can also put off a decision to another time to give your emotions a chance to subside.
- Do not delegate decisions with major ethics components, unless you have very good reason to trust the ethics of your subordinates.
- Understand the dangers of the slippery slope. Encourage dissent from those around you, and reward those willing to challenge your ethics decisions.
- Understand that emotions can override ethics in your decision making. Name the emotions you may expect to feel in tough situations and rehearse how you will deal with them when they come up.
- Before you make a decision, set time aside specifically to recall your "should" self.
- Evaluate options simultaneously, not sequentially. The latter allows you to make an ethical choice without comparison to more ethical alternatives.[113]
- Commit to ethical action publicly, so that there is more pressure to live up to a standard.

While success may bring special dangers to hierarchical leaders, as we have discussed, the general principles apply to anyone who is advancing in their career, since advancement always gives one perks (and opens up dangers) that come with increased responsibility.

The Importance of Balance

One of the chief downsides of enhanced leadership and professional advancement is the tendency to overwork, to lead an unbalanced life. There are at least two ways this can happen. When it does, bad behavior by good people is more likely.

First, in our 24/7, always-on-call, high-speed world, it is easy to succumb to the seemingly ceaseless demands of one's job. The stress is intense and doing a job ethically can be undercut due to this pressure. In a 2007 study by the firm Deloitte & Touche, 91 percent of respondents said that employees were more likely to behave ethically at work when they have work-life balance.[114] Since extreme workplace stress can cause dissatisfaction, it is not surprising that the same survey found that 60 percent of workers cite job dissatisfaction as one of the main reasons people behave unethically at work.

The leader must set the tone and model the practices that prevent an imbalance in workers lives. Gen. Colin Powell cautioned against leaders who are "busy bastards." They don't realize what the long hours they spend at work - and usually expect of others - can do to morale, effectiveness, and ethics. As he put it:

> *"When it was necessary to get a job done, I expected my subordinates to work around the clock. When that was not necessary, I wanted them to work normal hours, go home at a decent time, play with the kids, enjoy family and friends, read a novel, clear their heads, daydream, and refresh themselves. I wanted them to have a life outside the office. I am paying for the quality of their work, not for the hours they work".*[115]

Second, an imbalance in favor of work can lead us to fail to live up to our ethical standards because we have nothing else in our lives that seems to matter. Work becomes too emotionally important; we cannot conceive of life without it.

There is a scene in the film *Remains of the Day*, based on the Kazuo Ishiguro novel by the same name, in which Miss Kenton, the housekeeper, tells her boss, Mr. Stevens, that she will resign if Lord Darlington does not reverse his decision to fire two German, Jewish girls who report to her. It is the mid-1930s, and Lord Darlington is preparing to host international visitors in an effort to avert another world war. He feels that the presence of the Jewish girls would anger his German guests. Since, once let go, they could be forced to return to Germany where their lives could be in danger, Miss Kenton takes a stand, at least in her conversation with Stevens.

Sometime after this, Mr. Stevens, the butler and Miss Kenton's boss, asks her why she did not leave, since the Jewish girls had been forced out. "I'm not leaving," she says. "I have nowhere to go. I have no family. . . I'm frightened of leaving and that's the truth. All I see in the world is loneliness, and it frightens me. That's all my high principles are worth, Mr. Stevens."

Miss Kenton did not make an unethical decision. Lord Darlington did that. But neither did she live in accordance with her principles, because her work was her life. As she put it, "I have nowhere to go."

When your job is too important, when you depend on it too much, you are more likely to cut ethical corners to keep it.

Viewed from a slightly different vantage point, Miss Kenton made an ethical decision, but she lacked the ability to carry it out. As she found out, good intentions were not enough. What could she have done (without resigning)? To that we now turn.

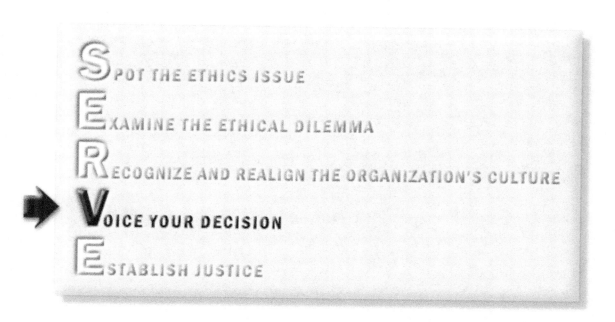

SPOT THE ETHICS ISSUE

EXAMINE THE ETHICAL DILEMMA

RECOGNIZE AND REALIGN THE ORGANIZATION'S CULTURE

VOICE YOUR DECISION

ESTABLISH JUSTICE

—9—
How do I put ethics decisions into words and actions?

—10—
Is it ever OK to lie as a public servant?

-9-
How Do I Put Ethics Decisions Into Words and Actions?

"Vision without execution is hallucination."   – Thomas Edison

In a now-classic formulation, civil servants faced with a disconnect between their values and those of the organization in which they work have three choices. They can *exit* the organization - quietly or with a public declaration. They can remain silent, choosing *loyalty* to superiors. Or they can *voice* their disagreement internally and seek a resolution. Leaving may change nothing and hence may allow unethical behavior to continue. Loyalty does the same, often sacrificing a broader public purpose in the process (and producing stress and feelings of guilt for doing nothing). Voicing ethical concerns seems like the best option, but *how* to do so is the challenge.[116]

Consider the case of Sarah, who was in a meeting when a co-worker, Dave, made inappropriate comments about women in general and some of the "hot" women in the office. Sarah was very uncomfortable. This was not the first time Dave had done this, but as before she said nothing. No one else in the meeting, including several men and two other women, called Dave on his behavior either.

Upset, Sarah pondered approaching her boss, Frank. She liked Frank, but she had begun to wonder if she wanted to stay in his organization if this was not dealt with. At the same time, she knew that the unit was under pressure to complete a number of major projects, and that Dave was involved in several of them. She sensed that Frank would be concerned that confronting the issue could disrupt the team at just the time where they needed to stay focused on work. All of this made her reluctant to press the issue. Yet, she sensed that if she waited for a better time, she might wait forever.

Sarah knew what she wanted to do - express her concern about Dave's sexist behavior, its impact on her and others, and enlist Frank's help in making Dave stop. But how exactly could she say all this in a way it would be heard? Would Frank get defensive, and if so what would she do then? Could she speak without making herself the issue because she was bringing this up just now? Not knowing how to speak up, time was slipping away - and she was getting more and more upset with herself.

Sarah is everywoman - and everyman - who at some point in a government career see an ethical issue, decide that they should address it, know what they want to do, but hesitate. The ethical decision may focus on people inside the organization, as in Sarah's case, or it may involve clients, customers, political leaders, or citizens. Regardless of who is impacted, as public servants we sometimes either don't know how to put our decision into words and actions, or we may fear speaking to higher level officials.

There are reasons, of course, why people hesitate to act on their ethical decisions. These situations don't come up that often, so they lack practice in how to do so. They may feel all alone - as Sarah does - because no one else is speaking up. They may feel that nothing will be done anyway, so why bother. They lack role models - who did voice their decisions well and "lived to tell the tale." Indeed, there seem to be plenty of stories, in the press and on the office grapevine, about those who spoke up and paid a price for it.

Voicing Your Values

All ethics decisions come with a desire to live out our values. Voicing those values is thus an essential skill. Making a decision in your head is not much good if you can't or don't do anything next. Dr. Mary Gentile and her colleagues at Babson College, with support from the Business and Society Program of the Aspen Institute and the Yale School of Management, have focused on just this need. Their project - "Giving Voice to Values" - offers considerable guidance on how to do just that.[117]

A central premise of "Giving Voice to Values" is that people *can* do so because they *have* done so. All of us, probably many times, have encountered situations - whether at work or in our personal lives - where we were asked to do something that conflicted with our values. More often than not, we found a way to resolve the problem that honored our values and was actually good for us, for those we cared about, and (if at work) for our organization. What we need to do, Gentile suggests, is learn from our successes.

Part of this process is getting to know ourselves better. What were our strengths in handing ethical issues in the past? What are our weak spots? How do we communicate best, using what styles or means of expression? How do we approach conflict? What is our tolerance for risk? By understanding ourselves, we can script ways to voice our values that are more comfortable for us and thus more likely to be used. We can also decide where we may need training or coaching to improve.

Part of the process is practice. In our working lives, we practice all kinds of things - presentations to large audiences, talks to our team, arguments to gain resources or convince top management on a needed course of action, etc. What we seldom practice, however, is the language we will use to confront ethical dilemmas. It may be hard to do this with colleagues in the workplace, but trying it with family members or with a coach outside of work is a good alternative.

Part of the process is also anticipating what reasons and rationalizations we will hear against the ethical course of action we have decided upon. According to Gentile, this means thinking about the stakeholders, what matters to them, how they will defend themselves, and how we will respond (and then, of course, verbally practicing our response). This involves as well, framing our ethical decision in terms that are most likely to be seen as having the organization's interests (not our own) at the forefront. For example, she suggests anchoring our argument in the long-term interests of the organization, in its broader purpose, in the total costs of the organization's proposed course of action (since many decisions are made without anticipating the downstream costs of ethical failures) and/or in the danger that taking an unethical path now may lead to further ethical compromises (in the way that one lie often leads to others to support it).

As the foregoing suggests, the "Giving Voice to Values" project concludes that there are "ethical enablers," both under our personal control and under the organization's control, that we can enlist in the script we create for ourselves. Some of these are shown in Box 9.1.

Box 9.1
Ethical Enablers

Under Your Control

- Finding allies
- Getting more information
- Understanding stakeholders
- Reframing the problem as an opportunity rather than a reproach
- How you select/sequence audiences
- Proceeding incrementally
- Questioning assumptions, rationalizations
- Finding a win-win solution
- Appealing to shared purpose/values
- Using your strengths

Within the Organizational Context

- Organizational policies, values, practices
- Organizational values on ethics, debate and discussion
- Existing mechanisms for open debate and discussion (e.g. dissent channels)
- Systems for raising questions (e.g. ombudsperson)
- Organizational history of doing the right thing
- Modeling by leaders of ethical behavior

Source: *Giving Voice to Values* (Gentile, 2012)

Returning to Sarah's problem with Dave, her co-worker, we can see ways she might approach her boss, Frank. Knowing that she does not like open confrontation and that Frank will have a large concern about accomplishing key projects, she decides to meet with Frank privately and to frame her conversation in the context of the overall needs of the organization - how Dave's behavior is actually slowing things down and making collaboration on the team difficult. Since she expects Frank may get defensive or at the least say "not now" to her concern, she asks her female co-workers if they share similar concern about Dave and if she might share that as part of her conversation with Frank. That way, she has allies and can argue that it is not just her productivity that is at risk. She also decides that she will not ask Frank to speak to Dave immediately but that she can wait until after the first major deadline, if she has Frank's commitment to do so then, thus presenting a "win-win" scenario. She knows that the organization has a firm, written policy against sexual harassment, and this will also be part of her conversation with Frank. Sarah decides to practice with her boyfriend, who she knows will be both supportive and helpful as he role-plays Frank and what Frank might say.

Sarah's situation is an example of a related issue in voicing values - speaking truth to power. In organizational life, and especially in public service, the need to do so can be critical to the commitment we make in taking the oath of office.

Speaking Truth to Power

On February 25, 2003, less than a month before the United States invaded Iraq to topple Saddam Hussein, Army Chief of Staff Erik Shinseki testified in front of the Senate Armed Services Committee. Asked by Sen. Carl Levin (D-MI) how many troops would be needed in an occupying force once the invasion succeeded, Shinseki responded: "I would say that what's been mobilized to this point, something on the order of several hundred thousand soldiers." Shinseki predicted that any postwar force would need to ensure safety in a country with "ethnic tensions that could lead to other problems."

Two days later, Secretary of Defense Donald Rumsfeld publicly disagreed, calling Shinseki's estimate "far off the mark." The same day, Rumsfeld's deputy, Paul Wolfowitz, said in regard to "higher-end predictions that we have been hearing recently" that "the notion that it will take several hundred thousand U.S. troops to provide stability in post-Saddam Iraq, are wildly off the mark."[118] Shinseki subsequently retired from the military after it was clear that he would not be appointed by Rumsfeld for a second term as Army Chief of Staff. He spoke the truth to power, and he appears to have paid a price. His "lesson" did not go unnoticed among military leaders.

In April 2006, when Shinseki's foresight had proved all too accurate and the U.S. strategy in Iraq was failing badly, retired Marine Corps Gen. Craig Newbold said in an article in *Time* that: "I offer a challenge to those still in uniform: a leader's responsibility is to give voice to those who can't—or don't have the opportunity to—speak . . . It is time for senior military leaders to discard caution in expressing their views and ensure that the President hears them clearly." In an article published by the Army War College in 2007, Leonard Wong and Douglas Lovelace questioned why a general had to be retired to call for those on duty to speak up.[119] What happened to speaking up when you were still in uniform?

The authors concluded in part that senior military leaders lacked an understanding of ways they could speak up and still remain loyal to civilian and military authority. Giving themselves the false choice of keeping quiet or resigning, they often did the first. They only gained their voice when safely in retirement. Speaking truth to power is no easy task, but it has been done. We can learn from that experience. What we learn is that it takes moral courage and a methodology to succeed.

Rushworth Kidder offers an elegant way to think about moral courage, as seen in Figure 9.1.[120]

Figure 9.1
The Elements of Moral Courage

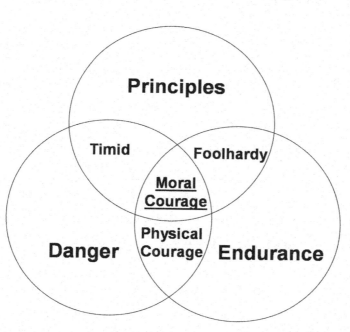

Figure: "Moral Courage and Its Contraries," (p. 184) from MORAL COURAGE by RUSHWORTH KIDDER. Copyright (c) 2005 by Rushworth M. Kidder. Reprinted by permission of HarperCollins Publishers.

Three elements are called into play, and only when all are engaged do we have moral courage. Displaying moral courage must be in service to moral *Principles*. Someone contemplating the need to demonstrate moral courage must also understand the *Dangers*. In an organizational setting, these may include loss of reputation, ostracism by colleagues, diminished access to power and resources, and even loss of one's job. Finally, moral courage requires *Endurance*, the willingness (and some thoughtful strategies) to persevere against danger in service to principles.

As Figure 9.1 suggests, two of these are not enough. Principles allied with Endurance while oblivious to the Danger is being foolhardy. We would not credit someone with moral courage who had no clue that they were putting themselves at any risk. In a similar vein, Principles allied with Danger but with no Endurance is the usual definition of timidity (or even cowardice). Finally, awareness of Danger and Endurance yet without any moral Principles may be physical courage (e.g. a bank robber) but we would not credit such a person with moral courage.[121]

Using this framework, we can credit Erik Shinseki with moral courage. He believed in the moral imperative of giving an honest professional opinion on a matter of grave national consequence. We can probably assume he knew that his testimony would not be welcomed by civilian Pentagon leadership (or the White House). Yet he persevered nonetheless, knowing that his effectiveness in his role, not to mention his tenure as Chief of Staff, was at risk.

By contrast, those senior officers who saw the unwarranted assumptions of easy success in Iraq and the dangers to their careers from speaking out while on active duty - and then kept silent - can be credited with timidity at best.

Endurance is best if it is more than just drawing a line in the sand. Box 9.2 presents the case of another Army Chief of Staff, George C. Marshall. As we saw earlier (Chapter 7), Marshall was known for confronting superiors in service to the mission. Read the case and think about how he does so, before reading further.

Clearly, Marshall draws on several of the techniques identified in "Giving Voice to Values." He knows himself and how he best approaches superiors. He has had practice in doing so and draws on that experience. He also employs the techniques of "social power."

Marshall has a position as Army Chief of Staff. It comes with power - the use of delegated authority, rewards, and other tools. But positional power is not enough. Key people do not report to him, or he is their subordinate. He cannot "order" the president to do anything. In service to his Oath of Office to defend the Constitution and to his moral values of honesty, integrity, and deferring to civilian authority, he needs to draw on other sources of power.

Box 9.2
Marshall Argues With Roosevelt

George Marshall was brought to Washington. D.C. in July of 1938 to join the Army's War Plans Division. His reputation as a master at logistics in World War I preceded him, but he was mostly unknown to President Roosevelt. On November 14, 1938, Marshall attended a White House meeting where FDR announced a decision to plan for a fleet of 10,000 planes, noting he would ask Congress for 20,000 but expected them to cut the request in half. After everyone else in the room agreed, he turned to Marshall, who was alarmed. "Mr. President, I am sorry, but I don't agree with that at all," Marshall said, concerned that the Army lacked enough trained pilots and munitions. As Marshall recalled, the president looked "startled" and the meeting ended. As everyone left, "they all bade me good-bye and said my tour in Washington was over."

Yet, on April 23, 1939, Roosevelt selected him to be the next Army Chief of Staff, jumping over 33 more senior generals. Marshall told FDR he would take the job only if he could speak his mind. "Is that all right?" Marshall asked. "Yes," Roosevelt replied, to which Marshall retorted: "You said 'yes' pleasantly, but it may be unpleasant." Marshall continued a cool relationship with the President, refusing to laugh at his jokes or go to Hyde Park. Marshall declined to state his party preference and would not even vote (on the assumption that voting could compromise his objectivity).

In early 1940, just weeks before the fall of Paris, the Appropriations Committee cut Marshall's request for new planes to 57 and cut $11 million needed to help defend 1,200 miles of Alaskan coastline. On May 10, 1940, Marshall met with Henry Morgenthau (Secretary of the Treasury), who told him that he might not get even $18 million he thought had been committed. He convinced Morgenthau to set up an appointment with the President. On May 13th, Morgenthau briefed the president on other matters, but Roosevelt did not want to hear from Marshall. As Marshall later recounted to his biographer, Forrest Pogue:

"Well, I know exactly what he would say," FDR said. "There is no necessity for me hearing him at all."

"Well, it was a desperate situation," Marshall recalled. "I felt that he might be the president, but I had certain knowledge which I was sure he didn't possess or didn't grasp. I thought the whole thing was catastrophic in its possibilities . . . So, recalling that a man has a great advantage, psychologically, when he stands looking down on a fellow, I took advantage, in a sense, of the president's condition. So when he terminated the meeting, I, not having had a chance to say anything, I walked over and stood looking down at him. I said, 'Mr. President, may I have three minutes?' And then, in a complete change of mood, and in a most gracious fashion, he said, 'Of course, General Marshall.'

Marshall then unleashed a torrent of facts and figures: The German army had 140 divisions, the United States only five; weapons were in short supply and critical new weapon systems were not even in production; and the country's industrial capacity had not yet been shifted to reflect the growing threat.

"I said, 'If you don't do something like that, and do it right away, and really do it today, I don't know what is going to happen to this country ...' I said, 'I don't know quite how to express myself about this to the President of the United States, but I will say this [this I said very forcefully] **that you have got to do something and you've got to do it today.**"*

Marshall left the room with a $79 million appropriation. A few days later, he requested and received an additional billion dollars.

"Social power" was first described in research by social psychologists John French and Bertram Raven in1959. As the concept has evolved, in a current formulation by organizational consultant John Whitlow, we can think of social power as the ability to influence others by using one or more of the following:[122]

- Interpersonal Power - emotional intelligence and related skills
- Associative Power - personal networks of key individuals and groups.
- Informational Power - knowledge and information in a particular area (business acumen)
- Expertise Power - command of a particular subject for an issue under discussion

Marshall draws on all four to speak the truth to power. His interpersonal power has built a relationship marked by trust and confidence from the president and Morgenthau, and he is astute in knowing how to approach Roosevelt in private and when he is most likely to be able to listen. His network, in the Administration and in Congress, is deep and effective, bolstering his credibility and justification for being heard. He is widely respected as a master of the military profession. His command of "a torrent of facts and figures" on the current military situation overpowers the president's reluctance. Marshall has also negotiated the nature of his relationship, from the very beginning, so that he can be objective and direct with Roosevelt.

Marshall is also a master at what Brig. Gen. John Johns (Ret.) calls "loyal dissent." This combination of both *loyalty* to superiors and *voice* in dealing with the ethical dilemma of confronting a conflict of values between the president and himself shows that one need not be silent to be loyal. Johns' "Guidelines for Loyal Dissent" offer a roadmap for speaking truth to power (see Box 9.3).

Note that, in these guidelines, *exit* - through resigning or even whistle-blowing - is still an option.

When All Else Fails

On November 18, 2004, Dr. David Graham, a 20-year employee and then the Associate Director for Science, Office of Drug Safety, at the Food and Drug Administration (FDA), testified in front of the Senate Finance Committee. He charged his own agency with inadequately protecting the public against the dangers of the arthritis drug, Vioxx, which he claimed his research showed was causing heart attacks and strokes. "I could have given a very mealy-mouthed statement," he told a reporter, "[b]ut then I would have been part of the problem."[123]

Indeed, for some time, Graham had been a thorn in the side of his own superiors. "You don't get rewards for doing the work that gets a drug taken off the market," he said. He consistently charged that the FDA was facing an ethical dilemma common to any agency that is charged with both supporting and regulating an industry.

Box 9.3
Guidelines for Loyal Dissent

1. Choose your issues carefully. Dissent tries the patience of superiors. Use your credits for dissent judiciously. Some criteria in choosing issues:
   a. How important is it?
   b. What are your chances of success?
   c. What are the costs to your career and family in challenging your superiors?
   d. Do you have a moral responsibility to challenge?

2. Do your homework and think it over! Do not shoot from the hip every time you disagree with a position taken by your superiors.

3. Clearly take ownership for your dissent.

4. Don't personalize the challenge: focus on the issue. Remember that reasonable people can honestly differ, sometimes with strong conviction, on issues.

5. Be objective and balanced in your analysis of the issue. Each of us is a product of our own unique experiences and we view the world based on those experiences. Try to put yourself in the shoes of the opposition, remembering that higher officials tend to view issues in a broader context.

6. Don't paint your superiors into a corner by challenging their judgment in public (or at a staff meeting unless the superior asks for a discussion of the issue), especially if they have taken a public stance.

7. Do not expect radical change in opposing views.

8. Know your boss. What are his/her central values and does the issue at hand relate to those central values? If so, change will be difficult.

9. Provide alternatives to the position you are challenging, i.e. don't be merely negative.

10. Choose your time to challenge. In general, try to get your oar in the water before a position has been announced.

11. Recognize when you have pushed to the limit. Bosses differ in their tolerance of dissent, even when it is loyal.

12. Always remember that you may be wrong, you may even be ideologically biased.

13. Accept defeat graciously, i.e. don't pout. On the other hand, if you cannot live with the decision from a moral standpoint, you have the option of going to higher authority, or ultimately resigning. (You may also feel justified in contacting Congress, interest groups, or the media. This may be loyal dissent in some instances, but it is often called "whistle blowing" and is judged by different criteria than what I am calling loyal dissent.)

Source: Dr. John Johns, Federal Executive Institute

Within a week, the FDA tried to remove Graham from further work on drug safety, only to back off when Sen. Charles Grassley, Chair of the Finance Committee, and the media intervened. FDA Commissioner Lester Crawford would later issue a memo to all staff indicating they were free to communicate with Congress. Merck, the maker of Vioxx, had already pulled the drug off the market when it knew it could not contravene Graham's research. The drug was later reinstated, however, with much greater restrictions on its use and how it could be marketed. Merck would eventually put up more than $1.3 billion to settle lawsuits and marketing charges against it. Graham, for his part, remained with the FDA and continued his work on drug safety.

Graham's case illustrates the importance of blowing the whistle when faced with an ethical dilemma that can be solved no other way - but also the pitfalls that may result. He was astute enough to seek outside support in his exercise of moral courage (including the not-for-profit Government Accountability Project), yet he also paid a price. While various whistleblower protections against retaliation are in place, there are countless examples of whistleblowers who lost their influence, were ostracized by colleagues and superiors, lost their jobs and/or suffered emotional as well as financial distress.

Whistle blowing, as the *Guidelines for Loyal Dissent* and the Graham case demonstrate, should be a last step, not only for the reasons already discussed but because it will most likely impact your family as well as you. Professor of political science, Carol Lewis, suggests a series of questions to ask before you blow the whistle (see Box 9.4).[124]

Box 9.4
Before You Blow the Whistle

1. Is the violation serious enough to warrant the risk to you and the organization?
2. Are you prepared for this action to become known, for heroism to mutate into betrayal?
3. Are you sure of your facts? Are you sure you're right?
4. Are you sure superiors are not trying to correct the situation?
5. Is your motive purely in the public interest?
6. Are you ready to accept the consequences if you are wrong?"

The first question can be the hardest and has two parts: (a) how can you judge if the issue is serious enough, and (2) even if it is, must you risk yourself and your organization?

As noted earlier, Leonard Wong and Douglas Lovelace of the U.S. Army War College in Carlisle, Pennsylvania, dealt with this problem. The asked the question: how do you know when to just salute? Their framework, with axis titles adjusted slightly to reflect a civilian as well as military workforce, is shown in Figure 9.2. It makes two major points. First, you need to array the threat to the public (in the military: national security) against the resistance to hearing the truth (in the military: resistance to military advice). Second, as Figure 9.2 shows, there are many ways to dissent short of blowing the whistle, acquiescing, or resigning in protest, though that remains an option.[125]

In conclusion, voicing one's values after deciding what to do regarding an ethics dilemma can be done by drawing upon a wide range of vehicles and techniques. The key is to speak thoughtfully and truthfully. Telling the truth - avoiding lying - turns out, however, to be more complex than it would seem.

Figure 9.2
How to Speak the Truth

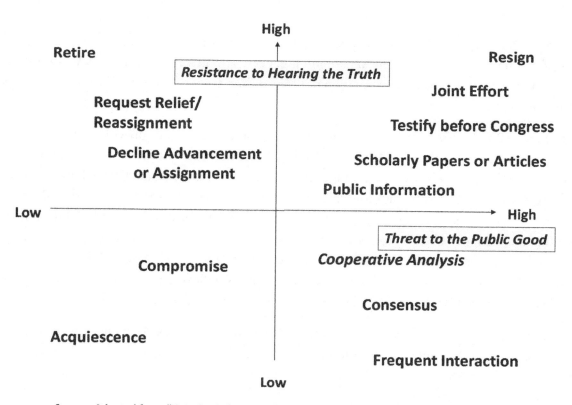

Source: Adapted from "Knowing When to Salute," Wang and Lovelace, Army War College

–10–
IS IT EVER OK TO
LIE TO A PUBLIC SERVANT?

"Integrity is the lifeblood of democracy, Deceit is a poison in its veins."
                                                                – Edward Kennedy

On March 12, 2013, James Clapper, the Director of National Intelligence, was asked a question by Sen. Ron Wyden of the Senate Intelligence Committee: "Does the NSA [National Security Agency] collect any type of data at all on millions or hundreds of millions of Americans?" "No, sir," Clapper replied.

On June 5, 2013, articles began appearing, using classified documents provided by Edward Snowden, a computer specialist working for an NSA contractor, that showed the NSA was doing just that. By June 21, Clapper had written Intelligence Committee Chairwoman Diane Feinstein that: "My response was clearly erroneous - for which I apologize." Shortly thereafter, he told MSNBC's Andrea Mitchell that "I responded in what I thought was the most truthful, or least untruthful manner, by saying no." Clapper went on to say that his testimony was not a lie because it all hinged on what the word "collect" means. He also claimed that he was caught in a situation where he was asked in a public forum about a classified data collection system. Needless to say, many Americans were angry. At least one Republican accused Clapper of perjury and demanded he resign.[126]

As Clapper's case suggests, when Americans believe public servants are lying, trust in government is the first casualty. Yet this case also illuminates the fact that those working in government sometimes struggle with whether, as well as how, they should tell the truth while doing their jobs. This struggle has been going on for a long time.

In *The Prince*, Machiavelli's classic guidance to rulers, he advised that:

"... how one lives is so far distant from how one ought to live, that he who neglects what is done for what ought to be done sooner effects his ruin than his preservation, for a man who wishes to act entirely up to his profession of virtue soon meets with what destroys him among so much that is evil." and " one must know how to colour one's actions and to be a great liar and deceiver."[127]

Machiavelli was not averse to leaders telling the truth. He just felt that some situations demanded that they lie. In contrast, philosopher and ethicist Sissela Bok argues that

"Trust is a social good to be protected just as much as the air we breathe or the water we drink. When it is damaged, the community as a whole suffers; and, when it is destroyed, societies falter and collapse . . . Trust and integrity are precious resources, easily squandered, hard to regain."[128]

Bok, for her part, is not totally averse to leaders telling a lie, though she would condone it only in very few situations that meet tight guidelines.

This struggle about truth-telling matters. Lying is not just an occasional issue for senior leaders who testify in Congress or who must struggle in the interests of "national security" about whether to tell the truth. As the data in Figure 10.1 show, government employees report that lying happens pretty frequently. Trust in government, including trust in one's organizational leaders, suffers as a result.

Figure 10.1

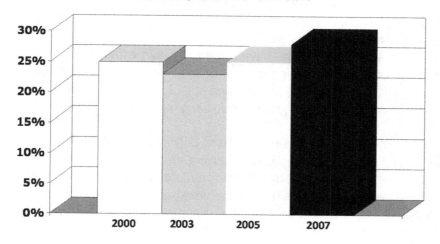

Lying in Government
% of Government Employees Who Report Observing Lying to Employees, Customers, Vendors or the Public

Source: National Government Ethics Survey, 2007, Ethics Resource Center, p. 3

As Bok argues, lies mean that citizens cannot trust the information they have been given, thus constraining the free and informed choice essential to democratic governance. When leaders lie to their workers - or government employees to each other - it leads to poor decision making at best and catastrophic accidents at worst. Lies even harm the liar, weakening his or her own moral compass and, for some, leading to a diminished sense of self.

What is a lie?

"Don't lie" would seem, then, to be sound advice for public servants. That assumes we know what a lie is. Consider the case of Dan in Box 10.1. Did Dan lie to Billy Fullerton? Decide for yourself before reading further.

Box 10.1
Dan Fisher and Serving Veterans

Dan Fisher is Director of the Southeast Claims Division in the Veterans Benefits Administration, and he has been under the gun from his boss, his agency head, and Congressional staff to cut the benefit claims backlog in his office – as have his counterparts for other regions of the country. Dan has tried, unsuccessfully, to convince his superiors that they are asking the impossible. He has had a 25% reduction in staff due to retirements and staff ceilings, which prevent replacements, and every time his staff does more outreach in the community, such as attending community meetings, they generate more claims. Last month, his boss suggested he stop doing outreach, but Dan feels that outreach is not only part of the job but essential as a public service. Dan, a veteran himself, has a particularly hard time with this request. "After all, veterans have a right to know what they are entitled to," he reasons, "especially given their sacrifice for their country." Nevertheless, his boss is now more insistent. When the latest – and still high – backlog numbers came in, his boss ordered him to refuse any more outreach meeting requests.

Dan scans his new emails and sees one from Billy Fullerton, President of the local VFW (Veterans of Foreign Wars) chapter, asking him (or one of his staff) to do a presentation at their next meeting to communicate what benefits VFW members are entitled to receive. Dan knows he has the time but types a brief response indicating that he appreciates the request but just has no one available in the near future. "Perhaps some other time," he says.

Clearly, Dan faces an ethical dilemma. He is torn between his desire to serve veterans by doing more public outreach and his boss's insistence that he stop doing that (to be fair to his boss, because of the latter's concern that not catching up on the claims backlog is not serving veterans well either). Dan does not want to lie to Billy Fullerton. But does he?

Some might argue that he lied because he said he has no time and clearly does. Some might argue that he has not lied because his boss has taken up all his and his staff's time with the demand to clear backlogged cases.

Consider another case, that of Mary Nash, in Box 10.2. Did Mary lie to the president of AMT? Again, decide for yourself before reading further.

Box 10.2
Mary Nash and AMT

Mary Nash manages a procurement office in a major federal agency. She recently signed eight contracts awarded to vendors for work for a program office in one of the agency's bureaus. This is a task order procurement. When a part of the bureau has a need for work covered under the procurement, Mary must choose at least three of the eight contractors and ask them for a bid on the specific piece of work. The bids are evaluated, and one is selected to receive a task order for the work. According to government procurement regulations, Mary must give each of the eight a fair opportunity to compete for task orders, which means in practice that she should invite bids from them on an equitable basis for work they are capable of performing.

After the contract was awarded, Mary's second level boss, a political appointee, verbally directed her not to give any work to AMT Management, one of the eight firms. He did not say the reason, and when Mary inquired, he just replied that he was "not comfortable" with them. Mary has followed this directive. It has been awkward, but at least so far she could fall back on the fact that AMT was not ideally suited, though perhaps it was capable, for any of the task orders generated thus far. As time passes, though, Mary is becoming increasingly uncomfortable. Her discomfort was magnified yesterday when the President of AMT Management called her to ask why, in over six months, her firm has never been given a chance to bid on a task order. "Your firm is clearly one of those whom we value as a partner in our work," Mary told AMT's President, "but the task orders to date have not played to AMT's particular strengths."

Mary also faces an ethical dilemma. She feels obligated, under the terms of a task order procurement, to spread the work around to qualified contractors. Her political boss has ordered her not to give AMT any work, a clear violation of procurement regulations. She feels the tug of loyalty to her boss (and perhaps a concern about her job) but also knows what the law requires. Up until now, she reasons, the issue has been hypothetical, because task orders have not been "ideally suited" for AMT. Faced with the AMT president's demand for fairness in the competitive process, she has answered him in the only way she can think to do so.

Some argue that she has already lied- even before the AMT president called her - by doing what she should not have done. They also argue that she lies to him now through the calculated but evasive statement that "Your firm is clearly one of those whom we value as a partner in our work, but the task orders to date have not played to AMT's particular strengths." Others argue that she has not lied because her statement is factually correct and that she (if not her political boss) does value AMT "as a partner in our work."

Considering both of these cases, we could argue that both Dan and Mary did not lie because their statements were technically truthful - similar to Clapper's insistence that he was truthful because the NSA did not "collect" information on individuals. Yet even if you accept this defense - and many would not - it is clear that something is not right here. It is clear to Dan and Mary as well. Were it not, they would not feel the emotional tug of ethical compromising.

Another way to look at the question is not just whether Dan or Mary "lied" but whether they could have been more truthful. Could Dan, for example, have told Billy Fullerton that he really wanted to speak to the VFW but could not in the foreseeable future because he just had to clear up the backlog? Could Mary have told the President of AMT that she would get back to him and then confronted her political boss to advise him that he was breaking procurement regulations and facing everything from a Congressional investigation to personal legal liability?

Sissela Bok defines a lie as statement with intent to deceive. First, it must make a statement, which could be a verbal act or a calculated act of silence. You have not lied if you are just thinking about deceiving someone. Second, you must have an intent. If you ask a young child: 'how much is 2 + 2?' and the answer comes back "5," the child has not lied because she has no intent to deceive you. She just doesn't know the truth.

Third, there must be deception. We do not need to struggle with the definition of "truth." In the courtroom, it is "the truth, the whole truth, and nothing but the truth." But Dan and Mary are not in a courtroom. They are under no obligation to share every detail of what appears in these two cases. They just need to meet the test that they do not make statements intended to deceive.

A "lie" is, after all, a very loaded emotional term, one from which we recoil in considering our own actions. As a result, we do not think of ourselves as lying. So we search for ways that make us comfortable that we are not doing so. One can imagine Dan and Mary going home the night of these events comfortable in the fact that "at least I didn't lie."

Bok's definition is a helpful guide. It can show us when we are about to lie. It can spur us to find ways to be more truthful - to make statements that are not intended to deceive. It can enable us to spot situations and voice our values when others in our organization are, or are about to engage in, lying.

Another way to see how ubiquitous (and to many confusing) the potential for lying is in government can be seen in Box 10.3. This is a set of techniques familiar to most in government (and many others as well).

Box 10.3
Presumed Alternatives to Lying in Government

Parsing the Definition of Words
Using Language Euphemisms
Feigning Memory Loss
Saying Nothing
Withholding Information
Suppressing Dissenting Views
Evading the Subject
Communicating Partial Truths
Distorting Data/Manipulating Statistics
Presenting Only One Side of an Argument
Leaking Selected Information
Using a False Analogy
Spinning the Story
Assuring Plausible Deniability

While we need not address each of these, illustrating a few will show how easily public servants can make a statement with an intent to deceive and think they are not lying.

During the height of the scandal involving President Clinton and Monica Lewinsky, a White House intern with whom Clinton had oral sex just steps away from the Oval Office, Clinton was asked to comment on a statement made by his attorney, that there "is no sexual relationship between Bill Clinton and Monica Lewinsky." Clinton defended the statement as being correct because at the time there was no relationship: "It depends upon what the meaning of the word 'is' is. If 'is' means 'is and never has been' that's one thing - if it means 'there is none,' that was a completely true statement." This is similar to Director Clapper's denial that he lied because it depends on what the term "collect" means. In both cases, public officials were cloaking an intent to deceive by *parsing the definition of key words*.

When officials in the George W. Bush Administration denied that they used "torture" with enemy combatants, they employed a *language euphemism* - "enhanced interrogation techniques" - to claim they were telling the truth. On June 17, 2008, William Haynes II testified in front of the Senate Armed Services Committee. He had left his position as General Counsel for the Department of Defense in March and was being questioned about the use of these enhanced interrogation techniques, whether he was aware of them, had discussed their legality with the White House, and/or had approved them. According to a press report, in two hours of testimony he said that he "did not recall" at least 23 times and that he "did not remember" at least 22 times.[129] Since it is not likely that he did not recall or remember all the things he was asked about - and could have offered to check his own records - *feigning memory loss* seems to have been used to avoid appearing to lie.

As noted previously, in the spring of 2014, a scandal erupted in the Department of Veterans Affairs (VA) when reports surfaced that employees were deliberately falsifying patient appointment wait times. For example, a veteran would request an appointment but be told he could not get one for at least a month. Rather than enter the "request date" in the system at that moment, the scheduler would wait until an appointment was available and then enter the request as if it had been made on that day, not weeks or months earlier. Thus, the data system was made to appear as if veterans were getting appointments as soon as they asked for them. This was clearly *distorting data*, with an intent to deceive. The lie got compounded when the regional health centers sent the false data to Washington, DC, withholding the truth of what was taking place. Still further, employees began to come forward saying they were threatened with retaliation if they told anyone in Washington, DC the truth. *Withholding accurate information* and *suppressing dissenting views* are methods of deceiving, though some may not think of themselves as lying when they use them.

As a final example, as reported in Bok's book. President Lyndon Johnson campaigned in the election of 1964 as the "peace candidate," charging his opponent, Barry Goldwater, with being too willing both to escalate the war in South Vietnam and to use nuclear weapons against communism. What Johnson never revealed was that, throughout the latter part of the campaign, he was secretly working with his advisors to massively expand the use of force against the North Vietnamese, which he did shortly after he won the election. In *saying nothing* about his plans, he thus deceived the voters. As Bok notes: "Deception of this kind strikes at the heart of democratic government. It allows those in power to override or nullify the right vested in the people to cast an informed vote in critical elections."[130]

Rationalization - Misperceiving Ourselves and Others

How it is that we end up using deception? Dan Ariely, a professor of psychology and behavioral economics at Duke University, asked himself the same question. In *The (Honest) Truth About Dishonesty*, he says the classic answer to when people choose to lie can be framed in the following logic equation:

Benefits of Lying > (Chance of Getting Caught x Penalty for Lying)

If the benefits of lying exceed the chance of getting caught times the penalty for lying, we are likely to lie. If that is correct, then we would always lie if there was absolutely no chance of getting caught or no penalty, and the bigger the benefits (in terms of how much they exceed the right side of the equation), the more likely we would be to lie.[131]

In his lab, he devised an experiment to test this. Study subjects were given a sheet of paper with a matrix as shown in Figure 10.2. Each cell of the five by four matrix had a series of numbers. The task was to find and circle the two numbers in each cell that added up to 10. The goal was to solve as many of these cells as possible in five minutes. Subjects were told they would be paid fifty cents for each cell they completed correctly.

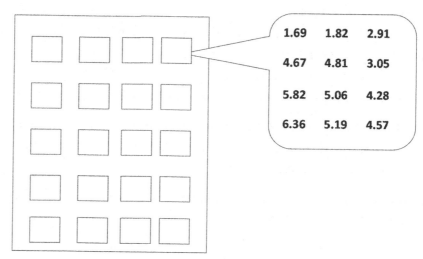

Figure 10.2
The Matrix Test

1.69	1.82	2.91
4.67	4.81	3.05
5.82	5.06	4.28
6.36	5.19	4.57

In the first trial, subjects completed the task and were asked to bring their sheet to the front of the room, where it was checked by a researcher, and then they were paid based on the number of correct cells. The average number of correct cells was four, so that the average payout was $2 per person. Note that there was neither an incentive nor possibility to cheat since a researcher would check the response sheet and determine the payout.

In the second trial, subjects were told to note the number they got correct, go to the back of the room and put their sheet in a shredder, and then go to the front of the room and tell the researcher how many they got right. This time, the ability to cheat (lie) was easy and it was impossible to get caught. The average correct jumped to six, earning $3 (the "shredder" sounded like it did its work but actually preserved each sheet undamaged for the research team). Note two things about this trial. First, lying did take place. Second, counter to the expectation of logic, the average did not jump dramatically (why not report 10 or 15 correct cells since a self-report with no way to check was at work?).

Subsequent trials upped the payout per correct cell to $1, $2, $5 and even $10. Yet the average self-report of correct cells stayed at six. In fact, at $10 it actually was lower than that. Ariely concluded that the logic equation could not be the prime driver. What took place, he concluded was a different, psychological equation. A person will lie only up to the point where their own self-image suffers. Hence, small gains somehow seemed OK, but to take a lot of money for what the subject knew was a lie just did not feel right. It did not square with the basic honesty the test subject felt he or she had.

Since the test subjects did lie when they could not be caught, they were engaged in a delicate balancing act regarding their self-esteem. Moral self-licensing, as we discussed in Chapter 8, may be at work. Subjects felt they were good people so this small transgression was easier to defend. Yet, at higher payouts, they could no longer defend (to themselves) lying. This suggests that we may have an inherent disgust about big lies, condemning all who tell them, including ourselves. It also suggests that if we can convince ourselves, through rationalization, that the lie is not really so bad - or not really a lie - then "the intent to deceive" becomes easier.

Ben Franklin captured the power of rationalization in his *Autobiography* when he noted that: "So convenient a thing it is to be a reasonable creature, since it enables one to find or make a reason for everything one has a mind to do."[132]

We have all been exposed to any number of ways to rationalize. Box 10.4 presents some of the most common in public service.

> ## Box 10.4
> ## Rationalization Arguments in Public Life
>
> I Had No Other Choice.
> It's Legal.
> It's Just Part of the Job.
> Everyone Does It.
> It Doesn't Hurt Anyone.
> It's Not My Responsibility. I'm Just Following Orders.
> It's All for a Good Cause (the "noble lie").
> I Don't Want to Hurt My Team/Boss.
> I Did it to Protect You.
> I Didn't Gain Anything Personally.
> I Deserve This for All I've Done.
> It'll Never Happen Again.

We probably recoil at some of these because they are so obvious and because we usually don't let others get by with them. Have your children ever succeeded with "everyone does it"? Do we let others off with "I'm just following orders"?

Yet some are seductive, under the "right" circumstances. "It's all for a good cause" gets said in a variety of ways, including "it's in the interest of national security" or "they'll be happy when they see the result." This rationalization relies on ethical consequentialism in its defense - the greatest good for the greatest number. While it may be true in some circumstances, we should be wary for two reasons. First, it violates both the "virtue" and "principles" points of the ethical triangle (see Chapter 3). Lying is not associated with virtuous character or acceptable as a universal maxim for guiding behavior. Second, making the "greatest good" argument requires being able to think of all those potentially affected over a very long timeframe in which consequences may occur. That's harder than it looks, since we usually think with much shorter moral horizons. President Johnson may well have invoked this defense as he secretly prepared to escalate the war in Vietnam, but it did not stand the test of time.

Note also, as Max Bazerman points out, that rationalization is something we sometimes use to ignore or excuse others' unethical behavior, not just our own. For example, through what he and his colleagues call "motivated blindness," we can excuse unethical behavior (as accounting firms did with

Enron) because we have a vested interest in ignoring a lie. We can also suspend our ethical judgment until we see whether an action produces a good or bad outcome, such as accepting the decision to go to war in Iraq until it appeared that it was failing, when all of a sudden we condemn it as unethical.[133]

It may appear that there are never situations in which a lie (whether outright, veiled, or rationalized) is justified. In the next section, we will suggest that there are. But first, there are some helpful practices to minimize lying, most suggested by Dan Ariely:

- Use reminders of the commitment to honesty

  When reminded of their obligation to tell the truth, people may be less likely to lie. Helpful reminders can take varied forms. Retaking the Oath of Office or signing forms that testify to our veracity in a given document (e.g. a financial disclosure form), report, or action can be useful. Leaders can emphasize the importance of truth-telling by setting an example, creating honesty as a core value in our organizations, rewarding truthfulness in public and private ways, and punishing those who lie.

- Decrease the distance between the actor and the act

  In another experiment, Ariely tested whether people thought it was acceptable to move their golf ball when a shot put them in a bad spot. Subjects were asked whether they would use each of three "solutions" and what they predicted others would do. Table 10.1 shows the results. As you can see, people thought themselves more honest than others, but the key finding was that it was easier to justify cheating the more physical distance you could place between yourself and the ball. This, hitting it with a club was deemed more "acceptable" than with your shoe, and actually picking it up with your hand was the least acceptable choice. Anyone in public service can relate to situations in which higher level officials have found it easier to ask subordinates to lie than do so themselves. As we saw in the case of *Challenger*, it was easier for the managers at MTI and NASA's Level 3 to rationalize a launch decision that would be finally made two levels above them and that did not have to be explained directly to the astronauts. The solution is to decrease the virtual and/or physical distance between the decision maker and those who will be affected by the decision.

- Prevent lying from becoming socially acceptable

  The more the culture of the group or organization tolerates lying, the easier it becomes for people to rationalize going along. In March 2013, Beverly Hall, the former superintendent of Atlanta's schools, and 34 others were indicted on multiple charges connected to changing students' answers on standardized tests to produce higher scores. The scores were related to decisions such as school reputation, staff bonuses, and teacher recognition and tenure. Hall herself had been feted at the White House and earned more than $300,000 in bonuses. One person could probably not have succeeded doing this alone, but when a like-minded group formed, it became more socially acceptable, easier to rationalize. Preventing this can be aided by the actions we discussed above as well as by anonymous surveys to measure the culture's toleration for lying, with appropriate follow-up action.

- Counter rationalizations

Asking unbiased others to check our reasoning and justification before we act is a useful defense against rationalization. When we sense that rationalization is being used by others, we can draw upon various ways to show the danger and consequences. As discussed in the Giving Voice to Values work of Mary Gentile and her colleagues, for example, we can point out examples of the slippery slope, the full costs if the lie is discovered, and other choices that do not involve lying.

Table 10.1
Propensity to Cheat in Golf by Moving Your Ball

Method of Cheating	Tendency to Cheat	
	Others	Oneself
With club	23%	8%
Kicking	14%	4%
Picking up	10%	2.5%
Source: The (Honest) Truth About Dishonesty, *by Dan Ariely, p. 64*		

Is It Ever OK to Lie in Public Life?

Some years ago, in a training program that included as a participant a covert CIA agent (who had changed his name for the purposes of the class), he described the hardest part of his job - making a split-second decision that could compromise one of his field agents and potentially lead to his capture, imprisonment or death. Would he lie to save that life? Absolutely, he replied. No one in the room questioned his response (or his need to use a false name in the class).

This is one of a small number of situations for which lying as a public servant is socially approved. In law enforcement, to use another example, lying to a suspect has been upheld in Supreme Court cases where it can be shown that the police did not coerce action or statements. For example, in *Frazier v. Cupp*, the Court held that a confession was voluntary and admissible even though the police had lied in telling the defendant that his accomplice had already confessed.[134] Witness protection programs, to take another example, are designed to lie about someone's identity to protect that person from harm.

Most public servants, however, will not confront such unusual and rare situations. Once again, Sissela Bok offers a useful way for the typical civil servant to confront this ethical dilemma. Her guidance is essentially a series of questions we can ask ourselves before we decide that it is acceptable to lie (see Box 10.5).

Box 10.5
Is It OK to Lie? - Questions to Ask

1. Is the lie essential to save a life or prevent imminent physical danger to others?
2. Will the lie damage human dignity? Preserve it?
3. Would the lie be viewed by the duped as equally justified?
4. Is there time to consider alternatives to lying?
5. Are there truthful alternatives?
6. Will the lie set a dangerous precedent - increase the chances for future lies?
7. Are there moral reasons that justify the lie?
8. What will be the impact of the lie on the liar? The duped? The broader society? Trust in government?
9. Has a public process been used in which reasonable people representing diverse viewpoints have set standards for when such a lie might be permissible?
10. Will I be able to explain the lie afterwards?

Source: Lying: Moral Choice in Public and Private Life *by Sissela Bok*

As we saw in the cases of Dan and Mary, for example, their responses failed almost all of these tests. Indeed, the number of situations that can survive the gauntlet of these ten questions will be small.

At the height of the Cuban Missile Crisis in October 1962, when President Kennedy was desperately searching for a way to get ICBMs (Intercontinental Ballistic Missiles) out of Cuba without launching a nuclear war, he decided to approve a backroom deal with Soviet Chairman Nikita Khrushchev. Kennedy would agree to remove missiles from Turkey (which were old and scheduled to be removed) if Khrushchev would remove the missiles from Cuba. Kennedy stipulated that the deal had to be kept secret (he did not want to appear to trade off European security for U.S. security) and that the missiles in Turkey would only come out after the Cuban situation was completely settled (he did not want the deal to appear as a quid pro quo). About a month after the crisis ended, Kennedy was asked a question at a news conference, and replied as follows:

> Q: Mr. President, in the various exchanges of the past three weeks, either between yourself and Chairman Khrushchev or at the United Nations, have any issues been touched on besides that of Cuba, and could you say how the events of these past three weeks might affect such an issue as Berlin or disarmament or nuclear testing?

> A: The President: No. I instructed the negotiators to confine themselves to the matter of Cuba completely, and therefore no other matters were discussed. Disarmament, any matters affecting Western Europe, relations between the Warsaw pact countries and NATO, all the rest – none of these matters was to be in any way referred to or negotiated about until we had made progress and come to some sort of a solution on Cuba. So that has been all we have done diplomatically with the Soviet Union the last month.

Kennedy clearly lied. Other matters had not only been discussed but had been negotiated. Was the lie justified?

The deal itself seems justifiable. It averted war and removed the missiles. Whether the lie about the deal is justifiable is a matter on which people may disagree. Had Kennedy told the truth in the press conference, we can imagine some of the possible consequences. Relations with Europe might well have been damaged, suggesting to the Soviets that it could drive a wedge in the West through aggressive tactics. Most people would probably have accepted the need for the lie if they had found out about it. There were probably no more-truthful alternatives. That even this type of situation gives one pause about the necessity of lying is as it should be. Lying may be necessary, but it should be neither easy nor frequent.

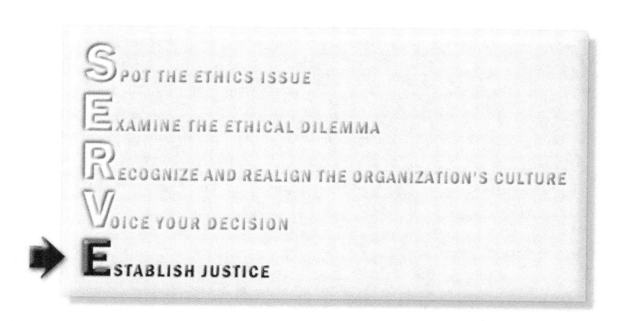

SPOT THE ETHICS ISSUE

EXAMINE THE ETHICAL DILEMMA

RECOGNIZE AND REALIGN THE ORGANIZATION'S CULTURE

VOICE YOUR DECISION

➡ **E**STABLISH JUSTICE

—11—
Why do I need to care about justice?

—12—
What is just and how do I act justly as a public servant?

–11–
WHY DO I NEED TO CARE ABOUT JUSTICE?

"Justice is the end of government. It is the end of civil society. It ever has been and ever will be pursued until it is obtained, or until liberty be lost in the pursuit."

- James Madison, Federalist #51

In the aftermath of the terrorist attacks of September 11, 2001, Congress enacted a Victims Compensation Fund. The fund operated between December 2001 and June 2004 (and was reauthorized in 2011) to provide money for economic and non-economic losses to individuals or relatives of deceased individuals and others who were killed or physically injured as a result of the attacks.

After the Gulf Oil spill in April 2010, under pressure from the Obama Administration, oil giant BP waived the $75 million cap on damages set in law and created a fund of up to $20 billion to compensate those who suffered losses as a result of the accident.

Both of these funds were administered by a Special Master, Kenneth Feinberg, a lawyer with wide experience in addressing the demands such tragedies create. Both of these funds were aimed primarily at helping those most significantly affected and secondarily at managing legal liability, to limit the long and stressful impact of lawsuits on victims and the tendency of lawsuits to damage companies and produce huge fees for lawyers. In short, both funds were efforts to address demands for justice.

Feinberg also managed The One Fund, a charitable group established by Boston Mayor Thomas Menino and Massachusetts Governor Deval Patrick, to compensate victims and survivors of the April 2013 Boston Marathon bombing. Reflecting on that experience, in a statement that could easily be applied to the 9/11 and Gulf Oil Spill funds, Feinberg said that: "I don't expect anyone to talk about fairness or justice when they've lost limbs, lost loved ones, had their lives turned asunder . . . The idea that anyone receives money and believes that justice has been done or that they have been treated fairly - I would be shocked if they felt that way . . . I hope they feel an acknowledgement that they received some compensation from fellow citizens. That's all."[135]

Yet an 'acknowledgement by fellow citizens' *is* an effort to provide some justice in tragedies that destroy the lives of innocent victims. In all three cases, there was a widely felt public need that victims and their families suffered unjustly. There was also a demand that those responsible be brought to justice. And there was a concern that efforts to do both should use procedures that were transparent, fair and efficient. These efforts in fact represent different definitions of justice.

Why Public Servants Need to Care About Justice

As James Madison noted, "justice is the end of government." The most clear-cut statement of this is in the Preamble to the U.S. Constitution, which begins: "We the People of the United States, in Order to form a more perfect Union, establish Justice . . ." Justice is the first substantive requirement of this "vision statement" which precedes the machinery of government established by the Constitution's seven Articles and 27 Amendments. That machinery is in fact designed to deliver justice. Over the course of years, justice has been the predominant work of American society under the Constitution, most notably, for example, in ending slavery, extending the franchise to minorities and women, and establishing a legal system to protect and expand the civil rights of individuals and groups.

The need for justice appeared in several of the *Federalist Papers*, written by James Madison, Alexander Hamilton, and John Jay to argue for ratification of the Constitution. In Federalist #10, Madison noted, reflecting on government under the Articles of Confederation and State constitutions, that "Complaints are everywhere heard . . . that our governments are too unstable, that the public good is disregarded in the conflicts of rival parties, and that measures are too often decided, not according to the rules of justice and the rights of the minor party, but by the superior force of the interested and overbearing majority." The Constitution, he argued, is the corrective to the injustice arising from "factions" that operate at the expense of what Madison called the "aggregate interests of the community."[136]

More recently, the Pledge of Allegiance, written in 1892 and formally adopted by Congress in 1942, recited in schools and in public ceremonies, reminds us of what our republic stands for, ending as it does with the words "with liberty and justice for all."

For many in government, it is easy to forget the call for justice, not because public servants don't care but because they are overwhelmed in their daily work with professional tasks, establishing and following procedures, and cutting costs. Their job descriptions, after all, do not contain the word "justice."

In *The Spirit of Public Administration*, professor H. George Frederickson notes that we too easily confound "government administration" with "public administration," putting the emphasis on governmental operations at the expense of the broader conception of the public that we are bound to serve:

> "*Narrow definitions of public administration tend to assume management values such as efficiency and economy. Broader conceptions of the public in public administration include these values but add the values of citizenship, fairness, equity, justice, ethics, responsiveness, and patriotism....the values associated with a broadened definition of the public are what ennoble the day-to-day practices of public work.*"[137]

Writing just before his successful campaign for the presidency, Jimmy Carter had sounded the same theme in his 1975 book, *Why Not the Best?*:

> "*. . . nowhere in the Constitution of the United States, or the Declaration of Independence, or the Bill of Rights, or the Emancipation Proclamation, or the Old Testament, or the New Testament, do you find the words 'economy' or 'efficiency.' Not that these words are unimportant. But you discover other words like honesty, integrity, fairness, liberty, justice, patriotism, compassion, love – and many others which describe what human beings ought to be. These are the same words which describe what a government of human beings ought to be.*"[138]

Both argue that there is a danger in pursuing the often-heralded path of neutral, disinterested competence in governing. If public servants deny they have a role in asking - and helping the public ask - what justice is and what it demands, then they leave that moral ground solely to others at best and turn their back on it at worst.

Between 1932 and 1972, the U.S. Public Health Service, working with the Tuskegee Institute, conducted a study on the natural progression of syphilis in rural African American men. Nearly 400 men had the disease but were neither informed of that fact nor treated, even when penicillin became available as a standard protocol. Of these, 28 died of syphilis, 100 died of related complications, 40 of their wives were infected and 19 of their children were born with congenital syphilis. Dr .John Heller, who participated in and later led the research defended it when the project became widely known with the simple statement that: "For the most part, doctors and civil servants simply did their jobs. Some merely followed orders, others worked for the glory of science."[139]

Public administration professors Guy Adams and Danny Balfour use the term "administrative evil" to characterize such manifestly unjust behavior. A chief antidote is to accept that justice demands much more from public servants.[140]

The requirement that public servants attend to the expectation for justice transcends national borders. On December 10, 1948, the United States was one of 48 nations that voted to adopt the Universal Declaration of Human Rights, whose own Preamble states that "recognition of the inherent dignity and of the equal and inalienable rights of all members of the human family is the foundation of freedom, justice and peace in the world . . ."[141]

All of these documents and declarations express a universal concern with justice, but where does that concern itself come from?

Justice as a Moral Intuition

In a now-classic experiment, called the Ultimatum Game, two people who are kept unknown to each other are paired for the distribution of a sum of money, say $10. One, called the "proposer," gets to offer a certain portion of the funds to the other, called the "responder," keeping the remainder. Both are told that they get the amounts in the proposed distribution only if the responder accepts the proposal. If the responder rejects the proposal, neither gets anything.

Box 11.1
Possible Distributions

Proposer Share	Responder Share
$10	$0
$9	$1
$8	$2
$7	$3
$6	$4
$5	$5
$4	$6
$3	$7
$2	$8
$1	$9
$0	$10

Imagine you are the proposer and are given the possible distributions in Box 11.1. What would you propose?

Now imagine you are the responder. What distribution(s) would you be willing to accept?

From a purely logical point of view, the responder should be willing to accept any distribution that offers more than $0 for the simple reason that walking away with something is better than walking away with nothing. Using similar reasoning, the proposer might be expected to offer only a small share to the responder, keeping most for himself. But that is not what happens.

In multiple studies across many nations, the average proposal is between a 60/40 and 50/50 split. The lower the offer, the greater the chance it is rejected, with nearly 70 percent of offers that are 80/20 or less being rejected. In short, most proposers have a sense that unfair offers will be rejected (leaving both players with nothing). Most responders are more concerned with punishing "unfair" offers by rejecting them than with getting at least some money for themselves. Even in a version of the game (the Impunity Game) where the responder is told that the proposer will get his share of the proposal no matter what the responder decides, the latter tends to reject unfair offers.[142]

A concern for fairness (and anger at unfairness) is clearly a driving force in the Ultimatum Game. This shows up in fMRI scans of the brains of responders. Unfair offers (defined as a proposed 80/20 or 90/10 split) produce activity in the anterior insula, the portion of the brain associated with pain, anger, and emotional disgust. Research also suggests that these emotions actually precede and overwhelm rational thinking (i.e. that some money is better than none).[143]

It is likely that this concern for fairness is hard-wired through evolution. As political scientist James Q. Wilson noted in his book, *The Moral Sense*, "It's not fair!" is one of the earliest utterances of young children. That sense of fairness grows more sophisticated with age. The need for cooperation within groups was essential for survival, and those who looked out only for themselves would have a hard time making it on their own and/or would be ostracized by the group.[144]

This moral intuition appears to operate not only in our own interest but on behalf of others. In one study, 19-month-old children watched scenes in which an animated figure tries to go up a hill and another animated figure either helps push the figure up or knocks it down. When asked to give a treat to one of the figures, the children tend to reward the good guy. When asked to take a treat away from one of them, they tend to take it away from the bad guy.[145]

In a study by researchers at the California Institute of Technology and the University of Illinois, participants faced an ethical dilemma. After reading short biographies of 60 children in an actual Ugandan orphanage, they were told that the orphanage would receive real money based on the decisions they made about how to distribute meals to the children. Subjects' brains were scanned while they made decisions. When they decided to take food away, such as by giving less food to some children so they could redistribute what food there was to ensure more could benefit, the part of the brain associated with emotions fired. As researcher Steven Quartz put it, "The emotional response to unfairness pushes people from extreme inequity and drives them to be fair . . . our basic impulse to be fair isn't a complicated thing that we learn."[146]

Justice and the Civil Servant

Consider the list of programs and policies in Box 11.2. What do these have in common?

> Box 11.2
> **An Array of Programs and Policies**
>
> Tax deduction for child care   Medicare
> All-volunteer Armed Forces   Affirmative action
> Competitive procurements   Employee bonuses
> Sentencing guidelines   Patents
> Administrative hearings   Social Security
> Health insurance mandate   Fines
> Student loans   Clean Air Act regulations

The typical response to this list is to note that they are all things enacted by government. Beyond that, they seem a pretty disparate group. What does Medicare have in common with sentencing guidelines, for example? By this point, the answer is probably clear. These, and a host of others we could add to the list, are efforts administered by public servants to establish justice. Let's look at one example in more detail.

In the late spring of 2014, the Justice Department sent electronic surveys to thousands of inmates, convicted and sentenced at least ten years ago for drug-related crimes. The survey invited prisoners to apply for clemency - and gathered information necessary to see if their petitions should be granted. The initiative arose out of a concern that many are in prison under sentences far harsher than they would get if convicted of the same offense today.

As Deputy Attorney General James M. Cole put it when the program was announced:

"For our criminal justice system to be effective, it needs not only to be fair, but it also must be perceived as fair. Older, stringent punishments that are out of line with sentences imposed under today's laws erode people's confidence in our criminal justice system."[147]

As Cole suggests, public servants cannot simply rely on the letter of the law to administer justice. These felons were convicted and sentenced under the law. Yet following the law without asking if it is still just can actually undermine the public's trust. The law and justice are not always the same thing.

Of course, public servants cannot simply use their personal sense of what is just to guide what they do. In this case, collecting survey data and establishing publicly announced and challengeable criteria (e.g. no release for those with connections to gangs, cartels or organized crime) must constrain the public official. Justice, like all of ethics, is a balancing act. It seeks the appropriate sweet spot between strict adherence to law and irresponsible license.

The public servant must have a finely honed understanding of justice - and some sophisticated skills - to navigate in the vast ocean of decisions that must be made. In August, 1974, newly sworn-in President Gerald Ford faced the need to both define and establish justice. In doing so, he had to figure out what being a just person meant. We can learn from what he did.

–12–

WHAT IS JUST AND HOW DO I
ACT JUSTLY AS A PUBLIC SERVANT?

"Injustice anywhere is a threat to justice everywhere."
– Martin Luther King, Jr.

On November 7, 1972, Richard Nixon was elected to a second term as President in a landslide victory over George McGovern. Gerald Ford, Minority Leader of the House of Representatives, from Michigan's 5th District, was elected to his thirteenth term that same night. He told his wife, Betty, that he would retire at the conclusion of that two-year term.

Yet, before the end of it, Gerald Ford was President. When Spiro Agnew, Nixon's running mate, was forced from office in October 1973 for taking bribes, Nixon nominated - and Congress confirmed - Ford as vice-president, following procedures in the 25th Amendment. When Nixon resigned the presidency on August 9, 1974, under threat of conviction in the Senate for obstructing justice in the investigation of the Watergate break-in, Ford took the Oath of Office. In his inaugural remarks, he said: "Our Constitution works; our great Republic is a government of laws and not of men. Here the people rule." In short, justice had been done.[148]

The speech might have ended there. Yet, in the very next sentence Ford added: "But there is a higher Power, by whatever name we honor Him, who ordains not only righteousness but love, not only justice but mercy." Ford then went on to ask the nation to "bind up the internal wounds of Watergate" and to pray for him and "for Richard Nixon and for his family." In these lines, Ford signaled that justice might not be simply a matter of attending to a legal requirement but could include some measure of healing and even forgiveness. What was "just" in the case of Richard Nixon turned out, for Ford, to be a complicated question.

There is scant evidence that Ford had decided to pardon Nixon upon taking office. No historical record shows a *quid pro quo* for Nixon resigning the presidency. Yet, by late August, Ford had become convinced that the priority work of the nation - which included ending the Vietnam War, fighting inflation, and reviving a stagnant economy - could not move forward as long as the country was consumed with the potential indictment, trial, and punishment of the disgraced president.

On Sunday, September 8, in the Oval Office, where about a dozen reporters had been hastily assembled, Ford read a speech that granted a "full, free, and absolute pardon" to Richard Nixon. Unlike his August inaugural remarks, which met a receptive and thankful audience, this speech was met with anger. His task was to convince the nation that pardoning Nixon was the right thing to do - that it was consistent with the demands of justice.[149] (For the full text of Ford's speech, see Appendix D.)

A glimpse of Ford's reasoning can be seen in the first paragraph, where he announced that he had "come to a decision" of which he was "certain in my own mind and conscience that it is the right thing to do." Indeed, he used the word "conscience" a total of eight times in the speech. A few paragraphs later, he noted that "[T]he Constitution is the supreme law of our land and it governs our actions as citizens." Then he added that "[O]nly the laws of God, which govern our consciences, are superior to it." This is a striking statement in which he puts what his conscience tells him is right above even the normal operation of the criminal justice system - though we need to keep in mind that he had, by law under Article II, Section II of the Constitution, the power to issue the pardon. His act was legal, using that definition of justice.

Mindful that exercising his pardon power would probably not justify the act in the minds of the public, Ford presented a number of arguments, each based on a particular conception of justice.

- "I have been advised that many months and perhaps more years will have to pass before Richard Nixon could obtain a fair trial by jury . . ." is an argument that fairness and due process are considerations. That argument was stated more boldly when Ford suggested that "the courts might well hold that Richard Nixon had been denied due process . . ."

- ". . . a former President of the United States, instead of enjoying equal treatment with any other citizen . . . would be cruelly and excessively penalized in preserving the presumption of innocence or in obtaining a speedy determination of his guilt . . ." is an argument couched in terms of the requirements of the 6th and 8th Amendments and the demand, again, that Nixon be treated fairly.

- "During this long period of delay . . . ugly passions would again be aroused . . . My concern is the immediate future of this great country . . . the greatest good of all the people of the United States . . . it is my duty, not merely to proclaim domestic tranquility but to use every means that I have to ensure it." In these words, Ford made the case that demands for the prosecution of Nixon must be weighed against the wider needs of the nation - that there is a conception of justice that transcends purely legal considerations of guilt and punishment. Indeed, "domestic tranquility" is a phrase taken directly from the Constitution's Preamble. By invoking it, Ford argued that he was concerned about justice for the nation not simply with the expectation that Nixon be put on trial.

Clearly, Ford had an expansive and complex view of the demands of justice. Just as clearly, at least in the short run, he was not persuasive. He dropped 22 points in opinion polls within two weeks of the speech, and calls/letters to the White House ran 6:1 against the pardon. The Republican Party lost 40 seats in the House and 5 in the Senate in the November elections that year. Ford narrowly beat Ronald Reagan at the 1976 Republican National Convention, but he lost the presidency to Jimmy Carter. But justice is not a popularity contest. History has been kinder to Ford than his contemporaries. In 1999, he was given a Congressional Gold Medal for helping heal "a nation in torment" as well as a Presidential Medal of Freedom. In 2001, he received a Profile in Courage award from the John F. Kennedy Presidential Library specifically for issuing the pardon.

Acting justly, as Ford's case illustrates, is not always a simple matter. As Box 12.1 shows, there are many conceptions of justice, and in any given situation, the demands of some may conflict with others. In Ford's case, the demands of the public for *retribution* conflicted with Ford's sense that *utility* - the greatest good for the greatest number - demanded that the nation heal and move on with its critical business. Ford was also interested in assuring *procedural justice*, which he argued might be nearly impossible since, as he put it, "[T]here are no historic or legal precedents to which I can turn in this matter, none that precisely fit the circumstances of a private citizen who has resigned the Presidency . . ."

Ford was also concerned with *restorative justice*, though this is not evident in the speech. He directed his staff to inform Nixon that he would get a pardon only if he agreed to make a public acknowledgment of wrong doing and turn over all his papers and tapes (for which legal ownership in 1974 did not clearly rest with the government). Ford also seemed intent on justice as *virtue*, as we can see in his struggle in both his inaugural remarks and pardon speech with balancing the demands of justice with mercy and with his own conscience.

As Box 12.1 demonstrates, each conception of justice is associated with questions that may be asked to explore how to apply it in a given situation.[150] In using these questions, keep in mind that there may be multiple perspectives on what justice means in a given situation and different answers to the same question, magnifying the public servant's task in establishing justice.

Box 12.1
Conceptions of Justice

Justice Defined As:	Questions to Ask:
VIRTUE	• What is the end or purpose for which a policy, program, or action is aimed? • What virtues does it promote and should they be honored? • What makes for good character and a good society?
UTILITY	• What is the greatest good for the greatest number? • What maximizes human happiness? Does the pleasure outweigh the pain?
RIGHT PRINCIPLE	• Is this the right thing to do, regardless of the consequences? • Am I using people as ends in themselves and never as means to an end?
FAIRNESS (DISTRIBUTIVE JUSTICE)	• On what basis do we distribute society's benefits? On the basis of need? contributions? equality? • Is the distribution of rights and benefits fair? • Do all have the same basic rights? equal opportunities?
LIBERTY	• Do we maximize individual liberty – as long as it does not harm others? • Do we reward individual talent, virtue, contribution, effort, and costs incurred?

PROCEDURE	• Are processes that resolve disputes and allocate resources:
	  o Transparent – open to all parties to observe and participate?
	  o Fair and representative– all parties have been treated the same way?
	  o Using accurate and correctible information?
	  o Without bias?
	  o Marked by due process – observe rules and regulations in place, both in spirit and letter?

RESTORATION	• Are injured people:
	  • Fairly compensated for loss?
	  • Compensated, where possible, by people who have injured them?
	• Are people who committed crimes:
	  • Required to compensate the victims/make them whole?
	  • Effectively reintegrated into society?

RETRIBUTION	• Are punishments:
	  • Arrived at through lawful evidence?
	  • Morally correct?
	  • Fair and fully deserved?
	  • Proportionate to the crime?

As another illustration, we can see that affirmative action will be considered restorative justice (and perhaps distributive justice) by some as a recompense for the sins of slavery and discrimination. Yet it may be seen as a violation of justice as liberty by others, who believe that it penalizes some whose merit is not rewarded because benefits have been given to people who have not earned them. Still further, as we have seen in multiple court cases, the administration of affirmative action policies and programs is fraught with issues of procedural justice.

The application of justice is not just a matter for presidents and court justices, however. Consider the case in Box 12.2. How would you analyze and resolve this issue?

Though on the surface this is a medical and management decision, it is an ethical dilemma in which the administration of justice plays a significant part in at least the following ways:

- Justice defined as *utility* raises the question: what is the greatest good for the greatest number? One could argue that spending $175,000 on one patient, who may not live even the six months projected, cannot be justified given the larger number of patients who could be served by the same funds. On the other hand, would other patients facing life-ending choices view this decision as a precedent, and how would that affect their trust and care? How would doctors react to whatever decision is made?

- Justice as *right principle* asks: how can we make a decision that respects human dignity? In this conception of justice, the outcome of the treatment (i.e. whether it actually works at all) is irrelevant. What matters is the intention of those entrusted with her care. They will respect the dictates of justice only if they can adopt a principle that they would adopt for all people, similarly situated, at all times.

- Justice defined as *fairness* asks at least two questions: how do we distribute limited hospital resources among all the needs we have? how do we ensure that all patients have equal rights in the way we make such decisions? Another way to frame this is a thought experiment: if we parachuted into this hospital from another world, not knowing if we would land with a medical condition as dire as this patient or just for some minor illness, would we be comfortable being a patient, given how the hospital makes decisions such as this?[151]

- Justice defined as *procedure* asks: do we have a process in place for making this medical decision that has at least the following attributes: (a) transparent (i.e. public, open to inspection and critique); (b) representative (i.e. participation by all affected parties (patient, patient's family, doctors, administrative staff); (c) uses the best available information, whose accuracy can be tested; (d) without bias (i.e. there is no impact on the decision of such nonmedical factors as the patient's age, race, sex, religion); and (e) marked by due process (e.g. the patient or patient's representative has the right to participate and appeal).

- Justice defined as *virtue* asks what kind of society we want to be and, for those in the medical profession, what kind of caregivers they want to be. As with the other perspectives on justice, these are not easy questions and thus demand thought and discussion.

With justice in mind, the hospital needs to ensure that all these factors are adequately addressed. An "ethics" or "patients rights" committee is one way this can be done. Absent such forethought, each decision like this one gets addressed ad hoc, which is unacceptable from the standpoint of the government's requirement to "establish Justice" (not to mention that such an unpredictable approach is likely to lead to inconsistent decisions that call into question the hospital's staff, management, and quality of care).

> ### Box 12.2
> ### Do We Withhold Treatment?
>
> A patient in a Veterans Hospital has lung cancer. At present, she is not expected to live more than six months. Her doctor, however, has informed her that there is an experimental drug that might prolong her life for an additional six months, though the drug has no hope of curing her. The drug regimen would cost $175,000. The patient wants the medication - her son's graduation from high school is eight months away - and the doctor has recommended using it.
>
> The doctor's recommendation must be approved by higher levels. The Chief Financial Officer must certify that funds are available for this purpose, and the Chief of Staff (the hospital's top medical official) must sign off that this is medically appropriate.
>
> The hospital is under intense cost pressures. Since the wind-down of the wars in Iraq and Afghanistan, the number of patients, many with severe medical problems, has grown almost exponentially. It is near the end of the fiscal year, and the hospital's budget for next year is not at all clear as Congress has not passed the Department's appropriation.
>
> As Chief Operating Officer for the hospital, you have been told about this situation. The final decision may well be yours if it cannot be resolved by lower level staff.

Embedding Attention to Establishing Justice in Organizational Operations

Most agencies will not face such life and death decisions, and the medical profession has a long history of attending to issues of ethics and justice. How can the typical government agency and manager build a just organization?

Issues of justice and fairness, after all, usually do not present themselves with headlines using those words. Without a sensitivity to justice and mechanisms to address it, public servants will either fail in their work or be caught (embarrassingly) off-guard when they are besieged by angry citizens.

Consider, for example, the following headlines:

- "Army Corps of Engineers Opens Floodgate on Swollen Mississippi River," May 15, 2011[152]

- "Why are So Many Children Trying to Cross the U.S. Border?," July 23, 2014[153]

- "FAA Approves Limited Use Of Drones For Utility Company," July 12, 2014[154]

- "DoD Hashing Out New Civilian Performance Appraisal System," August 4, 2014[155]

In every instance, justice is a central issue. The Corps of Engineers deliberately flooded thousands of square miles (destroying farms and homes) in order to prevent much more serious flooding in New Orleans and other downstream cities. How did it balance the competing demands for fairness, restorative justice, and procedural justice from all affected? As children from Central America swelled border towns in the Southwest, how did the government respond to the humanitarian crisis while also addressing the legitimate concerns for the welfare of the children (right principle and fairness) and compensation of cities and towns all across America who were asked to house these children (restorative justice)? How will the FAA establish procedures that assure everything from fair access to the use of drones to penalties for drone accidents or the violation of its own policies? How will the Department of Defense erect a performance appraisal system that is seen as fair by employees, given that a previous attempt during the Bush Administration was so roundly criticized that Congress killed it?

While everything in this book provides tools and ideas for addressing such considerations, there are at least five additional practices that those who want to be faithful to the Constitution's promise to "establish Justice" can consider.

- Make Seeking Justice an Explicit Role Expectation for Individuals and Organizations

  Strategic plans, operational goals and objectives, job descriptions, performance plans and daily work processes all contribute to seeking justice in government organizations. Yet they rarely articulate justice as a stated end in a way the focuses people on how well they are achieving it.

One way to correct this is to build it into the role expectation for public servants. A "role" is not the same thing as one's "job." Among professional actors, for example, one's *job* might be to perform a part in a play, but one's *role* is how one chooses (and is directed) to bring that part alive with emotional engagement and performance artistry. In government, many people with similar job descriptions perform those jobs very differently, often because they see their roles (or are supervised) differently. The public knows the difference between a call center representative who loves her job and the people she helps and one who just wants to get callers off the phone and go home.

In the 1990s, Ramona Trovato was a research and development specialist in the Environmental Protection Agency (EPA). Her job was to determine environmental standards for exposure to contaminants. At the time, these were all based on their impact on adults. But she saw her role more broadly. She began an effort to account for the impact of contaminants on children, knowing that what they eat, drink, and breathe relative to their weight could lead to a greater adverse impact on their health than the same levels of contaminants for adults. Children are now included in how EPA addresses this issue, a direct result of Trovato seeing that justice would not be served unless she saw her role as more than her job description.[156]

As noted in Chapter 1, the American Society of Public Administration (ASPA) has a Code of Ethics. Principle #4 and its associated practices illustrate one approach to articulating a social justice role for public servants. Such a role and practices can be incorporated in how agencies define the work of public servants:

> "**4. Strengthen social equity.** *Treat all persons with fairness, justice, and equality and respect individual differences, rights, and freedoms. Promote affirmative action and other initiatives to reduce unfairness, injustice, and inequality in society.*
>
> a. Provide services to the public with impartiality and consistency tempered by recognition of differences. Ensure that all persons have access to programs and services to which they are entitled under the law and maintain equitable standards of quality for all who receive the programs and services.
>
> b. Provide equal treatment, protection, and due process to all persons.
>
> c. Oppose all forms of discrimination and harassment and promote affirmative action, cultural competence, and other efforts to reduce

disparities in outcomes and increase the inclusion of underrepresented groups."

Others ways to draw attention to justice as a role for public servants are to engage employees in periodic discussion of the core purposes of their organizations and how they are (or are not) realized in daily work. Leaders can also establish rewards, other types of recognition, celebrations and ceremonies to honor organizational and individual efforts on behalf of citizens in meeting the goal of fostering justice in daily work.

Clearly, there are ethical boundaries that must be observed. We cannot, for example, turn seeking justice into a matter of purely personal preference. As discussed in Chapter 2, public servants who see themselves as "trustees" of the public good need to balance that with seeing themselves as "delegates" as well. This balance can be struck if a key role expectation for public servants is to manage an inclusive process by which different conceptions of justice on a particular topic are allowed to be expressed by stakeholders. Government employees then become facilitators of a public conversation about justice in society rather than solitary, isolated, and potentially biased decision makers. A government official will need to make a decision at some point, but ideally it will emerge from the democratic processes of engagement, knowledge sharing, debate, and consensus seeking. Central to performing in this way is the balancing of advocacy and inquiry that we discussed in Chapter 3.

- Increase the Sensitivity and Skills of Public Servants to Foster Justice

Articulating a role expectation is a start, but it is like a New Year's Resolution without sufficient emotional commitment or an action plan to carry it through. The problem for most public servants is that they work in large bureaucracies often separated by wide chasms of organizational, geographical, and interpersonal distance from those impacted by their decisions. They tend to be more educated and make more money than the average American, and their functional specialties can further isolate them from the daily life of those they serve. This is not their fault, but it is a problem to address.

The result of this physical and organizational isolation can be a psychological and emotional distance that pushes the impact of injustice out of sight and mind. Paul Piff and his colleagues, for example, found that upper-class individuals were more likely than lower class individuals to make unethical decisions in lab situations such as lying in a negotiation, endorsing unethical behavior at work, and taking valued goods from others. Their conclusion was that: "Upper-class individuals' relative independence from others and increased privacy in their professions may provide fewer structural constraints and decreased perceptions of risk associated with committing unethical acts. . . . A reduced concern for others' evaluations and increased goal-focus could further instigate unethical tendencies . . ."[157]

Research by Francesca Gino and colleagues shows that we judge behavior as more unethical when there is a clearly identifiable victim. For example, subjects in their experiments judged poor medical care as more unethical when the (hypothetical) patient was given a name (i.e. "Chris") then when referred to without one (i.e. "this person").[158] This is similar to our different reactions to news that "several people were killed" versus seeing the name, image, and hearing the personal story of one victim. The danger in bureaucracies is that injustice can be nameless - we never know specific individuals harmed by our actions (or failure to act). Gino and her colleagues also found that we tend to judge the same act as ethical or unethical depending on the outcome. That is, if a wrong behavior does not produce a harmful result, we are less likely to consider it unethical (i.e. "no harm, no foul"). Of course, in bureaucracies, a long time can elapse between the unjust action of a public servant and the downstream negative impact on a citizen. Sometimes the actor (agency) may never get feedback that what they have done caused harm and was unjust.

The potential danger of emotional distancing also showed up in a series of experiments by Elinor Amit and Joshua Greene. They found that when people were able to visualize the harm done to a victim in a scenario, they were more likely to focus on individual rights rather than to think in terms of the greatest good for the greatest number.[159] While "greatest good" judgments are certainly appropriate in some cases, the implied danger for public servants is that the broad goal of a policy, program, or piece of legislation takes precedence over its harmful impact on individuals when we cannot "see" that impact.

One way to ensure that public servants do not become emotionally as well as organizationally isolated from those they serve is through creative educational programs. Perhaps the most classic example of public service injustice was the participation of Nazi government workers in the Holocaust. Adolph Eichmann was aided by thousands more - public servants who lost their moral anchors. Could that happen here? The FBI Academy trains 1,000 new special agents each year. Since 1999, to make sure they keep justice and morality in their minds, that training has included a visit to the Holocaust Museum in Washington, D.C. In 2004, a special version of the program was also created for intelligence analysts. The program is a joint partnership between the museum and the Anti-Defamation League.

In addition to touring the exhibits, agents are confronted in the classroom with rigorous questioning. As one instructor put it to the agents: "What makes you different? What, at the end of the day, is going to keep you anchored? What keeps you from sliding down the slippery slope? What keeps you from abusing your power?" Special Agent Douglas Merel, a teacher of ethical leadership for the Academy, described the purpose of the program this way: "It makes our people think about morality, ethics, and how to maintain those during turbulent times."[160] Such training in ethics and the demands of justice is all too rare in government agencies.

So too are ways to bring government workers and leaders, who are not on the front lines every day, into contact with citizens impacted by their decisions. Some other approaches to doing so are: (a) ensuring public servants travel to and meet with those they serve; (b) having staff at all levels, including managers and executives, spend a few hours a month handling the phones on call-in help lines to expose them first-hand to the kinds of issues and problems that their efforts (often inadvertently) create; (c) monitoring social media for comments about organizational policies, programs, and services and inviting citizen reactions to these on government social media sites; (d) conducting town-hall, Web chat, and other outreach efforts to listen to citizens; (e) using newspaper or online coverage of the organization in staff roundtable discussions about the impacts of their work on others; and (f) using advisory boards and commissions to bring outside perspectives into organizational decision making.

- Ensure that Government is Representative

On Saturday, August 9, 2014, an unarmed black teenager, Michael Brown, was shot several times and killed by a white police officer on a street in Ferguson, Missouri. Some eyewitnesses claimed that Brown had done nothing to provoke the shooting, but Darren Wilson, the officer involved, maintained that Brown had struggled with him, trying to get his gun. Tensions quickly escalated as news of the shooting spread, and several nights of protests and looting followed.

A few protestors hurled rocks, bottles, and Molotov cocktails. Police responded with smoke bombs, tear gas, and rubber bullets, and they deployed armored vehicles. The situation calmed down (unfortunately only temporarily) nearly a week later, but only after the governor asked the State Highway Patrol to take over from town and county police. State Highway Patrol Captain Ron Johnson, a black man who grew up near Ferguson, announced that he would also protect the right of protestors to march peacefully, and he joined in the march with them.[161] Protests continued through the fall though in diminished form. But on November 24, 2014, a grand jury declined to indict officer Wilson. Protesters again stormed into the streets of Ferguson, with some looting and burning local businesses and torching police cruisers. Protests also spread to scores of other cities across the nation.

Several demands for justice were clearly at issue. The police stated that they were protecting the public (the greater good) both in the incident and when protests and looting began. The protestors, including Brown's parents and the local NAACP, demanded retribution for (in their judgment) the unprovoked murder of the teen. Fairness was a demand of all parties. Captain Johnson tried to restore calm so that procedural justice could sort all of this out. But procedural justice (the grand jury process) was itself viewed as compromised in the person of the prosecutor, the grand jury itself, and the belief among the black community that it ignored the fact that sufficient evidence existed to at least bring the case to trial.

What inflamed the situation was clearly the fact that the victim was black and the officer who shot him was white. But racial tensions were not new to Ferguson. St. Louis County, the surrounding jurisdiction, is largely white. Ferguson's black population had grown in recent years, moving from about half to two-thirds of the residents. Yet the 53-person Ferguson police force had only three blacks, and the city's mayor and police chief were both white.[162] Further, the prosecutor who took the case to the grand jury was white (and his father, a police officer, had been killed by a black man). The grand jury itself was three-fourths white.

In a perfect world, the racial composition of the police force, district attorney, and grand jury should not matter. Justice should be blind. But Ferguson - like many other communities in America - is not a perfect world. Establishing justice, as this case demonstrates, can be that much harder when the public service and those who act on its behest are not representative of those they serve.

Representativeness offers many benefits in the pursuit of justice. It helps government understand the language, history, culture, needs and grievances of the people it serves. It demonstrates fairness in hiring. It encourages citizen access to people who are "like me" to air their concerns. It makes government seem more legitimate by decreasing, as we saw above, the social and psychological distance between citizens and public servants. All of these do not guarantee justice is served, but the perception of justice is harder to demonstrate without representativeness.

Representativeness means more than just racial, ethnic, and gender diversity. A government workforce that, in former President Clinton's phrase, "looks like America," should also include, for example, representative percentages of people with disabilities, non-English-speaking language skills, sexual orientation, and differing ages, among other characteristics. Beginning with the civil rights era of the 1960s, such representativeness has increasingly become a concern of government, but it is still a work in progress. At the federal level, for example, Hispanics and Latinos are still significantly under-represented, despite the fact that this segment of the American population is growing dramatically.

Clearly, the hiring process is the principle way to ensure representativeness among the full-time and part-time government workforce. But other methods exist to give whoever works for government a more sensitive understanding of under-represented groups, such as training programs, community outreach, and the use of advisory boards to bring in needed perspectives.

- Ensure that Government Contractors Promote Justice

Representativeness as a goal also needs to apply to contractors, who increasingly do more of the government's work, have direct contact with citizens in delivering services, and are thus the face of justice (or injustice) in places as diverse as airports, prisons, parks, and security details.

Estimates of the size of the contractor workforce vary, but there may be as many as four contract employees for every federal civil servant, and the amount spent on government contracts was more than three times the amount spent on government employee payroll in fiscal year 2010, according to political science professor Paul Light.[163]

Yet efforts to hold government contractors to high ethical standards are at least as difficult, if not more so, than what is done to ensure ethical behavior among government employees. Contract workers are much harder to oversee directly. While contractors are required to have a code of ethics and conduct ethics training, holding them accountable for unethical behavior requires both an investigatory capability on the part of government procurement personnel (and others, for serious offenses) and an often long and uncertain process of administrative hearings and disbarment.

When we turn to the question of establishing justice, not just observing minimal ethical standards, the task becomes harder. Contractors take no oath to the Constitution and are not steeped in a public service ethic. Ensuring they have that commitment and perspective, especially when it may run contrary to the profit motive that drives private sector operations, is a task that is as necessary as it may be difficult.

Nevertheless, civil servants who care about justice have an obligation to work with contractors on this issue. This can be done through, for example, incorporating provisions in the Statement of Work that governs contractor work processes and employee training, careful monitoring of contractor operations, and surveys of those served by contractor personnel to spot instances or trends that threaten the commitment to justice that government must meet.

- Promote Justice Within the Government Workforce

If we want public servants to promote justice in America, we should also make sure that they are being treated fairly themselves. Perceptions of unfairness or favoritism at work are associated with higher levels of burnout, more dissatisfaction with supervisors and co-workers, less effort in accomplishing work tasks, more EEO complaints, and a lesser likelihood of recommending their organization as a place to work. All of these undercut the achievement of organizational goals, which include establishing justice.[164]

As the data in Table 12.1, from the federal government's annual workforce survey, demonstrate, perceptions of unfairness in a range of personnel practices exist among segments of the workforce. In a 2013 study by the Merit Systems Protection Board, 28 percent of employees reported that their own supervisor practice favoritism (in such actions as social interactions, work assignments, and training and development), while 53 percent said that other supervisors do so.[165] Whether objectively true, perceptions are reality in the minds of those who have them. As is true with the public we serve, a sense of unjust treatment destroys trust inside government organizations as well. When applied to the demand that federal agencies "establish Justice" in America, such perceptions generate cynicism and make that task harder.

A variety of mechanisms exist within agencies to foster fairness in the treatment of government workers and ensure that laws to ensure just treatment are followed. Such approaches include Equal Employment Opportunity offices, diversity programs, training for supervisors and managers, assessments of workforce culture with actions to address identified weaknesses, Executive Orders to focus on hiring a representative workforce, and regulations prohibiting discrimination, sexual harassment, and a range of other prohibited personnel practices. When these mechanisms are used, with commitment and vigor, they advance the course of justice within the government workforce. Supervisors must also be held accountable for demonstrating behavior, such as the actions in Box 12.1, that promotes workplace justice.

Table 12.1
Perceptions of Fairness Among Federal Civil Servants

Survey Question	% Positive Response (Strongly Agree/Agree)
My performance appraisal is a fair reflection of my performance.	68.2%
Promotions in my work unit are based on merit.	32.0%
Arbitrary action, personal favoritism and coercion for partisan political purposes are not tolerated.	50.3%
Prohibited Personnel Practices (for example, illegally discriminating for or against any employee/applicant, obstructing a person's right to compete for employment, knowingly violating veterans' preference requirements) are not tolerated.	65.1%
Pay raises depend on how well employees perform their jobs.	19.5%
Awards in my work unit depend on how well employees perform their jobs.	38.0%

Ethics, in the pursuit of justice, is by its nature always a work in progress. So, too, is the desire to recruit into government service those who take this goal as a duty and seek its achievement in their work. When we have people like that in public service, they help restore honor to the profession and those who labor for the public's benefit each day.

RESTORING HONOR TO PUBLIC SERVICE

"... since public administrators have the day-to-day control over the vast public bureaucracy, because they can use the rule-enforcing power of the government and because they do not come up for election, they incur special moral obligations. They must be more than value-neutral technicians running the apparatus of government. ... The professional obligation of public administrators begins with their duties as virtuous citizens ... when one accepts the calling of public administrator, one also accepts the responsibility of transcending that ordinary virtue to seek honor."

- David K. Hart

Americans often view public servants as a necessary evil. They administer essential programs, but it seems that nearly every day they make some mistake, dutifully reported by the media. We thank them occasionally, especially in times of natural disasters, tolerate them much of the time, and often get angry at them. In a nation founded on distrust of government, public servants have come to accept such treatment as the inevitable accompaniment to their jobs.

This is healthy neither for the nation nor the public service. In 1789, when George Washington took the oath as president, public service was an honored obligation of gentlemen. Today, most Americans associate honor with military service but tend to view those who enter the civil service as "feds" and "bureaucrats" and think that the "best and the brightest" either are in, or should go into, the private sector.

This book has been devoted to highlighting the importance of ethical leadership among public servants. The nation needs such behavior, and those who work for government must meet that expectation. Doing so will help address the gap in trust between the public and its servants. This concluding chapter argues that being an ethical public servant will also help restore honor to the public service and those who labor in it. That is also a needed outcome.

"Ethical behavior" is too often seen - by the public and by public servants themselves - as the absence of wrong doing. Ethics standards and laws proscribe certain behaviors. They say much less about how an ideal public servant ought to behave. While the preceding chapters try to fill this gap, the word "ethics" simply cannot do full justice to the need for right conduct in government or to the achievements of a truly exemplary public servant. "Ethics" does not fully capture the essence of what we need. "Honor" may serve us better.

In June 1940, the French government surrendered to Adolph Hitler's forces. In Article 19 of the armistice, France agreed to "surrender on demand all Germans named by the German government in France." This launched a roundup of German and Jewish refugees, who were then taken to Nazi extermination camps. The American government, which wanted to limit immigration and also maintain good relations with the new Vichy government in France, refused most requests to issue visas to refugees. However, that did not stop Hiram Bingham IV, the American Vice Counsel in Marseilles.

On his own authority, Bingham issued 2,000 travel visas and fake passports. He also worked with others to help refugees escape, including painter Marc Chagall and political theorist Hannah Arendt. As he related on a tape not found until the 1990s, "My boss, who was the consul general at the time, said: 'The Germans are going to win the war. Why should we do anything to offend them?' But, I had to do as much as I could."

In 1941, after complaints from German and French officials, Bingham was pulled from his post and transferred to Portugal and then Argentina. In the latter country, he reported on the Argentine practice of giving safe harbor to Nazi war criminals. When the State Department refused to investigate, Bingham resigned in protest in 1946.

Bingham's actions drew praise from those he helped. Yet, they would not earn acclaim in the United States until more than half a century later. Bingham rarely spoke of what he did. He died in 1988. On June 27, 2002, Secretary of State Colin Powell presented a "courageous diplomat" award posthumously to his children.

Hiram Bingham was a man of honor who brought honor to the public service. Belatedly, we recognized both. We can produce and need to honor more such public servants.

What Happened to Honor?

"Honor" is, as noted, embedded in military culture. It is a declared standard, an aim of military education, and a practice regularly sought and evaluated. The "Medal of Honor" has come to represent the highest level of sacrifice among those in uniform, and recipients are recognized in a White House ceremony.

There is no comparable attention to honor in the civil service. "Honor" is not on lists of competencies or organizational values. It is not a subject of study. Performance evaluations do not assess it. There is no presidential award for people like Hiram Bingham. The closest would seem to be the "President's Award for Distinguished Civilian Federal Service," inaugurated by President Eisenhower in 1957. Most Americans (including most civil servants) have never heard of it. Its criteria do not speak of "honor," and it has been given only twice in the past dozen years. When "honor" is used at all in the civil service, it seems reserved for those killed in the line of duty (e.g. the Wall of Honor instituted in 2013 by the U.S. Office of Personnel Management). They indeed deserve to be called honorable, but honor needs a much broader audience and set of practitioners.

When the 56 signers of the Declaration of Independence said that "we mutually pledge to each other our Lives, our Fortunes, and our sacred Honor," they were putting at risk their immortal character as well as their bodies and possessions. Honor was "sacred" to them, associated as it was with a reputation earned through virtuous actions arising from a sense of duty to their country. The fact that they made a pledge to each other recognized that honor comes not just from internal self-direction but from earned external respect.

Over the next dozen years, the Constitution followed the Declaration, and evolutionary government replaced revolutionary warfare. As the eighteenth century gave way to the nineteenth, considerations of constitutional design gave way to tasks of governmental administration. Government by gentlemen gradually gave way to government by citizens. Democracy pushed aristocracy aside. "Fitness of character," which was Washington's central consideration in appointing people to positions in government, took second place to the demand for technical competence. Working for government became less a calling - a sense of duty as an obligation of citizenship - and more a job. Character and honor no doubt still mattered, but they were seldom explicit criteria. As the nineteenth century ended, they receded even further from conscious consideration in favor of "neutral competence" as the hallmark of the admirable civil servant.[166]

Honor took a back seat not just in government but in society at large. Some of this was associated with democratization, in which an "honor culture" seemed an aristocratic anachronism (and occasionally dangerous, as in the practice of dueling).[167] There may have been other causes as well, such as the growing emphasis on individual rights and self-fulfillment in American culture at the expense of the demands of duty and the need for recognition for honorable behavior.[168]

The reasons matter for our purposes less than the effects. Honor appeared less as a goal or source of guidance for one's daily behavior. The term "honor" came to be associated more with less exalted aspects of human actions. One might be asked to "do the honors" at a meal or event. We might "honor our partner" in square dancing, honor an invitation, or have the honor of going first. Merchants "honor" a credit card. The terms "Your Honor" and "The Honorable" still precede the names of some judges and many government officers, but they recognize the position, not necessarily the behavior (as those who so dislike Congress will readily admit). Fame, which in the eighteenth century was the high opinion of others eagerly sought by those consumed with acting honorably, has given way to the desire for celebrity. Big accolades (and big money) go more often to those in the entertainment field than to those in public service. Even many in public life seem smitten with the desire for celebrity status.

As honor receded in importance, laws and regulations to proscribe certain behaviors among those who work for government gained more attention, in part to fill the gap. The excesses of the "spoils system" beginning with and following the administration of Andrew Jackson, corrupt practices in Civil War procurement, and other abuses resulted over the past 150 years in a veritable encyclopedia of "thou shalt nots" for those who labor in public service. In this way, ethical behavior replaced honor as the touchstone for public servants. Something was no doubt gained; but something was also lost.

Can Honor Be Recaptured as a Standard for, and Characteristic of, Public Service?

Honor has not died out, but it has clearly become less visible as both expectation and acknowledged behavior. However, the Founding period did not own "honor." To behave with honor is a human capability, as accessible to those who serve today's president as to those who served George Washington.

In early 1942, George C. Marshall, then Army Chief of Staff, saw the need for civil administrators in conquered territories though at that time in World War II there were no conquered territories. With foresight, Marshall created a School of Military Governance at the University of Virginia and set about training civilian and military people for the task. On March 1, 1943, after the State Department turned down his entreaties to take leadership of the effort to govern areas captured by the Allies, Marshall established a Civil Affairs Section in the War Department. He selected Brigadier

General John J. Hilldring to head this office. As Hilldring recounted in later years, here is what Marshall said on turning the task over to him:

> *"I'm turning over to you a sacred trust and I want you to bear that in mind every day and every hour you preside over this military government and civil affairs venture. Our people sometimes say that soldiers are stupid . . . Sometimes our people think we are extravagant with the public money, that we squander it, spend it recklessly. I don't agree that we do. We are in a business where it's difficult always to administer your affairs as a businessman can administer his affairs in a company . . . But even though people say we are extravagant, that in itself isn't too disastrous . . .*
>
> *But we have a great asset and that is that our people, our countrymen, do not distrust us and do not fear us. Our countrymen, our fellow citizens, are not afraid of us. They don't harbor any ideas that we intend to alter the government of the country or the nature of this government in any way. This is a sacred trust that I turn over to you today . . . And I don't want you to do anything, and I don't want to permit the enormous corps of military governors that you are in the process of training and that you are going to dispatch all over the world, to damage this high regard in which the professional soldiers in the Army are held by our people, and it could happen, it could happen, Hilldring, if you don't understand what you are about . . . This is my principal charge to you, this is the thing I never want you to forget in the dust of battle and when the pressure will be on you, and the pressure will be on you."*[169]

Marshall is giving an assignment, the most basic leadership task. Both he and Hilldring are not on the front lines of combat; they inhabit the bureaucratic offices of the Pentagon. Though military officers, they are concerned with civil administration and might as well have been in the State Department (had it chosen to take on this assignment). But Marshall stepped well beyond the confines of routine job performance - and insisted Hilldring do the same.

Marshall saw his role in the full scope of a Constitutional officer. He knew that the future of the conquered territories (hence peace in Europe and the security of the United Sates) depended on wise administration. He understood that the American people cast a wary eye on the exercise of power. Yet he also knew that the Army held their trust - a "sacred trust" - if it did not squander it. He made Hilldring aware that this trust, the "high regard" of the American people, was the most valued product of his work, his "principal charge." Marshall, a man of honor, reminded Hilldring how important honor was - and that achieving it would not be easy, because "the pressure will be on you."

Two Views of Public Service

The Bingham and Marshall examples suggest that excellent professional performance is necessary but not sufficient to restore honor. Both men had a job to do, but their conception of their work went beyond its technical aspects. They were twentieth century government officials, but they had not lost sight of eighteenth century Constitutional values. Rather than leaving the founding period behind, they made it a part of their philosophy of leadership. This integration of founding understandings with contemporary action is highlighted in Table P-1, which presents two ways to think about one's role as a member of the public service.

The most common view falls under "Civil Service as Program Administration." Excellence is defined as achieving legislated goals and Administration objectives through professional competence, adhering to law and regulation, and using the best techniques available. One's time horizon is focused on present demands. Serving the public is the aim. The civil servant views his work as a job in the course of a career (in and perhaps outside of government). Sound performance earns financial rewards, promotions and perquisites. Poor performance results in the failure to gain - or the loss of - these benefits of office. To some, this may seem a rather pedestrian view of public service, but if everyone in government performed according to this understanding, the results of governmental administration - and the public's trust - would no doubt improve.

The problem with "Civil Service as Program Administration" is not that it is wrong but that it is too limiting. When we don only this hat, it is as if we are wearing a virtual reality device that has one of its other dimensions turned off.

If we add "Public Service as Responsible Citizenship" to the role definition, we strengthen the possibilities for honor. The cases of Bingham, and Marshall highlight this.

The first important distinction between those two aspects of the role is in the column headings themselves. "Public" is broader than "civil" as H. George Frederickson notes:

> *"The first casualty of the administrative state is the gradual loss of the concept of the public in public administration . . . it was for good reason that [Woodrow]Wilson and others called it public rather than government administration. . . . Narrow definitions of public administration tend to assume management values such as efficiency and economy. Broader conceptions of the public in public administration include these values but add the values of citizenship, fairness, equity, justice, ethics, responsiveness, and patriotism . . . the values associated with a broadened definition of the public are what ennoble the day-to-day practices of public work."*[170]

Table P-1
Two Approaches to a Guiding Philosophy for the Public Servant

	PUBLIC SERVICE AS RESPONSIBLE CITIZENSHIP	CIVIL SERVICE AS PROGRAM ADMINISTRATION
Guiding Documents	Declaration of Independence and the U.S. Constitution	agency-specific law and regulation
Ethical Touchstone	Oath of Office (moral obligation)	Code of Ethics (regulatory and legal observance)
Orientation to Public Service	public service as a calling, public servant as trustee	government employment as a job, government employee as delegate
Orientation to the U.S. Constitution	a work in progress, toward the achievement of the Preamble's promise	a rulebook and a guide to permissible action
Goal	the success of the "American experiment" in republican government	program effectiveness/efficiency
Justice Achieved Through	benevolence, charity, love	adherence to law and program success
Key Metaphor	the public as a commons	government as a business
Time Orientation	past, present, and future	the short-term present
Key Audience	citizens	customers
Key Expectation of the Public	responsible and engaged citizenship	consumer of government goods and services
Approach to the Public	engage and learn	serve and guide
Engagement in Political Management	high - in service to the common good and regime values	low - in service to neutral competence
Focus for Education of the Public Servant	Constitutional thinking, regime values, ethical behavior	professional expertise and administrative excellence
Risk from Failure	shame	loss of power, pay, and perquisites

"Public servants" see themselves as citizens who occupy roles in the government. "Civil servants" see themselves as employees working for government. As Frederickson also notes:

> *"If, in our education for and practice of public administration, we define ourselves only as government employees, we prepare the seedbed for careerism and individualism."*[171]

Civil service as a "job" treats working for the people in much the same manner as working for Walmart. Public service as a calling brings forth passionate commitment to republican government and anchors work in moral values and the common good.

Program administration focuses on agency-specific laws and regulations as guiding documents. Responsible citizenship looks to the founding values of the Constitution and the Declaration of Independence. This is what Marshall meant in reminding Hilldring of the role of the military in the broader society. The primary ethical touchstone of the public servant is the Oath of Office, a solemn pledge that demands moral thought and action. Program administrators focus primarily on the requirements of the Code of Ethics, to which they neither raise their hands nor publicly pledge their fidelity. Satisfying the requirements of the Code of Ethics results from knowing you have done no prohibited action. Satisfying the Oath of Office results from a constant questioning of yourself and others about your ability to meet the Preamble's promise.

Public servants see themselves as trustees of founding values. They are in a job, of course, but that is just one consideration. While they accept that they have only delegated authority, they think beyond what they are permitted to do to what their oath requires them to do. This may sound idealistic, but idealism is an aid to acting honorably. In their description of the difference between the German civil service that aided in the Holocaust and the Danish public service that sheltered and rescued its Jewish citizens, Hart and Frederickson note the importance of such idealism:

> *"The first step must be to rid ourselves of the notion that idealism has no place in the bureaucracy. . . . public servants must be both moral philosophers and moral activists, which would require: first, an understanding of, and belief in, American regime values; and, second, a sense of extensive benevolence for the people of the nation."*[172]

If, as James Madison noted, "[J]ustice is the end of government," the public servant as responsible citizen sees justice as more than adherence to law and programmatic achievement. The public servant must ask if what she is doing serves the ends of justice, not just legal requirements. Driven by justice, achieved through benevolence, charity and love of others, is what made Bingham's work so honorable.

Critics of government, including many inside agencies, are fond of citing the need to adopt the outlook, values, and practices of the best private sector businesses. The program administrator will give this attention, for there is something to be learned and gained by doing so. But the public servant will question the applicability of the business model and know its limits. The values of efficiency and effectiveness are paramount in the private sector, but they are among other, competing and often more important values in the public sector. The goal for the public servant as responsible citizen is the success of what the Founders called the "American experiment" - the success of republican government. That is the "bottom line."

The audience for the public servant is citizens, not customers. Citizens need to be actively engaged. Customers need only consume (and pay for through taxes) government's goods and services. The public servant, knows that passive citizenry is not the ideal to seek because it makes the civil servant's job easier but the danger to avoid because it distances the public from its responsibility to share in governing. Political scientist Louis Gawthrop highlights this important aspect of the public servant's work:

> "In addition to ensuring that the laws are faithfully executed, it must also become the primary responsibility of the permanent career service, at all levels of government, to ensure the vitality of citizenship in an active citizenry fully engaged in the art of government . . ."[173]

Dan Fenn, a professor at the John F. Kennedy School of Government, captures this aspect of the public servant role well (Box P-1). "We need to see as part of our jobs the never-ending search for new and effective ways to build public participation into our decision-making processes," he notes, with the twin benefits that the citizen learns how to engage in governing and gains more understanding about how hard that work is for those who do it every day.[174]

As Marshall realized, the public servant also has a time horizon that differs from the program administrator. If he had focused only on winning the coming battles in North Africa, the Army would never have been prepared to govern captured cities and towns in Europe a year later. The resulting chaos would have tied down troops in controlling unrest and weakened the belief of freed people that democratic governance was possible and preferable. Thus, Marshall thought years ahead (even more so when he entered civilian service as Secretary of State and conceived the Marshall Plan for the recovery of Europe). He also thought about history, as he once told students at Princeton: "In order to take a full part in the life which is before you, I think you must in effect relive the past so that you may turn to the present with deep convictions and an understanding of what manner of country this is for which men for many generations have laid down their lives."[175]

Box P-1
The School Board Dodge

"Suppose I am one of five people on an elected school board. Someone comes up to me at a party . . . and says: "I really think we should have four years of Latin in our high school curriculum."

"Recalling my own behavior, probably I would say something like: "Interesting idea!" Going through my mind, however, would be: "Oh, Lord, I hope she doesn't pursue this. I have enough on my plate already."

"Then suppose a week later she calls me and says" You know, I have been talking with friends of mine and there is a group of ten of us parents who really think four years of Latin is important . . . what do you think?" What I think is that I wish she'd forgotten it; what I think is, "How do I handle this?" But what I say is: "Okay, I'll look into it for you."

"I make the calculation that she isn't going away. I call the superintendent, who tells me we're short of classrooms and have no teachers capable of doing the job. Dutifully, I pass this along to my friend, hoping that will end it. But no. "Well. I'm sure there are logistical issues," she says, "But we think this is so important."

"Recalling my own public career, I would figure out some bob or weave - unfortunately Probably ask her to put it on paper . . . blah, blah, blah."

"What I could do is sit down with her and say: "Let me walk through this process with you. First, as you know, I am only one of five members. There have to be three to move ahead with this. But then there is the superintendent. He actually runs the schools, and, though formally he works for us, we wouldn't push something like this without his cooperation. Whatever the legal lines may be, the actual power to get things done is divided here between us and the professional staff. They implement . . . And then he has the principal and the teachers' views to take into account. Beyond that, we would have to displace another language to make room for the fourth year of Latin. . . . I could then guide her through the process."

"I could have done that sort of thing in my career - but I didn't. I could have searched for chances to explain the realities to people. But I didn't."

"What happens when we pull the curtain away like that? All of a sudden we don't look so powerful."

"But would it build understanding? Would it build trust? Would it mean that in future interactions with other public servants, my friend would be both more effective and more realistic? Would it be a better way to bring people to a recognition of just how our system works . . . I think so, and I wish I had done it."

Source:, "Conclusion" by Dan Fenn, Jr.in
The Trusted Leader: Building the Relationships That Make Government Work *(2011)*

Marshall suggests, as does the role of public service as responsible citizenship, that education for public service must include but go beyond learning professional and technical tasks. The program administrator who does not understand the Constitution, the political theory of the Federalist Papers, the power and ongoing relevance of the anti-Federalist view, regime values, and how to behave ethically - to cite some prominent examples of content - can be a danger to the public. He risks acting without understanding that he is not just a technical specialist but one who must deliver democracy.

Bingham illustrates another central point. He acted against orders because he would have felt shame had he not done so. The loss of the perquisites of office was the price he paid. They were not unimportant to him, but they were not all that mattered either.

Marshall and Bingham, of course, were products of the twentieth century, as Washington and Madison were products of the eighteenth. Honor as a characteristic of a public servant is, their examples suggest, just as possible today as it was then (see Box P-2). [176] Before we turn to the challenge of how to reinvigorate honor, it is important to emphasize that the two views discussed here are not mutually exclusive. They need each other. As noted, the program administrator without Constitutional understanding and fidelity risks undermining the very republican government he is sworn to protect. Just as surely, the public servant who cannot perform in her role as a program administrator risks having admirable ends but failing miserably in means.

How Do We Restore Honor in Public Service?

Serving the public is honorable work, but ensuring that its practitioners serve honorably and are recognized for doing so requires attention at three levels. First, the public servant will need to be driven by an internal compass that incorporates both roles described above and that desires the esteem of others for doing so. Second, the civil service will need a culture in which acting honorably becomes a cherished and more explicit goal. Third, the nation will need to confer honor, much more publicly, on those who live up to the demands that constitute honor (as expressed in the roles of responsible citizenship combined with program administrator).

In 2002, Pasquale D'Amuro, chief of counterintelligence at the FBI, told FBI agents based in Guantanamo Bay, Cuba, that they were not allowed to use or be associated with abusive interrogation tactics. The use of snarling dogs, sleep deprivation, sexual humiliation and other methods were, in his judgment, antithetical to the core values of the Bureau and the U.S. Constitution. From a practical standpoint, D'Amuro also believed that traditional FBI techniques were better.

Box P-2
Ed McGaffigan: Public Service as Calling

The longest-serving commissioner of the Nuclear Regulatory Commission (NRC), Ed McGaffigan was appointed by a Democratic president (Clinton) in 1996, reappointed in 2000, and reappointed again, by a Republican president (Bush) in 2005. By his own admission, McGaffigan dedicated his life to public service after being inspired, as a seventh grader, by President Kennedy's Inaugural challenge to "ask not what your country can do for you - ask what you can do for your country."

After earning a degree in physics and two master's degrees, he joined the State Department. He served in the White House, in the U.S. Embassy in Moscow, and then for Sen. Jeff Bingaman for more than a dozen years. His government experience was thus both broad and deep even before he joined the NRC. McGaffigan did not step down from that latter post until melanoma forced his exit in late 2006. He died less than a year later.

During a ceremony honoring him before he stepped down, a fellow commissioner noted that "[H]e can quote the most obscure regulations, and give exact details on how they were written," a tribute to the "civil servant as program administrator" in McGaffigan's service. By all accounts, he improved NRC and developed a reputation for scientific excellence.

But being commissioner was more than a job and more than the application of technical expertise for McGaffigan. He was also a "public servant as responsible citizen." "He invests his entire character is this mission," his chief of staff, Jeff Sharkey, said of him. When his wife died in 1999, McGaffigan was still on Capitol Hill the next day, testifying before Congress: "What we do is go on," he said. "It's part of the duty thing." After his passing, NRC Chairman Dale Klein said of him: "He always took the view of what is best for the American people, not what might bring attention to himself." Former NRC Chairman Nils Diaz said:"Ed, above all, wanted to serve our nation with distinction and with a passion to do what was better for the common good."

In May 2008, the Justice Department's Inspector General released a report on interrogation and detention policies at Guantanamo and other sites. It noted that FBI agents, with very few exceptions, followed this guidance, and it applauded the FBI for "its conduct and professionalism."[177]

Coming on the heels of the September 11th attacks - and the intense pressure to gain intelligence to avert any further terrorism directed against Americans - we can guess at the pressure the FBI was under. Objecting to these interrogation tactics, whether from a desk in Washington, D.C. or a post in the prison at Guantanamo Bay, cannot have been easy. Yet D'Amuro's decision, and the actions of his agents in the field, were honorable, as the IG's report notes. Their behavior reminds one of Cicero's advice to his son in the former's classic (and last) essay on public duty, *DeOfficiis*:

> *"In carrying out such enterprises, some run the risk of losing their lives, others their reputation and the good-will of their fellow-citizens. It is our duty, then, to be more ready to endanger our own than the public welfare and to hazard honour and glory more readily than other advantages."*[178]

To restore honor, individual public servants will have to do at least the following, which this case illustrates:

- Put service to the nation above considerations of personal gain (or loss);[179]
- Treat the Oath of Office as a moral obligation;
- Perform their professional and technical duties ethically and with excellence;
- Understand the importance of character to public service and to earning the public's trust;
- Practice the virtues of integrity, truthfulness, ethical conduct and fidelity to Constitutional values until they become ingrained habits;
- Understand, through study and reflection, the nation's founding documents in their historical context and as an expression of an enduring and still unfulfilled promise;
- Form a studied conception of justice, which includes being able to think about what constitutes the public interest and the good society;
- Consider, in daily actions, the long-term interests of the nation; and
- Call attention to and seek redress of unethical conduct of others in public service who, through their actions, dishonor public service.

These behaviors are meant to incorporate the expectations of both the responsible citizen and the program administrator, as described above. D'Amuro and his agents, for example, had to be professionally competent as well as Constitutionally engaged.

The Civil Service: Fostering a Culture of Honor

It is hard for civil servants to behave honorably in a culture that ignores that standard. If honor is a declared aim of military service, and much is done to inculcate that, the civil service needs corresponding attention to honor. Those charged with management of the civil service as an institution will need to:

- Alter the core definition (and competency lists) of what it means to be a public servant, with a much greater emphasis on the public servant as responsible citizen;
- Reinvigorate the education of public servants, both prior to entry and during career advancement, with the ethos of responsible citizenship, including:
  o Attention to character during the recruitment and selection process;
  o Education in Constitutional thinking, values, and the demands of the Oath of Office;
  o Training in ethical thinking and leadership - that goes well beyond the current focus on what one *can* and *cannot* do - to address how to resolve dilemmas about what one *should* do; and
  o Provision of moral exemplars for public servants.
- Revise the language and documentation used for those who leave the public service, differentiating in writing that one leaves either as an "honorable departure" (instead of "resignation"); or as a "dishonorable separation" (instead of "fired");
- Provide awards and very public recognition of those who act honorably. This must extend beyond current awards for program administration (of which there are many) to include awards for responsible citizenship and ethical action (of which there are too few); and
- Establish mechanisms of internal self-policing by the public service profession to detect and sanction those who fail to live up to the standards of responsible citizenship. Without naming dishonor and casting shame, honor has less meaning.

A Nation That Honors Its Public Servants

Those in our armed forces make sacrifices in (and too often *of*) their personal lives that most civil servants are never asked to make. They deserve all the honors we bestow upon them. Nonetheless, we should not forget that many civilian workers in federal law and border enforcement, in our intelligence services, and in conflict zones abroad, as three examples, make similar sacrifices. All civil servants who meet the test noted above also serve honorably. None of these civil servants deserve the denigration, or the infrequent and insufficient recognition, to which they are subject when they do so. Honoring civil servants need not diminish the honor accorded to our military. Honor of public servants is not a zero-sum game. Disrespect of the civil servant must itself become dishonorable.

Achieving this will require action from within the government as well as from the media and other groups outside government. Three steps are especially necessary:

- Identify and publicly recognize civil servants who are moral exemplars, through awards from the highest levels of agencies, from nongovernment groups, from the media, and the President;
- Honor, through a U.S. burial flag and public ceremony, all those civil servants who give their lives in service to their country;
- Provide support - emotional and physical - for those "morally injured" due to their faithfulness to the demands of responsible citizenship as public servants.

In an atmosphere of "civil service bashing," even many in senior leadership positions in government seem reluctant to publicize honorable behavior. Press coverage is too seldom sought for agency-specific and government-wide ceremonies, even when these are held. That reflects a lack of courage and must be corrected with sufficient and public recognition. Such recognition is also needed from Congress, non-governmental groups and the media.

In a typical year, about 150 civil servants are killed while on duty.[180] Until 2011, the nation honored none of them with a burial flag. The Civilian Service Recognition Act of that year allowed agency heads to provide a flag, upon request, for those killed due to a criminal act, an act of terrorism, a natural disaster, or "other circumstances as determined by the president." In 2013, the U.S. Office of Personnel Management instituted a "Wall of Honor" to memorialize the names and of those civil servants who die due to circumstances covered by the act. Some agencies have comparable "walls of honor." Such practices should be routine in all agencies, and the award of flags should be routine in all cases where civil servants die due to work-related causes (without the time-delaying necessity of submitting any of those requests to the president).

When civil servants act honorably, they sometimes do so at great personal cost. In the military, the concept of "moral injury" (as distinct from physical injury) has been defined as "failing to prevent, bearing witness to, or learning about acts that transgress deeply held moral beliefs and expectations."[181] In a military setting, for example, a soldier might shoot in self-defense and kill an innocent civilian as a result. While acting appropriately given the situation, the soldier might still feel profound sorrow upon violating his sense of the kind of person he wants to be. This "moral injury" could plague a soldier for years to come.

Those in the civil service can also experience moral injury. In some cases, this may be produced in those engaged in law enforcement, security, and intelligence work. But it can also happen to others who witness government actions that violate their moral values and Constitutional beliefs. Whistleblowers are frequently affected in this way. So might others be who observe and object to wrongdoing, are ignored, or even find themselves unwitting participants to illegal or immoral acts.

A nation that honors its public servants will provide support when the behaviors of responsible citizenship and program administration produce moral injury. While the military and the Department of Veterans Affairs have begun to give attention to this problem for those on active duty and veterans, there is no comparable attention (much less admission of the problem) in the civil service. Civilian government agencies should provide comparable counseling and support, yet at present they can't be counted upon to do so. This may be because they have not accepted, or staffed for, this role. It can also be because those who are morally injured have either not come forward or are the very ones who have taken issue with some agency action and have been shunned for doing so. The response of agency superiors to the morally courageous has, unfortunately, often been ostracism or retaliation, not psychological support. Private and not-for-profit groups who represent the interests of the civil service, especially those concerned with supporting ethical behavior, will need to help fill this gap.

Conclusion

As he left the Constitutional Convention in September 1787, Benjamin Franklin was asked by some local citizens what kind of government it had created. He replied, "A republic, if you can keep it." Keeping it is the task of all of us, but it is a charge clothed in the twin demands of ethics and honor for the public servant. It must begin with a dedication to fellow citizens by those who are, first and foremost, citizens themselves. Public servants can hope for support and respect from a thankful public. But they should not count on it. They can hope for assistance from their organizations and leaders. But they should not count on that either. What they should count on is what they can control themselves - meeting the highest standard of duty and fidelity to the Constitution and the people. The test must involve constant self-reflection and improvement. Whether it generates thanks or not, it is the test that the admired Roman Emperor Marcus Aurelius set for himself:

> *"When the camp had gone to sleep, the emperor, who was late to bed and early to rise, sat at his table and took stock, not of battles, sieges, and fortunes, of which there is little mention, but of himself, his state of mind, his lapses from justice or from speaking the truth or from command of his temper. He used these night hours to conjure up the ideals he had set before himself as a man and as a ruler of men, to see them more clearly, to consider what they demanded of him, to consider what he was in light of what he might have been and in reason ought to be."[182]*

When public servants do that, ethics and honor will follow.

Appendices

—A—
The American Society for Public Administration (ASPA) Code of Ethics

—B—
An Ethics Decision Making Model

—C—
Ethics Web Sites

—D—
Ford's Speech to the Nation Announcing the Pardon of Richard M. Nixon

—E—
Practice Ethics Cases

—F—
Ethics and Public Service: An Annotated Bibliography

—APPENDIX A—

THE AMERICAN SOCIETY FOR PUBLIC ADMINISTRATION (ASPA) CODE OF ETHICS*

The ASPA Code of Ethics is a statement of the aspirations and high expectations of public servants. These practices serve as a guide to behavior for members of ASPA in carrying out its principles. The Code and these practices are intended to be used as a whole and in conjunction with one another. An ethical public servant will consider the full range of standards and values that are relevant to handling a specific matter and be committed to upholding both the spirit and the letter of this code.

ASPA members are committed to—

1. **Advance the Public Interest.** Promote the interests of the public and put service to the public above service to oneself.
   a. Seek to advance the good of the public as a whole, taking into account current and long-term interests of the society.
   b. Exercise discretionary authority to promote the public interest.
   c. Be prepared to make decisions that may not be popular but that are in the public's best interest.
   d. Subordinate personal interests and institutional loyalties to the public good.
   e. Serve all persons with courtesy, respect, and dedication to high standards.

2. **Uphold the Constitution and the Law.** Respect and support government constitutions and laws, while seeking to improve laws and policies to promote the public good.
   a. Recognize and understand the constitutional, legislative and regulatory framework in which you work and fully discharge your professional roles and responsibilities.
   b. Promote constitutional principles of equality, fairness, representativeness, responsiveness and due process in protecting citizens' rights and promoting the public good.

c. Develop proposals for sound laws and policies and for improving or eliminating laws and policies that are unethical, counterproductive, or obsolete.

d. Respect and safeguard protected and confidential information.

3. **Promote democratic participation.** Inform the public and encourage active engagement in governance. Be open, transparent and responsive, and respect and assist all persons in their dealings with public organizations.

a. Be open and transparent while protecting privacy rights and security.

b. Recognize and support the public's right to know the public's business.

c. Involve the community in the development, implementation, and assessment of policies and public programs, and seek to empower citizens in the democratic process, including special assistance to those who lack resources or influence.

d. Assist members of the public in their dealings with government and respond to the public in ways that are complete, clear, and easy to understand.

e. Promote timely and continuing dissemination of information about government activities to the community, ensuring a fair and transparent process and educating citizens to make effective contributions.

4. **Strengthen social equity.** Treat all persons with fairness, justice, and equality and respect individual differences, rights, and freedoms. Promote affirmative action and other initiatives to reduce unfairness, injustice, and inequality in society.

a. Provide services to the public with impartiality and consistency tempered by recognition of differences. Ensure that all persons have access to programs and services to which they are entitled under the law and maintain equitable standards of quality for all who receive the programs and services.

b. Provide equal treatment, protection, and due process to all persons.

c. Oppose all forms of discrimination and harassment and promote affirmative action, cultural competence, and other efforts to reduce disparities in outcomes and increase the inclusion of underrepresented groups.

5. **Fully Inform and Advise.** Provide accurate, honest, comprehensive, and timely information and advice to elected and appointed officials and governing board members, and to staff members in your organization.

a. Provide information and advice based on a complete and impartial review of circumstances and needs of the public and the goals and objectives of the organization.

b. Be prepared to provide information and recommendations that may not be popular or preferred by superiors or colleagues.

6. **Demonstrate personal integrity.** Adhere to the highest standards of conduct to inspire public confidence and trust in public service.

    a. Exercise integrity, courage, compassion, benevolence, and optimism.

    b. Maintain truthfulness and honesty and do not compromise them for advancement, honor, or personal gain.

    c. Resist political, organizational, and personal pressures to compromise ethical integrity and principles and support others who are subject to these pressures.

    d. Accept individual responsibility for your actions and the consequences of your actions.

    e. Guard against using public position for personal gain or to advance personal or private interests.

    f. Zealously guard against conflict of interest or its appearance. Disclose any interests that may affect objectivity in making decisions and recuse oneself from participation in those decisions.

    g. Conduct official acts without partisanship or favoritism.

    h. Ensure that others receive credit for their work and contributions.

7. **Promote Ethical Organizations:** Strive to attain the highest standards of ethics, stewardship, and public service in organizations that serve the public.

    a. Work to establish procedures that hold individuals and the organization accountable for their conduct and support these procedures with clear reporting of activities and accomplishments.

    b. Act as stewards of public funds by the strategic, effective, and efficient use of resources; by regularly reexamining the efficacy of policies, programs, and services; and by seeking to prevent all forms of mismanagement or waste.

    c. Encourage open expression of views by staff members within the organization and provide administrative channels for dissent. Protect the whistle blowing rights of public employees, provide assurance of due process and safeguards against reprisal, and give support to colleagues who are victims of retribution.

    d. Seek to correct instances of wrongdoing or report them to superiors. If remedies cannot be assured by reporting wrongdoing internally, seek external sources or agencies for review and action.

    e. Support merit principles that promote excellence, competence, and professionalism in the selection and promotion of public officials and employees and protect against biased, arbitrary, and capricious actions.

    f. Promote proactive efforts to increase the representativeness of the public workforce and the full inclusion of persons with diverse characteristics.

g. Encourage organizations to adopt, distribute, and periodically review a code of ethics as a living document that applies principles of this code and other relevant codes to the specific mission and conditions of the organization.

8. **Advance Professional Excellence:** Strengthen personal capabilities to act competently and ethically and encourage the professional development of others.

   a. Keep up-to-date on emerging issues, practices, and potential problems that could affect your performance and accomplishing the mission of your organization.
   b. Provide support and encouragement to others to upgrade competence and participate in professional activities and associations.
   c. Allocate time and resources to the professional development of students, interns, beginning professionals, and other colleagues.

   * Approved by the ASPA Council on March 16, 2013. This code was reprinted with permission from the American Society for Public Administration.

−Appendix B−

An Ethics Decision Making Model*

This model and set of questions is designed to help you think about an ethics issue you face. Some questions may be more relevant than others for your particular issue, but in most cases almost every question will offer a useful perspective for thinking through the dilemma.

As shown below, the very first consideration is whether the issue you face is a "right vs. wrong" or a "right vs. right" question. In the first instance ("right vs. wrong"), the presumption is that there is a law or regulation that proscribes the wrong choice. This is not truly an ethics "dilemma" because one choice is morally wrong. Ethical action in this case means doing the right thing.

The rest of the model applies to "right vs. right" choices, ethics dilemmas where two or more courses of action are permissible and you are trying to determine what is the best action to take.

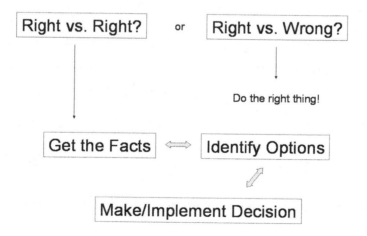

* The questions in this model draw upon a wide range of books and writers who have grappled with how to address ethics issues. See, for example: Badaracco (2002), Cooper (1998), Gentile (2012), Lewis (1991), Kidder (1995), Svara (2014), and Werhane (1999).

Get the Facts

1. DEFINITION:
    a. In everyday language, how do you define the ethics issue? What's the dilemma?
    b. Is it really a "right vs. right" issue?

2. STAKEHOLDERS and STAKEHOLDER VALUES:
    a. Who are the relevant stakeholders (including yourself): inside the organization? outside?
    b. What are their values and perspectives in regard to the issue? How do they see the issue?
    c. Are concerns about justice involved? If so, which stakeholders have which concerns?

3. STAKES:
    a. What are the stakes for you? For others?
    b. What are your motives regarding this issue? Your intentions?

4. CONFLICTS:
    a. What values are in conflict (e.g. personal, organizational, societal) for you? For others?
    b. What moral principles are in conflict for you? For others?

5. FACTS:
    a. What are the relevant facts? Are they really facts or just assumptions?
    b. What's the relevant history to this situation? How did it emerge? What else has been done in the past that is relevant to resolving it? What got you to where you are with this ethical issue?
    c. What are the applicable laws? regulations? formal policies/procedures?
    d. What are the relevant precedents?
    e. How might others see the facts of the situation? What facts would matter to them and why?

6. ASSUMPTIONS:
    a. What assumptions are you making about any of the above that need to be checked out? How can you do so?
    b. Are your motives, loyalties and/or assumptions affecting how you define the "facts" of the situation?
    c. What assumptions would others make about the situation? How do those assumptions differ from your own?

Identify Options

7. RESPONSIBILITY:
   a. Who has the obligation to address the issue?
   b. If not you, what will you do to move the issue onto others' agendas?
   c. If more than you, how will you get others involved?
   d. To who are you obligated on this issue? Where should your loyalties be?

8. RESULTS:
   a. What objectives/results do you seek in addressing the ethical issue?
   b. What results matter to other stakeholders?

9. OPTIONS:
   a. What options exist for addressing the ethical issue:
      i. Using a "universal rule of right conduct" (deontological) perspective (i.e. the rule that you would be willing to see any action you take crafted as a universal law applicable to all people all of the time)?
      ii. Using the "greatest good for the greatest number" (teleological) perspective (i.e. the rule that you decide based on what produces the greatest benefit for the greatest number of people)?
      iii. Using the "golden rule" perspective (i.e. the rule that you should "do unto others as you would have them do unto you")?
      iv. Using the "virtue" perspective (i.e. what would a good person do?)?
   b. How can you appropriately invite others (especially those affected) into generating and thinking about options?
   c. What options do/might they add?
   d. Are you considering all the options – or did you filter some out without enough attention to them?
   e. How might your mental biases (e.g. errors of attention, motivated blindness, threats to your status, anchoring biases, attribution bias, etc.) be impacting your ethical thinking?
   f. Are your most promising options sufficiently detailed (e.g. time, place, resources) for you to think carefully about them?

10. IMPACTS:
    a. What are the likely downstream effects (positive and negative) of your most promising options?
       i. On achieving the results you seek?

    ii.   On you? Your career?

    iii.   On other stakeholders?

    iv.   On your organization?

    v.   In the short term? Long term?

Make and Implement Decision

11. MAKE A DECISION:
   a. What core value matters to you in reaching a decision? Which is the one that matters most?
   b. What core values matter most to other stakeholders?
   c. What option(s) seem(s) best? Are these:
      i. Legal?
      ii. Feasible to implement?
      iii. Likely to be effective? (i.e. meet your desired results?)
      iv. Likely to pass the "smell test?" the "Washington Post" test? the "grandchildren" test?
      v. Addressing your most important core value in this situation?
      vi. Emotionally satisfying? If something about it is rubbing you the wrong way, what is it and why?
      vii. Likely to be perceived as appropriate years from now?
   d. Is your decision as disinterested as possible? That is, if you did not know how the decision would affect your personal interests, would you still make the same call?

12. PREPARE TO IMPLEMENT:
   a. Who is likely to be injured by your decision?
   b. How might you prevent or mitigate harmful effects?
   c. Who is likely to oppose your decision? How will you deal with their opposition? Consider any of the follow questions that may be relevant:
      i. How can you get them to think about long term as well as short term concerns and benefits?
      ii. How can you get them to consider the broader purpose they seek to serve?
      iii. How can you frame the proposed course of action so that it appears less costly than other options, considering both short and long-term costs of acting or not acting?
      iv. How can you gain allies?
   d. How will you implement and communicate (i.e. voice) your decision:

i.   With those directly affected?

ii.   With other interested parties?

e. How can you create a support system for implementation:

i.   For you and the stress involved?

ii.   For others affected?

13. IMPLEMENT AND ASSESS:

a. How will you judge the long-term consequences and the effectiveness of your decision?

b. When will you revisit the decision to assess its impact on the situation, yourself, and others? How will you do so?

—Appendix C—

Ethics Web Sites

This list has been compiled to *illustrate* the wide range of organizations that exist to help you act ethically. The list is by no means comprehensive; many other useful sites exist. The list is divided into two categories: (a) sites that are operated by government and (b) sites operated by university or non-profit organizations.

Government Ethics Web Sites

Office of Government Ethics
www.usoge.gov

The U.S. Office of Government Ethics (OGE) aims to foster high ethical standards for executive branch employees and strengthen the public's confidence that the Government's business is conducted with impartiality and integrity. OGE is a source for education and assistance on all ethics laws, rules, and regulations. It also enables connections to agency-specific ethics Web sites, especially through its Program Excellence and Awards Program.

The President's Commission for the Study of Bioethical Issues
www.bioethics.gov

This is an advisory panel of the leaders in medicine, science, ethics, religion, law, and engineering. The Commission advises the president on bioethical issues and seeks to identify and promote policies and practices that ensure scientific research, health care delivery, and technological innovation are conducted in a socially and ethically responsible manner.

NIH Department of Bioethics
http://www.bioethics.nih.gov/home/index.shtml

This NIH department is committed to interdisciplinary and inter-institutional collaboration, with a focus on bringing medical, legal, philosophical, and scientific disciplines to bear on contemporary questions in bioethics.

The Vice Admiral James B. Stockdale Center for Ethical Leadership, U.S. Naval Academy
http://www.usna.edu/Ethics/

The Center seeks to accomplish its mission ("transform ethical leadership development worldwide") through studying important emerging ethical leadership issues, consulting with high-level leaders, developing new ways to strengthen and accelerate ethical leadership development, dissemination via lectures, print publications, and multi-media, made available on the Web, and through connecting people, programs, and experiences.

Defense Industry Initiative on Business Ethics and Conduct (DII)
http://www.dii.org

This non-profit organization combines the efforts of 77 companies to foster a culture for and the practice of ethics and integrity in all business dealings with the United States Department of Defense.

Council on Government Ethics Laws
http://www.cogel.org/

This is a group of government ethics officials who work in the fields of governmental ethics, freedom of information, elections, lobbying, and campaign finance.

Private/Non-Profit Web Sites

Ethics Resource Center
www.ethics.org

Originally established by the former director of the Office of Government Ethics, the Ethics Resource Center focuses on ethics research and education in both business and government.

Edmond J. Safra Center for Ethics, Harvard University
www.ethics.harvard.edu

The center focuses on teaching and research related to ethics in public life.

Josephson Institute of Ethics
http://josephsoninstitute.org

The Josephson Institute conducts programs and offers consulting services for leaders including legislators and mayors, high-ranking public executives, congressional staff, editors and reporters, senior corporate and nonprofit executives, judges and lawyers, and military and police officers.

Carnegie Council on Ethics & International Affairs
http://www.cceia.org/

The Carnegie Council's mission is to be the voice for ethics in international policy. The Council convenes forums and creates educational opportunities and information resources for an international audience of teachers and students, journalists, international affairs professionals, and concerned citizens.

Center for Public Integrity
http://www.publicintegrity.org/

The Center for Public Integrity is a nonprofit organization dedicated to producing original, responsible investigative journalism on issues of public concern. Its mission is "To serve democracy by revealing abuses of power, corruption and betrayal of public trust by powerful public and private institutions, using the tools of investigative journalism."

International Center for Ethics, Justice and Public Life, Brandeis University
http://www.brandeis.edu/ethics/

The mission of the International Center for Ethics, Justice and Public Life is "to develop effective responses to conflict and injustice by offering innovative approaches to coexistence, strengthening the work of international courts and encouraging ethical practice in civic and professional life."

Institute for Global Ethics
www.globalethics.org

The Institute promotes ethical behavior in individuals, institutions, and nations through research, public discourse, and practical action.

Government Accountability Project
www.whistleblower.org

This organization focuses on enhancing occupational free speech for both government and private sector workers. It has a large focus on supporting whistle blower protections.

The Hastings Center
http://www.thehastingscenter.org/Default.aspx

The Hastings Center focuses on bioethics in five areas: health and health care; children and families; aging, chronic care and end of life; emerging science and conceptions of self; and human impact on the natural world.

Center for the Study of Ethics in the Professions, Illinois Institute of Technology, Chicago, IL
http://ethics.iit.edu

This site contains links to ethics issues and ethics codes in a wide range of professional fields (e.g. agriculture, business, computing, engineering, finance, government/military, health care, law, management, and science).

Computer Ethics Institute
http://computerethicsinstitute.org/home.html

The Computer Ethics Institute focuses on current and emerging ethics issues in the field of information technology.

Ford's Speech to the Nation Announcing the Pardon of Richard M. Nixon September 8, 1974

Ladies and gentlemen:

I have come to a decision which I felt I should tell you and all of my fellow American citizens, as soon as I was certain in my own mind and in my own conscience that it is the right thing to do.

I have learned already in this office that the difficult decisions always come to this desk. I must admit that many of them do not look at all the same as the hypothetical questions that I have answered freely and perhaps too fast on previous occasions.

My customary policy is to try and get all the facts and to consider the opinions of my countrymen and to take counsel with my most valued friends. But these seldom agree, and in the end, the decision is mine. To procrastinate, to agonize, and to wait for a more favorable turn of events that may never come or more compelling external pressures that may as well be wrong as right, is itself a decision of sorts and a weak and potentially dangerous course for a President to follow.

I have promised to uphold the Constitution, to do what is right as God gives me to see the right, and to do the very best that I can for America.

I have asked your help and your prayers, not only when I became President but many times since. The Constitution is the supreme law of our land and it governs our actions as citizens. Only the laws of God, which govern our consciences, are superior to it.

As we are a nation under God, so I am sworn to uphold our laws with the help of God. And I have sought such guidance and searched my own conscience with special diligence to determine the right thing for me to do with respect to my predecessor in this place, Richard Nixon, and his loyal wife and family.

Theirs is an American tragedy in which we all have played a part. It could go on and on and on, or someone must write the end to it. I have concluded that only I can do that, and if I can, I must.

There are no historic or legal precedents to which I can turn in this matter, none that precisely fit the circumstances of a private citizen who has resigned the Presidency of the United States. But it is common knowledge that serious allegations and accusations hang like a sword over our former President's head, threatening his health as he tries to reshape his life, a great part of which was spent in the service of this country and by the mandate of its people.

After years of bitter controversy and divisive national debate, I have been advised, and I am compelled to conclude that many months and perhaps more years will have to pass before Richard Nixon could obtain a fair trial by jury in any jurisdiction of the United States under governing decisions of the Supreme Court.

I deeply believe in equal justice for all Americans, whatever their station or former station. The law, whether human or divine, is no respecter of persons; but the law is a respecter of reality.

The facts, as I see them, are that a former President of the United States, instead of enjoying equal treatment with any other citizen accused of violating the law, would be cruelly and excessively penalized either in preserving the presumption of his innocence or in obtaining a speedy determination of his guilt in order to repay a legal debt to society.

During this long period of delay and potential litigation, ugly passions would again be aroused. And our people would again be polarized in their opinions. And the credibility of our free institutions of government would again be challenged at home and abroad.

In the end, the courts might well hold that Richard Nixon had been denied due process, and the verdict of history would even more be inconclusive with respect to those charges arising out of the period of his Presidency, of which I am presently aware.

But it is not the ultimate fate of Richard Nixon that most concerns me, though surely it deeply troubles every decent and every compassionate person. My concern is the immediate future of this great country.

In this, I dare not depend upon my personal sympathy as a long-time friend of the former President, nor my professional judgment as a lawyer, and I do not.

As President, my primary concern must always be the greatest good of all the people of the United States whose servant I am. As a man, my first consideration is to be true to my own convictions and my own conscience.

My conscience tells me clearly and certainly that I cannot prolong the bad dreams that continue to reopen a chapter that is closed. My conscience tells me that only I, as President, have the constitutional power to firmly shut and seal this book. My conscience tells me it is my duty, not merely to proclaim domestic tranquility but to use every means that I have to insure it. I do believe that the buck stops here, that I cannot rely upon public opinion polls to tell me what is right. I do believe that right makes might and that if I am wrong, 10 angels swearing I was right would make no difference. I do believe, with all my heart and mind and spirit, that I, not as President but as a humble servant of God, will receive justice without mercy if I fail to show mercy.

Finally, I feel that Richard Nixon and his loved ones have suffered enough and will continue to suffer, no matter what I do, no matter what we, as a great and good nation, can do together to make his goal of peace come true.

Now, therefore, I, Gerald R. Ford, President of the United States, pursuant to the pardon power conferred upon me by Article II, Section 2, of the Constitution, have granted and by these presents [sic] do grant a full, free, and absolute pardon unto Richard Nixon for all offenses against the United States which he, Richard Nixon, has committed or may have committed or taken part in during the period from July (January) 20, 1969 through August 9, 1974.

In witness whereof, I have hereunto set my hand this eighth day of September, in the year of our Lord nineteen hundred and seventy-four, and of the Independence of the United States of America the one hundred and ninety-ninth.

PRACTICE ETHICS CASES

For those in public service, ethics is a practical, not a philosophical, issue. Thus, ethical thinking and action can be improved by working on practical cases. When done in a small group, where multiple views are encouraged, skill growth is even greater.

The cases that follow are all drawn from "real-life" events. Some come directly from news stories. Others come from interviews with managers and executives (though names and agencies are always made up to preserve the confidentiality of the interviews).

As you consider each case, draw on the tools and ideas in this book. Consider such questions (see Appendix B) as:

- What is the ethics issue?
- Who is responsible for addressing this issue?
- What values are in conflict?
- What are the facts in the case? assumptions?
- Who are the stakeholders and how do they see the ethical dilemma?
- Does the desire for justice appear in this case? If so, how?
- What options exist for resolving the dilemma?
- What option seems best, and how would you act?
- What opposition might you get and how will you address it?

The Impending Layoffs

"I wish I could tell you more," Sarah said to Bill Locke, her administrative assistant, as she rose to end the meeting. No truer words had ever been spoken, not that it made her feel any better. She _did_ wish she could tell him more, but she had not. Faithful to her own boss's request, Sarah had not divulged details of the coming layoffs - even that there would be some.

It was pretty widely known, of course, that the unit had suffered a major budget cutback. "And anybody who can put two and two together must know that we can't support all the people we now have with only two-thirds of last year's budget." Sarah thought. "But that doesn't mean that everyone knows it," Sarah also realized, "and it kills me to have to turn people like Bill away without telling them everything _I_ know." Bill was a single parent, and losing his job would be devastating. And just last week, she heard that Esther, a human resources specialist she admired a great deal, was thinking of finally buying a first home for her growing family. "Would she still be doing that," Sarah wondered, "if I had told her the truth?"

She had not lied, exactly, she reasoned. She just hadn't disclosed all the details that management knew – that there would be layoffs, that they would occur in about three months, and that they would be aimed at reducing twenty percent of the staff, perhaps a little less if they could subtly encourage enough people to take early retirement before then. It did not help her to know that she was not alone in facing all this. Supervisors in other units had been given the same guidance from top management. But what if they broke down and told their employees while she held firm to the management line?

Sarah was torn between her desire to say more and the clear message from her boss: "We've got work to complete around here," her boss had told her. "How can we do that if everyone is wondering if they'll have a job? Morale would plummet." Top management also felt convinced that open acknowledgement of the need for layoffs might lead the best employees to take jobs elsewhere, a further threat to current work.

Hoping to put this out of her mind for a while, Sarah turned to her waiting emails, only to see one from Mary Fisher, titled "Layoff Rumors Flying! – What's Going to Happen?"

What should Sarah do?

Educating the Public

In 2002 and 2004, the Environment Protection Agency (EPA) paid the Weather Channel a total of $40,000 to produce and broadcast several videos about ozone depletion, urban heat problems, and the dangers of ultraviolet radiation as part of the Bush Administration's effort to educate the public about climate change. The contract called for the Weather Channel to create four two-minute "video capsules" on the topics and air them several times during peak viewing periods. EPA would have the right to review scripts and suggest content, but the Weather Channel retained editorial control.

When the project's funding source came to light, EPA encountered criticism from some who charged them with violation of the federal ban on "covert propaganda." Melanie Sloan, executive director of Citizens for Responsibility and Ethics in Washington, a nonprofit advocacy group, said, "The way they've presented it makes it look more independent than it in fact is, and that's misleading." "It would be totally fine for there to be a community service message on these topics. All it would have to say - much more clearly – is that this was paid for by the government," she said.

All four videos display EPA's logo at the end of the segment as well as a line of text that reads: "This has been a co-production of the Environmental Protection Agency & The Weather Channel." The tag line does not say EPA paid for the segments, and the segments are narrated by Nick Walter, a Weather Channel employee and meteorologist, who functions as the reporter for the videos.

"We're being completely up front," said Eryne Witcher, an EPA spokeswoman when questioned about the video segments. "An important role for EPA is to educate the public on key issues," she noted.

Is there an ethical issue here? If so, how could it have been resolved?

A Minor Request

Tim Braxton was confused and getting testy. He had just hung up from a call with an analyst with the Government Accountability Office (GAO) and told her, again, that the information she wanted was not being sent – at least not yet. His growing frustration was not with GAO, though they had certainly played the "I gotcha" game with him before. He was certainly not their best friend. No, this time, his irritation was directed at his own Policy Division, who had had the GAO-requested information he gathered for more than a month but had not passed it on to GAO.

It all had started routinely enough. Since Tim's branch was responsible for a $450 million contract soon to be awarded, it was not uncommon for GAO – as well as the agency's own Inspector General (IG) - to track the design and management of such a large contract. Not surprisingly, then, GAO had asked to see emails and other documents that supported the branch's work plan. GAO wanted to assess the branch's risk analysis on the contract and contract management process. Tim thought it was both straightforward and reasonable to comply. He had nothing to hide and, in fact, felt that the material asked for would prove just what GAO wanted to know: that the branch was doing a good job at handling the risk analysis.

Tim was taken back, however, as was his boss, when the head of the Policy Division – to whom the documents were required to go on their way to GAO – said that they would not be sent forward any time soon, if at all. When Tim pressed them for an explanation, they "politely" informed him that it was their job, not his, to decide what to send and when to send it. They added that they did not want to make it easy for GAO, because that would just generate more requests to see more documents, and the Policy Division was determined not to let GAO see the organization's every move.

Tim thought this was shortsighted. He felt that GAO had a right to the material and could enforce that right in the end. Denying the request was just making a bad relationship with an organization they didn't need to give them any trouble. He wondered if there was something else behind the division's stonewalling, though he could not fathom what that might be.

So Tim was caught between the proverbial rock and a hard place. He could not satisfy GAO, his own Policy Division was mad at him, and his own employees were not happy either. They could not see what the problem was and knew that they would pay the price if GAO decided to throw its Congressional weight around. Once the contract was actually awarded, they could be expected to camp out in even greater numbers to exercise their oversight role.

In pondering what to do, Tim had considered asking the Policy Division to give GAO at least the less innocuous of the material - emails just giving the agendas of meetings held and not the results. Tim had done this exact thing a couple years before, not seeing anything wrong with it, and had taken a little heat for it after the fact. But it still seemed like a reasonable idea. He even floated this at one point as a "trial balloon" to a contact he had in the division, and they didn't seem to like this idea either. In fact, this friend got irritated with Tim, and he remembered wondering why such a good friendship now seemed so fragile.

What, if anything, should Tim do?

The Muffling of a Surgeon General*

In early July, 2007, former Surgeon General Richard Carmona told the House Oversight and Government Reform Committee that the Bush Administration had pushed him to hold back or weaken public health recommendations because they conflicted with political goals.

For example, he said, the Administration had urged him to "water down" a report on the dangers of secondhand smoke, and it would not allow him to use the bully pulpit of his office to address such topics as stem cells research, emergency contraception, or sex education.

Carmona even suggested that he was told to refrain from going to the Special Olympics because of its ties to the Kennedy family. "I was specifically told by a senior person, 'Why would you want to help those people?,'" he testified. While Carmona did not name the Kennedys, he was asked after the hearing if that is who he meant. "You said it, I didn't," he replied.

Carmon was not the only one to complain of political pressure or interference with the job of the surgeon general. Dr. David Satcher, who served in that post under President Clinton, and Dr. C. Everett Coop, who was surgeon general under President Reagan, also testified to being subjected to political pressure.

Emily Lawrimore, a Bush White House spokeswoman, responded to Carmona's testimony by saying that "It's disappointing to us if he failed to use this position to the fullest extent in advocating for policies he thought were in the best interest of the nation."

Should Carmona have spoken up more forcefully while he was still Surgeon General? How could he have done so?

Are scientists who work for government subjected to political pressures on their work or public statements? If so, how could they address that?

---

* Drawn from: "Surgeon General Sees 4-Year Term as Compromised," *The New York Times*, July 7, 2007. Carmona left his post in July 2006, at the end of his term.

The Switcheroo

Bodri Chopra had had a great vacation. It was so refreshing to get away with his wife and three young children. They had never been to the Grand Canyon, and they were thrilled with the views, the hiking, and just being together away from the stress of the daily grind. So it was with some anger that he discovered, on returning to the office yesterday, that the attorney he had hired for his unit in the Office of General Counsel just before he went on leave was not actually going to work for him after all.

Sheila Tate had all the right qualifications - third in her class at Georgetown Law School, associate editor of the law journal, a two-year stint working on Capitol Hill in the very area - securities law - that his office needed help. She had been due to start work the same day he returned, and he had laid out a careful orientation week for her.

Yet, when he came into the office on Monday, he was surprised that Sheila was not there waiting for him. He had set up a 9 am appointment with her when he hired her. When he asked his staff if anyone had seen her, he was told that she was in his boss's office.

Bodri had worked for Ed Harper for two years. They had a good relationship, so he assumed that Ed was having a courtesy conversation to welcome Sheila to the organization. He could not have been more wrong.

In fact, he soon learned from Sheila that she was working for Ed - full-time. She seemed a little embarrassed that he did not know. As she related, Ed had approached her last week, wanting her to work for him instead. She assumed that Ed had communicated this to Bodri, though he couldn't imagine how she could think that since he had been on leave.

Technically, of course, Bodri knew that Sheila could work for whomever she wished. But this didn't seem right. As his anger mounted, he wondered if he was just being over-sensitive or if there really was something else going on.

What should Bodri do?

Animal Rights and Economic Needs*

The U.S. Meat Animal Research Center in Clay Center, Nebraska, federally-funded by the U.S. Department of Agriculture, got some unwelcome publicity in January 2015 courtesy of an exposé by the *New York Times*. In operation for half a century, the center is charged with helping farmers who produce beef, lamb, and pork earn a good profit. To serve that mission, the center conducts research aimed at increasing livestock yields and reducing production costs. This includes attention to containing disease and ensuring food safety.

Some of the center's research, the focus of the *Times* article, has raised ethical questions, even from those in the meat production business. For example, an effort to increase pig yields has resulted in litters of up to 14 piglets, but many newborns die because they are too frail or are crowded in pens and crushed by their mothers. In an effort to raise lamb production while lowering costs, the center's researchers have conducted experiments, named "easy care," that aim to allow ewes giving birth to do so in the fields, rather than in barns, yet many of the lambs cannot survive the outdoor conditions and/or are abandoned by their mothers.

Normally, the Animal Welfare Act of 1966 would govern such experiments, but the authorizing legislation specifically exempted farm animals used in research to benefit agriculture. The center has resisted suggestions that it comply with such procedures, including pleas that it join organizations that scrutinize experiments. Further, according to the *Times*, "[T]he center's parent agency, the Agriculture Department, strictly polices the treatment of animals at slaughterhouses and private laboratories. But it does not closely monitor the center's use of animals, or even enforce its own rules requiring careful scrutiny of experiments."

The Department maintains that the center meets its requirements on experimental approval through use of review committees. Yet the *Times* study, using documents obtained under the Freedom of Information Act, found that "of 850 experimental protocols since 1985 . . . approvals were typically made by six or fewer staff members, often including the lead researchers for the experiment." Committee minutes were almost absent - just six sentences from one single session were turned over to the *Times* for the past ten years. A study of the protocols found that "the words "profit" or "production efficiency" appear 111 times, "pain" comes up only twice."

The center, in its defense, points to the good it does. According to the *Times* article: "We're just as concerned about the humane treatment of animals as anyone else," said Sherrill Echternkamp, a scientist who retired from the center in 2013. Still, she added: "It's not a perfect world. We are trying to feed a population that is expanding very rapidly, to nine billion by 2050, and if we are going to feed that population, there are some trade-offs."

The center has about 44 scientists and 73 technicians for its population of about 30,000 animals. The scientists do not have medical degrees yet regularly perform surgery. It has only one veterinarian, who is not a scientist (down from six who were scientists on staff two decades ago). The one vet complained in 2011 and 2012 about animal treatment, including barns so stuffed with pigs that they could not be cleaned and were breeding disease. At the same time, the center's budget has limited funds to provide better shelters.

What are the ethics issues in this case? Who should do what to address them?

* "In Quest for More Meat Profits, U.S. Lab Lets Animals Suffer," by Michael Moss, *The New York Times,* January 20, 2015

—APPENDIX F—

ETHICS AND PUBLIC SERVICE
AN ANNOTATED BIBLIOGRAPHY

This annotated bibliography includes a sampling of books on ethics and public service. The books are not philosophical tomes. They are oriented to practicing ethics in organizational life. The books are organized according to the SERVE model, though clearly some books could fall in more than one of the five areas the model represents.

Spot an Ethics Issue

Arendt, Hannah, **Eichmann in Jerusalem: A Report on the Banality of Evil,** New York: Penguin Books, 1964.

> Arendt covered the trial of Adolph Eichmann in Jerusalem, and this account of the trial and administrative life of the notorious civil servant who orchestrated the Nazi "final solution" is a powerful reminder of what the absence of moral thinking can mean in bureaucratic life.

Gawthrop, Louis, **Public Service and Democracy: Ethical Imperatives for the 21st Century,** New York: Chatham House Publishers, 1998.

> Career civil servants are not elected, yet they are involved every day in decisions that affect the public welfare. Since we can't vote them out of office, how do we ensure that they do what they should do? Gawthrop argues that democracy can only be preserved when public officials imbue their thinking and action with three core moral values - faith, hope, and love – and when they truly accept that they are their "brother's keeper." Effective public service, he maintains, requires a moral center not just following the law.

Phillips, Donald T. and Admiral James M. Loy, **Character in Action: The U.S. Coast Guard on Leadership**, Annapolis, MD: The Naval Institute Press, 2003.

> During Hurricane Katrina, the U.S. Coast Guard was heralded for rescuing more than 30,000 people. This book highlights the core values and leadership principles that made such success possible. The Coast Guard aims to develop character. Their emphasis on values, teamwork, and preparing each "coastie" to do the right thing are not only exemplary but essential in a service where much of the work is doing by young crews on small boats under trying circumstances.

Rohr, John, **Ethics for Bureaucrats: An Essay on Law and Values**, New York: Marcel Dekker, Inc, 1989.

> This book is a search for an ethical approach for public servants. Rohr argues that traditional efforts fall short, including focusing on conflict of interest rules, the Ethics in Government Act, resigning in protest, and whistle blowing. None of these offer enough guidance or latitude for the many daily decisions public officials must face. Instead, he argues that civil servants should study Supreme Court cases because it is in court decisions that the way to act in accordance with the regime values that guide our Constitution gets clarified. Much of the book focuses on taking critical Court decisions, extracting the principles they address and raising questions about how civil servants could carry those principles into their own thinking.

Rohr, John, **Public Service, Ethics, and Constitutional Practice**, Lawrence: University Press of Kansas, 1998.

> Bureaucrats are not isolated from the policy process just because they are un-elected. So how do we ensure they don't abuse their power? Rohr maintains there are several things we must do, the first of which is to anchor their thinking in regime values – those Constitutional values that shape society. We can achieve this through an educational process that focuses on the meaning and expectations of their Oath of Office, institutional literacy (understanding the statutory foundation, administrative history, and key court cases for their agency), and reminding them of the political vision of the President and their commitment to political neutrality.

Examine the Ethical Dilemma

Ciulla, Joanne, **The Ethics of Leadership**, Toronto: Thomson/Wadsworth, 2000.
> Ciulla weaves classical texts (Aristotle, Mill, Kant, Lao Tsu, etc) with contemporary writing and short case studies into a book meant for use in the classroom or for self-study. The book covers topics central to leadership and ethics, including power and self-interest, the public and private morality of leaders, and exploration of the two predominant ethical streams in western thought – the ethics of duty by Kant and the ethics of utilitarianism by Mill, and the relationship between leader and followers.

Cooper, Terry, **The Responsible Administrator: An Approach to Ethics for the Administrative Role**, 4th Edition, San Francisco: Jossey-Bass, 1998.
> Cooper first presents a model for addressing ethical questions and then tackles ethics at a very practical level for the individual and the organization. At the individual level, he addresses such questions as: what are the public administrator's obligations and who is she/he accountable to? He also addresses common conflicts administrators face, such as conflicts of power, conflicts among various roles they play, and conflicts of interest. At the organizational level, Cooper focuses on how managers can create ethical cultures, covering such topics as the role of ethics laws and rules, codes of conduct and how to safeguard ethical autonomy.

Herbert, Wray, **On Second Thought: Outsmarting Your Mind's Hard-Wired Habits**, New York, NY: Crown Publishing, 2010.
> Evolution has hard-wired certain patterns of thought and action - heuristics – into us. They form the default setting of how we will make decisions, unless we over-ride them with conscious thought. But such thought takes energy – and the ability to spot our heuristic thinking. Wray covers twenty different mental heuristics, how they may have emerged in our evolutionary history, how they appear in everyday life, and the potential and pitfalls of defaulting to them.

Kahneman, Daniel, **Thinking Fast and Slow**, New York, NY: Farrar, Straus and Giroux, 2011.
> A Nobel economist, Kahneman focuses on the psychology of decision making. He suggests that we all have a typical, quick way of addressing many of the decisions we face (thinking fast) that often works well but that can get us into trouble when its application of common mental heuristics do not fit the situation. In such cases, we need to think slow – use our full

brain capacity to reason through to the right decision. Kahneman offers a series of such situations, how to spot them, and what to do to prevent decision making errors.

Kidder, Rushworth, **How Good People Make Tough Choices: Resolving the Dilemmas of Ethical Living,** New York: Fireside, 1995.

Kidder maintains that the tough choices in life are not moral temptations (choices between right and wrong) but ethical dilemmas (choices between right and right, between courses of action all legal but not necessarily all morally equivalent). He presents a framework for thinking through ethical dilemmas that includes clarifying the value conflicts involved, generating options, and applying ethical principles to determine the best course of action.

Lewis, Carol and Gilman, Stuart, **The Ethics Challenge in Public Service: A Problem-Solving Guide.** San Francisco: Jossey-Bass, 2012.

Lewis and Gilman take a comprehensive look at ethics and public service. This book is a very practical, down-to-earth approach to ethics for those in public service, written to focus on practice not theory.

Richter, William L. and Burke, Francis, Editors, **Combating Corruption, Encouraging Ethics: A Practical Guide to Management Ethics,** Lanham, MD: Rowman and Littlefield Publishers, 2007.

The editors have combined an excellent set of short readings/excerpts and case studies to cover a wide range of topics, such as ethical foundations, responsibility and accountability, fraud, waste and corrupt practices, lying, abuse of authority, and strategies to build trust and create an ethical culture in government organizations. The chapters can be read in any order, and many of the excerpts (and the thought-provoking questions the editors provide with them) are excellent for discussion in the work setting.

Rock, David, **Your Brain at Work: Strategies for Overcoming Distraction, Regaining Focus, and Working Smarter All Day Long,** New York, NY: Harper Business, 2009.

Rock is one of the leaders in the new field of neuroscience and leadership. In this volume, he explores how the brain functions and the impact of its physical limits on our ability to make decisions. He pays special attention to strategies for addressing these limits. While the book's focus is on decision making, its conclusions and strategies have implications for ethical decision making as well.

Werhane, Patricia, **Moral Imagination and Management Decision Making,** New York: Oxford University Press, 1999.

Why do good managers make bad, unethical decisions? Werhane suggests that it is often because they are locked into a particular conception of their role, a particular narrative of how the world works, a particular mental model that makes it almost impossible for them to see things from any other vantage point. She argues that moral imagination, the ability to see a situation from different perspectives and to create and consider alternatives for appropriate action is essential to managerial decision making which is both effective and moral.

Recognize and Modify the Organization's Culture

Adams, Guy B. and Balfour, Danny L, **Unmasking Administrative Evil**, New York, NY: M.E. Sharpe, 2004.

> The authors examine how it is that ordinary people in organizations can engage in unethical and evil acts. Examples discussed include, among others, the German bureaucracy during the Holocaust, the use of German scientists in the American space program, and the twin space shuttle disasters of *Challenger* and *Columbia*. Concluding chapters explore ways to confront and end such practices in the public service.

Denhardt, Kathryn, **The Ethics of Public Service: Resolving Moral Dilemmas in Public Organizations**, New York: Greenwood Press, 1988.

> Denhardt addresses four core purposes: the need for ethical deliberation in administrative decisions, procedural and normative guidance in making these decisions, how to foster ethical organizations, and how to hold public officials and their organizations accountable. She argues that ethical action requires ethical content, an ethical process, and moral courage. She demonstrates the many ways organizations can make ethical action difficult and how leaders can do a more effective job of creating ethical environments.

Zimbardo, Philip, **The Lucifer Effect: Understanding How Good People Turn Evil**, New York: Random House, 2007.

> Zimbardo was the lead researcher in the Stanford Prison Experiment which randomly assigned healthy, psychologically stable college men to be prisoners and guards and discovered how each internalized their roles with disturbing results. Zimbardo recounts the experiments and learnings from that effort and then uses them as a jumping off point to examine the abuses in the real-life prison at Abu Ghraib. His broad conclusion: "bad apples" usually result from a "bad barrel" - that we have to look at the situation and the system in which people are placed to understand how they can do evil things.

Voice Your Decision

Ariely, Dan, **The (Honest) Truth About Dishonesty: How We Lie to Everyone – Especially Ourselves**, New York, NY: Harper, 2012.

> If we were purely rational, we would lie whenever the potential gain is greater than the chance of being caught and attendant punishment. Ariely, drawing on a variety of experiments, finds instead that we usually lie only to the extent that we can convince ourselves that we are still a good person. Having demonstrated that psychology plays a key part in whether and how much we lie, he then goes on to show what other factors may encourage or discourage lying (cheating). For example, we cheat more when we see others do so and when we have a conflict of interest. Our lying diminishes if we sign a pledge that we will be truthful and if we read the Ten Commandments (even for atheists).

Badarraco, Jr., Joseph, Jr., **Leading Quietly,** Boston: Harvard Business School Press, 2002.

> While the heroic, larger than life, leader is sometimes needed in society, Badarraco argues that most situations demand and are best addressed through the quiet leader, a person who does the right thing without fanfare but effectively. He maintains that there are eight tactics quiet leaders use as well as three traits – restraint, modesty, and tenacity – that characterize their actions.

Bok, Sissela, **Lying: Moral Choice in Public and Private Life,** New York: Vintage Books, 1978.

> When can a lie be justified? What is the impact of lying on the liar as well as those duped by the lie, including the broader society? Bok addresses these questions in detail and crafts a powerful argument that lying is rarely justified, even in public life. She maintains that when public officials lie to citizens, they attack the foundation of democracy: informed consent of the governed.

Gentile, Mary C., **Giving Voice to Values: How to Speak Your Mind When You Know What's Right**, New Haven, CT: Yale University Press, 2010

> We could be more ethical if we felt more comfortable and had more skill in speaking and acting on what we know we should do. Lacking such confidence, ethical decisions lie dormant, even though we don't want that. Gentile offers ways for us to get better in acting on our ethical values, through such approaches as realizing under what conditions we *have* acted on them before, using our personal strengths (when we are best at

speaking and taking action), scripting how we will address reasons and rationalizations of others for why we should not act, and rehearsing – out loud – what we will say.

Kidder, Rushworth, **Moral Courage**, New York: William Morrow, 2005.

Thinking through ethical dilemmas is necessary but not sufficient to being an ethical person. We also need moral courage. Moral courage is not the same as physical courage, because many situations do not require bravery in battle or in the face of mortal danger. In fact, according to Kidder, moral courage is required far more often, and it consists of deciding on the core principles and values that matter, understanding the dangers (to reputation, livelihood, etc) that may attend acting morally, and having the endurance to act and persist despite obstacles.

O'Leary, Rosemary, **The Ethics of Dissent: Managing Guerrilla Government**, Washington, DC: CQ Press, 2006.

O'Leary explores territory that is more common than often admitted: government employees who "work, sometimes quietly, sometimes not – against the wishes of their superiors." She labels them "guerrillas," and her book explores why they exist, how they work, and how organizations can – if they wish – decrease the tendency for this kind of behavior. O'Leary sees both the ethical high road of the employee who acts out of a principled concern for the public interest and the ethical low road of the government guerrilla motivated more by a personal agenda masquerading as high moral principle. Much of her book consists of detailed case studies, from which she draws conclusions about guerrilla tactics and methods to allow dissent and disagreement in organizations to prevent the need for guerrillas.

Sunstein, Cass, **Why Societies Need Dissent**, Cambridge: Harvard University Press, 2003.

The pressure to conform is powerful and injurious in many situations in public and private life. Sunstein surveys the psychological research that explains the power of strong individuals and group culture and the practical evidence in real-life situations that show how conformity sways decision making. While ethics is not a core purpose of this book, his explanation of conformity and steps one can take to lessen its negative impact on thinking and action offer a powerful reminder that the best leaders and organizations find ways to encourage and use dissent to improve their decision making.

Establish Justice

Denhardt, Janet and Denhardt, Robert, **The New Public Service: Serving, not Steering**, New York: M.E. Sharpe, 2003.

> The authors trace the evolution of public service across three time periods. "The Old Public Administration" represents that time when the role of the civil servant was the neutral, scientific implementation of policy dictated by elected and appointed officials. The citizen was the passive recipient. "The New Public Management" emerged when it became clear that administration inevitably involved some policy making, and the role of the civil servant became reliance on market mechanisms to allow the citizen to be a customer. "The New Public Service" sees the role of the civil servant as fostering democracy through active engagement of citizens in both the creation and implementation of policy. While not a book on "ethics" per se, *The New Public Service* demands an ethical orientation of the public administrator that focuses on thinking about what it means to create the good society and civic virtue.

Rohr. John, **To Run a Constitution: The Legitimacy of the Administrative State**, Lawrence, KS: The University Press of Kansas, 1986.

> This is a classic text on how the field of public administration developed and why career public officials occupy an important and Constitutionally legitimate role in public policy formulation and execution. Rohr argues that the framers thought extensively about administration and that career public officials provide the long-term, deliberative, and broad representativeness of society that the founders felt was essential to the success of the Constitution. He shows how the role of public administrator evolved and how public officials must act to serve the public interest.

Sandel, Michael J., **Justice: What's the Right Thing to Do?**, New York, NY: Farrar, Straus and Giroux, 2009.

> Based on Sandel's wildly popular Harvard University course, "Justice," this book is a very readable and thought-provoking exploration of different historical and philosophical interpretations of what constitutes justice, as well as their strengths and weaknesses. Sandel uses contemporary ethical problems to illustrate how each approach to justice would address them.

REFERENCES

Adams, Guy B. and Balfour, Danny L. 2004. *Unmasking Administrative Evil*. Armonk, NY: M.E. Sharpe.

Appiah, Kwame Anthony. 2010. *The Honor Code: How Moral Revolutions Happen*. New York, NY: W.W. Norton & Company.

Ariely, Dan. 2012. *The (Honest) Truth About Dishonesty: How We Lie to Everyone - Especially Ourselves*. New York, NY: Harper.

Aurelius, Marcus. 1964. *Meditations*. London, UK: Penguin Books.

Badaracco, Jr., Joseph. 2002. *Leading Quietly: An Unorthodox Guide to Doing the Right Thing*. Cambridge, MA: Harvard Business School Press.

Bazerman, Max. 2014. *The Power of Noticing: What the Best Leaders See*. New York, NY: Simon and Schuster.

Biech, Elaine, Editor. 2011. *2011 Pfeiffer Annual, Consulting*. San Francisco, CA: Wiley.

Bok, Sissela. 1979. *Lying: Moral Choice in Public and Private Life*. New York, NY: Vantage Books.

Bowman, James. 2006. *Honor: A History*. New York, NY: Encounter Books.

Brockman, John, Editor. 2013. *Thinking: The New Science of Decision-Making, Problem-Solving, and Prediction*. New York, NY: Harper-Collins.

Carter, Jimmy. 1975. *Why Not the Best?* Nashville, TN: Broadman Press.

Chabris, Christopher and Simons, Daniel. 2010. *The Invisible Gorilla and Other Ways Our Intuitions Deceive Us.* New York, NY: Crown.

Cicero. 1913. *De Officiis.* English Translation by Walter Miller. New York, NY: Macmillan.

Cooper, Terry L. 1998. *The Responsible Administrator: An Approach to Ethics for the Administrative Role,* 4th Edition. San Francisco, CA: Jossey-Bass.

Cooper, Terry L. and Wright, N. Dale. 1992. *Exemplary Public Administrators: Character and Leadership in Government.* San Francisco: Jossey-Bass

Ethics Resource Center. 2007. *National Government Ethics Survey: An Inside View of Public Sector Ethics.* Washington, DC: Ethics Resource Center.

Franklin, Benjamin. 2007. *The Autobiography of Benjamin Franklin.* Washington, DC: Regnery History.

Frederickson, H. George. 1997. *The Spirit of Public Administration.* San Francisco, Jossey-Bass.

French, J. and Raven, B. 1959. *The Bases of Social Power. In Studies in Social Power,* D. Cartwright, Ed. Ann Arbor, MI: Institute for Social Research.

Gawthrop, Louis C. 1998. *Public Service and Democracy: Ethical Imperatives for the 21st Century.* New York, NY: Chatham House.

Gentile, Mary C. 2012. *Giving Voice to Values: How to Speak Your Mind When You Know What's Right.* New Haven, CT: Yale University Press.

Goodwin, Doris Kearns. 2005. *Team of Rivals: The Political Genius of Abraham Lincoln.* New York, NY: Simon & Schuster.

Greene, Joshua. 2013. *Moral Tribes: Emotion, Reason, and the Gap Between Us and Them.* New York, NY: Penguin Press.

Groopman, Jerome. 2007. *How Doctors Think.* New York, NY: Houghton Mifflin.

Hallihan, Joseph. 2009. *Why We Make Mistakes.* New York, NY: Broadway Books.

Hirschman, Albert O. 1970. *Exit, Voice, and Loyalty: Responses to Decline in Firms, Organizations, and States.* Cambridge, MA: Harvard University Press.

Janis, Irving l. 1982. *Groupthink*. Independence, KY: Cengage Learning.

Janis, Irving L. 1989. *Crucial Decisions: Leadership in Policy Making and Crisis Management*. New York, NY: The Free Press.

Kahneman, Daniel. 2011. *Thinking, Fast and Slow*. New York, NY: Farrar, Straus, and Giroux.

Kidder, Rushworth. 1995. *How Good People Make Tough Choices: Resolving the Dilemmas of Ethical Living*, New York, NY: Fireside.

Kidder, Rushworth. 2006. *Moral Courage: Taking Action When Your Values are Put to the Test*. New York, NY: William Morrow Paperbacks.

Lehrer, Jonah. 2009. *How We Decide*. New York, NY: Houghton-Mifflin.

Lewis, Carol W. 1991. *The Ethics Challenge in Public Service: A Problem-Solving Guide*. San Francisco, CA: Jossey-Bass Publishers.

Machiavelli, Niccolo. 1984 Edition, Daniel Donno, Translator. *The Prince*. New York, NY: Bantam Classics.

Mackenzie, G. Calvin. 2002. *Scandal Proof: Do Ethics Laws Make Government Ethical?*, Washington, DC: The Brookings Institution.

Maier, Mark. 1995. "Red Flags," "Smart People," Flawed Decisions:" Morton Thiokol and the NASA Space Shuttle Challenger Disaster." Orange, CA: Chapman University.

McConnell, Malcolm. 1987. *Challenger: A Major Malfunction*. New York, NY: Doubleday.

Mosher, Frederick C. 1968. *Democracy and Public Service*. New York, NY: Oxford University Press.

Newell, Terry, Reeher, Grant, and Ronayne, Peter. 2011. *The Trusted Leader: Building the Relationships That Make Government Work, Second Edition*, Washington, DC: CQ Press.

Newell, Terry. 2013. *Statesmanship, Character, and Leadership in America*. New York, NY: Palgrave Macmillan.

O'Leary, Rosemary. 2006. *The Ethics of Dissent: Managing Guerrilla Government*. Washington, DC: CQ Press.

Petraeus, David H., Amos, James F., and Nagl, John A. 2007. *The U.S. Army – Marine Corps Counterinsurgency Field Manual*. Chicago, IL: The University of Chicago Press.

Phillips, Donald T. and Admiral James M. Loy. 2003. *Character in Action: The U.S. Coast Guard on Leadership,* Annapolis, MD: The Naval Institute Press.

Phillips, Donald T. and Admiral James M. Loy. 2008. *The Architecture of Leadership.* Annapolis, MD: The Naval Institute Press.

Plous, Scott. 1993. *The Psychology of Judgment and Decision Making.* New York, NY: McGraw-Hill.

Pops, Gerald M. 2009. *Ethical Leadership in Turbulent Times: Modeling the Public Career of George C. Marshall.* Plymouth, UK: Lexington Books.

Powell, Colin and Koltz, Tony. 2012. *It Worked for Me: In Life and Leadership.* New York, NY: Harper-Collins.

Rawls, John. 2001. *Justice as Fairness: A Restatement.* Cambridge, MA: Belknap Press.

Report of the Columbia Accident Investigation Board, Volume I, August 26, 2003. http://www.nasa.gov/columbia/home/CAIB_Vol1.html

Report of the President's Commission on the Space Shuttle Challenger Accident, June 6, 1986. http://history.nasa.gov/rogersrep/genindex.htm

Rock, David. 2009. *Your Brain at Work: Strategies for Overcoming Distraction, Regaining Focus, and Working Smarter All Day Long.* New York, NY: Harper Collins.

Rohr, John. 1989. *Ethics for Bureaucrats: An Essay on Law and Values*, Second Edition. New York, NY: Marcel Dekker.

Senge, Peter, Ross, Richard, Smith, Bryan, Roberts, Charlotte, and Kleiner, Art. 1994. *The Fifth Discipline Fieldbook: Strategies and Tools for Building a Learning Organization.* New York: Doubleday.

Svara, James H. 2014. *The Ethics Primer for Public Administrators in Government and Nonprofit Organizations.* Burlington, MA: Jones and Bartlett Learning.

Tuchman, Barbara W. 1984. *The March of Folly: From Troy to Vietnam.* New York, NY: Random House.

Vaughan, Diane. 1996. *The Challenger Launch Decision : Risky Technology, Culture, and Deviance at NASA.* Chicago: University of Chicago Press.

Werhane, Patricia H. 1999. *Moral Imagination and Management Decision Making*. New York, NY: Oxford University Press.

Wilson, James W. 1993. *The Moral Sense*. New York, NY: The Free Press.

Winik, Jay. 2006. *April 1865: The Month That Saved America*. New York, NY: Harper Perennial.

Wray, Herbert. 2010. *On Second Thought: Outsmarting Your Mind's Hard-Wired Habits*, New York, NY: Crown Publishing.

ENDNOTES

Introduction

[1] "Safety Lapses Raised Risks in Trailers for Katrina Victims," Spencer Hsu, *Washington Post*, May 25, 2008; "FEMA Knew of Chemical in Trailers," Spencer Hsu, *Washington Post*, July 20, 2007; "Class-Action Suit Against FEMA Trailer Manufacturers Settled for $42.6 Million," Mike Bruner, NBC News, September 28, 2012,
http://investigations.nbcnews.com/_news/2012/09/28/14140222-class-action-suit-against-fema-trailer-manufacturers-settled-for-426-million?lite

[2] Inaugural Address, January 20, 1981, http://www.presidency.ucsb.edu/ws/?pid=43130

[3] Federal Employee Viewpoint Survey, 2014,
http://www.fedview.opm.gov/2014/Reports/ResponseWPCT.asp?AGY=ALL&SECT=5

[4] National Government Ethics, Survey, 2007, p. 12,
http://www.ethics.org/files/u5/The_National_Government_Ethics_Survey.pdf

[5] "Managing Public Employees in the Public Interest," January 2013, www.mspb.gov/studies.

[6] CNN/ORC Poll. August 8, 2014, http://politicalticker.blogs.cnn.com/2014/08/08/cnn-poll-trust-in-government-at-all-time-low-2/ and the National Election Studies,
http://www.electionstudies.org/nesguide/2ndtable/t5a_1_2.htm

[7] "Americans Think Officials Knew About IRS Political Targeting: Nearly Half Consider Administration Ethics Subpar," Gallup Poll, June 1-4, 2013,
http://www.gallup.com/poll/162962/americans-think-officials-knew-irs-poltical-targeting.aspx

8 http://news.yahoo.com/blogs/ticket/irs-official-lois-lerner-not-done-anything-wrong-153037583.html

9 http://articles.washingtonpost.com/2009-02-06/news/36817325_1_tax-audits-irs-job-tax-returns

10 Warren Buffet From Omaha World Herald, February 1, 1994) http://www.character-education.info/Articles/Motivational-Character-Quotes.htm

11 Alexander Hamilton's Letter of Instructions to the Commanding Officers of the Revenue Cutters, June 4, 1791, http://www.uscg.mil/history/faqs/hamiltonletter.pdf

12 "One by One," by Adm. James M. Loy and Donald T. Phillips, Viewpoint, *Government Executive*, January 21, 2007, p. 63. See also: Phillips and Loy (2003) and (2008).

13 The cases in this book are almost always based on actual events that government workers have faced. Where those situations are public knowledge, the names of people and agencies are used. In other cases, the names and agencies, and sometimes other potentially identifying details, have been changed to respect the confidentiality promised to those from whom the cases have come.

14 James S. Bowman and Claire Connolly Knox, Ethics in Government" No Matter How Long and Dark the Night: Diverse Ethical Challenges Facing Public administrators," *Public Administration Review*, July/August 2008, pp.627-639.

Chapter 1

15 "Inspector General: GSA official's waste part of pattern," *Federal Times*, April 17, 2012; "GSA official's wife accompanied him on trips at taxpayer expense," *The Washington Post*, April 17, 2012; "Acting GSA chief calls Las Vegas spree 'completely unacceptable,'" *The Washington Post*, http://www.washingtonpost.com/politics/acting-gsa-chief-calls-las-vegas-spree-completely-unacceptable/2012/04/10/gIQAp2998S_story.html . Jeff Neely was indicted in 2014 for making fraudulent claims and false statements.

16 "Exposing the Truth of Abu Ghraib: Anderson Cooper Interviews Whistleblower Joe Darby," June 24, 2007, CBS 60 Minutes, http://www.cbsnews.com/8301-18560_162-2238188.html

17 *www.oge.gov/Laws-and.../Compilation-of-Federal-Ethics-Laws/*

18 http://dictionary.reference.com/browse/oath?s=t

19 http://en.wikiquote.org/wiki/Adolf_Eichmann

[20] http://en.wikipedia.org/wiki/Guatemala_syphilis_experiment

[21] Wilson, Woodrow, "The Study of Administration," *Political Science Quarterly*, Vol. 2, No. 2, June 1887, pp. 197-222.

[22] Rohr, John, *Ethics for Bureaucrats* (1989), p.7

[23] Gawthrop, Louis C., *Public Service and Democracy* (1998), p. 19.

[24] Quoted in Mackenzie, G. Calvin (2002) p. 174

[25]

http://www.aspanet.org/public/ASPA/Resources/Code_of_Ethics/ASPA/Resources/Code%20of%20Ethics1.aspx?hkey=acd40318-a945-4ffc-ba7b-18e037b1a858

[26] Taylor, John Wilson, "The Athenian Ephebic Oath," *The Classical Journal*, Volume 13, No. 7, April 1918, pp. 495-501. The oath contained some elements clearly not pertinent or appropriate in our time, such as a pledge to honor the Greek gods. Also, it is important to note, the oath could be taken only by men (not slaves or women) as only they were eligible for citizenship.

Chapter 2

[27] *The Washington Post*, August 3, 2002.

[28] Cliff decided to raise the dish, after taking a vote among his staff. The vote, however, was public and one staff member with very clear concerns was not able to express them. Further, Cliff probably could have handled the problem by telling NASA of the danger and asking it to delay the moon walk. By including them in the decision, he would have appropriately shared the responsibility for doing the right thing. In the end, Cliff got lucky; the dish did not collapse.

[29] Kidder, Rushworth (1995)

[30] See, for example, Cooper, Terry (1998), pp. 57-58.

Chapter 3

[31] This account is taken from "The Memo: How an internal effort to ban the abuse and torture of detainees was thwarted," by Jane Mayer, *The New Yorker*, February 27, 2006. By the end of the day, Haynes notified Mora that Secretary of Defense Donald Rumsfeld had suspended authorization for the use of the abusive techniques. Rumsfeld then established a working group

to review the policy. Mora was appointed to the group but would later learn that its report, which he was not allowed to see, supported continued use of the techniques. Mora left his position in January 2006 and would receive a Profile in Courage Award from the John F. Kennedy Presidential Library that same year.

[32] Badaracco (2002)

[33] One aspect of working through ethical dilemmas is to find how contrasting values can be reconciled with a creative solution.

[34] Kidder (1995)

[35] Nutt, Paul, "The Identification of Solution Ideas During Organizational Decision Making," *Management Science*, Volume 39, Issue 9, pp. 1071-1085, September 1993

[36] Werhane (1999), p. 13.

[37] Svara, James H., "The Ethical Triangle: Synthesizing the Bases of Administrative Ethics," Public Integrity Annual 1997, Lexington, KY: Council of State Governments and American Society of Public Administration, 1997, pp. 33-41. *Public Integrity* Annual 2, 1997. See also: Svara (2014).

[38] The three points of the ethical triangle correspond closely to three classical approaches to ethical thinking: virtues (Aristotle's virtue ethics), principles (Kant's categorical imperative), and consequences (Bentham's greatest good for the greatest number).

Chapter 4

[39] Isen, Alice M and Simmonds, Stanley F., "The Effect of Feeling Good on a Helping Task That is Incompatible with Good Mood," *Social Psychology*, Vol. 41, No. 4, pp. 346-349, 1978.

[40] Benjamin Franklin to Joseph Priestly, September 19, 1772, http://www.smartdraw.com/articles/blog/lettertopriestley.pdf (January 26, 2015)

[41] Greene, Joshua, Sommerville, Brian, Nystrom, Leigh, Darley, John and Cohen, Jonathan, "An fMRI Investigation of Emotional Engagement in Moral Judgment," *Science*, Vol. 293, 2001, pp. 2105-2108. See also Greene (2013).

[42] Greene suggests this example. Other research shows that, when people have damage to their ventromedial prefrontal cortex (the part of the brain that has to integrate emotion with reason),

they become pure utilitarians. They can and do sacrifice others in personal, moral situations because that's the "logical" thing to do. See: "Morality is a Slave to Emotion," March 23, 2007, Agence France-Presse.

[43] The "older" part of our brain (from an evolutionary standpoint) houses the center for emotions. The "newer" prefrontal cortex developed to its current complexity much later. This helps explain the finding that emotion is the basis of our initial reaction in an ethical dilemma and also why it may take longer to apply reason to moral dilemmas: the dorsolateral prefrontal cortex has to go into what Greene calls "manual mode" to deal with the otherwise purely "automatic" (emotional) mode of the older parts of the brain.

[44] Senge, Peter, Ross, Richard, Smith, Bryan, Roberts, Charlotte, and Kleiner, Art, (1994), pp. 242-246: "The Ladder of Inference."

[45] Eisenberger, Naomi and Lieberman, Matthew, "Why rejection hurts: a common neural alarm system for physical and social pain," *Trends in Cognitive Science*, Vol. 8, No.7, July 2004, pp. 294-300.

[46] "Peer Pressure? It's Hardwired Into Our Brains, Study Finds," *Science Daily*, http://www.sciencedaily.com/releases/2011/09/110906164312.htm (January26, 2015)

[47] Rock, David (2009). Glucose is used by the body to produce energy.

[48] It's not only thinking harder that takes energy but the demands on our bodies by stressful situations. Facing a mentally and emotionally demanding task – and ethical dilemmas qualify – can leave us drained. See also: Jabr, Ferris, "Does Thinking Really Hard Burn More Calories?," *Scientific American,* July 28, 2012. http://www.scientificamerican.com/article.cfm?id=thinking-hard-calories&print=true (January 26, 2015)

[49] Danzigera,Shai, Levab, Jonathan , and Avnaim-Pessoa, Liora, "Extraneous factors in judicial decisions," *Proceedings of the National Academy of Sciences*, Vol, 108. No. 17, April 2011, pp. 6889-6892.

[50] Ibid., p. 35

[51] Kahneman (2011)

[52] A Review of the FBI's Handling of the Brandon Mayfield Case, (Unclassified and Redacted) , Special Report, March 2006 , Office of the Inspector General, http://www.justice.gov/oig/special/s0601/PDF_list.htm (January26, 2015)

[53] There is a growing literature on mental biases and heuristics. See, for example, Chabris and Simons (2010), Groopman (2007), Hallihan (2009), Lehrer (2009), and Plous (1993). For a quick list of cognitive biases, see also: http://en.wikipedia.org/wiki/List_of_cognitive_biases (January 26, 2015)

[54] Bazerman (2014).

Chapter 5

[55] He also needs to put the decision into words when he meets with his boss, his peers, and potentially the director. This part, voicing the decision, is so important that we will come back to it in Chapter 8.

[56] For more on the Implications Wheel, go to: http://implicationswheel.com/ (January 26, 2015)

[57] Lewis, Carol (1991), p.179

Chapter 6

[58] See Dreifus, Claudia, "Finding Hope in Knowing the Universal Capacity for Evil," *The New York Times*, April 3, 2007 and Wilson, Jamie, "Eight years for US soldier who abused prisoners," *The Guardian*, October 22, 2004, http://www.theguardian.com/world/2004/oct/22/usa.iraq (January 26, 2015)

[59] Petraeus, David, Amos, James, and Nagl, John (2007)

[60] To see these and other data, go to www.fedview.opm.gov and search on the year in question.. For example, the 2014 results can be found at: http://www.fedview.opm.gov/2014/Reports (January 26, 2015)

[61] Ethics Resource Center (2007)

[62] The discussion of *Challenger* draws on two primary sources. These are the report of the "Presidential Commission on the Space Shuttle Challenger Accident," dated June 6, 1986 (http://history.nasa.gov/rogersrep/genindex.htm) (January 26, 2015) and "Red Flags," "Smart People," "Flawed Decisions:" Morton Thiokol and the NASA Space Shuttle *Challenger* Disaster," by Mark Maier, Chapman University, 1995.

[63] Presidential Commission report, Chapter IV, p. 72

[64] Maier (1995), p. 2

[65] Ibid, p.2

[66] Ibid., p.5

[67] Commission report, Appendix D

[68] Op cit

[69] Chapman (1995). p.8

[70] Op cit

[71] Commission Report, Chapter V, p. 104

[72] Report of the Columbia Accident Investigation (2003), Chapter 8, p. 199. See: http://www.nasa.gov/columbia/home/CAIB_Vol1.html (January 26, 2015)

[73] Vaughan (1996)

[74] Commission Report, Chapter VI, p. 161

[75] Commission Report, Chapter V, p. 101

[76] McConnell (1987), p. 109

[77] Commission Report, Chapter V, p. 104

[78] Commission Report, Chapter V, p. 94

[79] Maier (1995), p. 14

[80] Greene (2013), pp. 224-248

[81] http://en.wikipedia.org/wiki/Asch_conformity_experiments#Results (January 26, 2015)

[82] http://en.wikipedia.org/wiki/Milgram_experiment (January 26, 2015). While the Milgram experiment could not be repeated in the United States due to modern requirements for informed consent for experimental subjects, a version of it was repeated recently in France. Contestants in a TV show with a live audience were asked to shock a man in a box when he incorrectly answered questions put to him. They did not know that he was not wired to be shocked; they were told that he was. Eighty percent of the contestants kept zapping him even when he screamed in pain. This was an even higher percentage than Milgram observed, perhaps in this case because of the extra "encouragement" and social acceptance by the shouting audience ("Fake TV Game Show 'Tortures' Man, Shocks France," NPR, March 18, 2010, Eleanor Beardsley).

[83] Milgram, Stanley, "The Perils of Obedience". *Harper's Magazine*,247:1483 (1973:Dec.) p.62+

Chapter 7

[84] "Fact Sheet, VHA Integrated Ethics Program Selected for the Prestigious Harvard Award Competition," go to: http://www.ethics.va.gov/integratedethics (January 26, 2015) and click on "Top 25 Programs" under "Honors and Awards"

[85] Kraman, Steve S. and Hamm, Ginney, "Risk Management: Extreme Honesty May Be the Best Policy," *Annals of Internal Medicine*, Vol, 31, No 12, December 1999, pp. 963-967.

[86] VHA Handbook 1004.08, "Disclosure of Adverse Events to Patients," October 2, 2012, http://www.ethics.va.gov/Handbook1004-08.pdf (January 26, 2015). In 2014, the Department of Veterans Affairs was embroiled in a major ethical scandal because it was taking too long for veterans to get to see doctors and because staff were falsifying wait time data. While this did not appear to damage the quality of care once a patient actually got to see a doctor, it may well have resulted in some deaths due to delayed treatment. The falsification of wait time data will be dealt with in Chapter10, when we discuss lying in public life.

[87] National Government Ethics Survey, Ethics Resource Center, 2007, pp. 11-17, go to: http://www.ethics.org/files/u5/The_National_Government_Ethics_Survey.pdf (January 26, 2015)

[88] Supplemental Research Brief, 2009 National Business Ethics Survey, Ethics and Employee Engagement, p. 2, go to: http://www.ethics.org/files/u5/NBESResearchBrief2.pdf (January 26, 2015)

[89] The Power of Employee Engagement, U.S. Merit Systems Protection Board, September 2008, go to: http://www.mspb.gov/netsearch/viewdocs.aspx?docnumber=379024&version=379721 (January 26, 2015)

[90] The behaviors are mostly taken from the Organizational Ethical Climate Self-Assessment, an instrument developed and validated by the author. For a copy of the instrument, instructions on its use, and validation data, see: "Organizational Ethical Climate Self-Assessment," *The 2011 Pfeiffer Annual, Consulting*, San Francisco, CA.

[91] Goodwin (2005), p. 539.

[92] See Winik (2006) for a description of how Lincoln's magnanimity affected events leading up to and after the fall of the Confederacy.

[93] Cooper and Wright (1992), p. 13

94 Ibid, Chapter 12. Marie Ragghiatani's story is also told in the 1985 film, *Marie*.

95 "Survey: Employer's, Employees' Core Values Sometimes Don't Coincide," April 16, 2007, http://www.clomedia.com/articles/survey_employer_s_employees_core_values_sometimes_don_t_coincide (January 26, 2015)

96 Research by the author, using the Organizational Ethical Climate Self-Assessment (see note 90) at the Federal Executive Institute. Respondents were GS15 and Senior Executive Service leaders.

97 Newell, Terry, Reeher, Grant, and Ronayne, Peter (2011), p. 41

98 The Astronaut Code of Professional Responsibility may be seen at: http://www.jsc.nasa.gov/Bios/AstronautCodeEarthFINAL.pdf (January 26, 2015)

99 "Technical Conscience" – personal communication to the author

100 See the website of the National Constitution Center for assistance in doing this: http://www.constitutioncenter.org (January 26, 2015)

101 For Clancy's full testimony, go to: http://judiciary.house.gov/_cache/files/8f1ec6b9-0304-4776-9b74-eea42b2a600c/usss-clancy-testimony.pdf (January 26, 2015)

102 Janis (1982)

103 O'Leary (2006)

104 See: "Ethical Leadership: Fostering an Ethical Environment and Culture," p. 23, http://www.ethics.va.gov/ELprimer.pdf (January 26, 2015)

105 The survey has been published as "Organization Ethical Climate Self-Assessment," Beich, Elaine, Editor, The *2011 Pfeiffer Annual, Consulting* (2011).

106 "State Department honors three with 'constructive dissent' awards," *The Washington Post*, June 25, 2010, p. B03.

107 "Federal Appeals Board Has Major Concerns With Firing Provisions in New VA Law." August 7, 2014, by Eric Katz, http://www.govexec.com/management/2014/08/federal-appeals-board-has-major-concerns-firing-provisions-new-va-law/90887/?oref=govexec_today_nl (January 26, 2015)

108 For the Profiles in Courage Award, go to: http://www.jfklibrary.org/Events-and-Awards/Profile-in-Courage-Award.aspx (January 26, 2015). For the Giraffe Heroes Project, go to: http://www.giraffe.org/ (January 26, 2015)

Chapter 8

[109] Tuchman (1984), p. 85.

[110] Ludwig, Dean and Longenecker, Clinton, "The Bathsheba Syndrome: The Ethical Failure of Successful Leaders," *Journal of Business Ethics*, Vol. 12, pp. 265-273, 1993.

[111] "Tenbrunel, Ann E., Diekmann, Kristina, A., Wade-Benzoni, Kimberly A. and Bazerman, Max H., "Why We Aren't as Ethical as We Think We Are: A Temporal Explanation." Working Paper, 2007.

[112] Merritt, Anna C., Effron, Daniel A., and Monin, Benoit, "Moral Self-Licensing: When Being Good Frees Us to Be Bad," Social and Personality Psychology Compass, Volume 4, Issue 5, pages 344–357, May 2010

[113] Bazerman, M.H., Tenbrunel, A.A. and Wade-Benzoni, K., "Negotiating with Yourself and Losing: Making Decisions with Competing Internal Preferences," *Academy of Management Review*, 23(2), 225-241, 1998.

[114] "Leadership Counts: Deloitte & Touche USA 2007 Ethics & Workplace" survey results," while no longer available on their website, go to: http://www.clomedia.com/articles/survey_finds_strong_relationship_between_work_life_balance_ethical_behavior (January 26, 2015)

[115] Powell and Koltz (2012), p. 40.

Chapter 9

[116] See Hirschman (1970). In his initial formulation, which looked at ways to stop decline in businesses, organizations and states, Hirschman sees loyalty, coupled with voice, as a viable strategy. Silent loyalty, however, is not effective. In the formulation in this book, loyalty is assumed to be acquiescence, silent or otherwise. Voice is, however, not inconsistent with loyalty in the sense that one of the best ways to be loyal to an organization and/or superior is to constructively disagree with its decisions and actions when they violate ethical norms, which in themselves could threaten the effectiveness of the organization.

[117] Gentile (2012). See also the "Giving Voice to Values" website at: http://www.babson.edu/academics/teaching-research/gvv/Pages/home.aspx (January 26, 2015)

[118] USA Today, February 25, 2003 and http://www.nytimes.com/2003/02/28/us/threats-responses-military-spending-pentagon-contradicts-general-iraq-occupation.html (January 26, 2015)

[119] Leonard Wong and Douglas Lovelace, "Knowing When to Salute," Strategic Studies Institute, Army War College, 2007.

[120] Kidder (2006)

[121] Those who demonstrate physical courage often do so because they have moral courage, such as emergency services and law enforcement personnel and members of the armed forces.

[122] Whitlow, John. "Social Power: A Brief Overview," undated.

[123] "Face of the Year: David Graham," by Matthew Herper, *Forbes*, December 13, 2004. The account of David Graham has been taken from this article and the Government Accountability Project: http://www.whistleblower.org/vioxx-david-graham (January 26, 2015)

[124] Lewis (1991), p. 132.

[125] Wong, Leonard and Lovelace, Douglas, *Knowing When to Salute*, Strategic Studies Institute, U.S. Army War College, 2007.

Chapter 10

[126] "Intelligence director Clapper apologizes for erroneous statement to Congress," The Hill: July 2, 2013, http://thehill.com/policy/defense/308979-clapper-apologies-for-erroneous-statement-to-congress-on-us-data-collection (January 26, 2015). See also: http://www.usnews.com/news/articles/2013/07/02/national-intelligence-director-apologizes-for-lying-to-congress (January 26, 2015)

[127] Machiavelli (1984), *The Prince*, Chapters XV and XVIII.

[128] Bok (1979), p. 28.

[129] "Abu Ghraib? Doesn't Ring a Bell," by Dana Milbank, *The Washington Post*, June 18, 2008, p. A3.

[130] Bok (1979), p. 182.

[131] Ariely (2012).

[132] Franklin (2007), Chapter Four.

[133] Gino, Francesa, Moore, Don, and Bazerman, Max, "See No Evil: When We Overlook Other People's Unethical Behavior," Working Paper, 2008.

[134] See: http://en.wikipedia.org/wiki/Frazier_v._Cupp (January 27, 2015)

Chapter 11

[135] "Fund director lauds American impulse after tragedy," by Susan Page, *USA Today*, June 1, 2013/. See: http://www.usatoday.com/story/news/nation/2013/05/31/kenneth-feinberg-victims-compensation-boston-marathan-bombing-newtown-shooting/2375201/ (January 27, 2015)

[136] Federalist #10, http://thomas.loc.gov/home/histdox/fed_10.html (January 27, 2015)

[137] Frederickson (1997), p.5

[138] Carter (1978), p. 116.

[139] "Tuskegee Syphilis Experiment," http://en.wikipedia.org/wiki/Tuskegee_syphilis_experiment#Study_details (January 27, 2015)

[140] Adams and Balfour (2004)

[141] Universal Declaration of Human Rights, http://www.un.org/en/documents/udhr/ (January 27, 2015)

[142] "Irrational markets: people reject free money out of anger," by John Timmer, June 29, 2009, http://arstechnica.com/science/2009/06/irrational-markets-people-reject-free-money-out-of-anger/ (January 27, 2015)

[143] "The neural basis of economic decision-making in the ultimatum game," Alan Sanfey et al., *Science* ,.Vol. 300, No.5626, pages 1775-1778, June 13, 2003.

[144] Wilson (1993)

[145] Brockman (2013), p. 349.

[146] "How Fairness is Wired in the Brain," by Elisabeth Nadin, *Science Daily*, May 8, 2008, http://www.sciencedaily.com/releases/2008/05/080528140226.htm (January 27, 2015)

[147] "Justice Department outlines criteria for clemency," *The Washington Post*, April 24, 2014, p. A2

Chapter 12

[148] For the full text of Ford's inaugural remarks, go to: http://www.presidency.ucsb.edu/ws/index.php?pid=4409 (January 27, 2015)

[149] For a full treatment of the speech, see: Newell (2013), Chapter 7.

[150] Different conceptions of justice are also associated with long philosophical traditions and writings. "Virtue," for example, has been explored since Aristotle. "Utility" was developed by Jeremy Bentham and John Stuart Mill. "Right principle" was crafted in detail in the work of Immanuel Kant, while justice as "fairness" has been most recently elaborated by John Rawls. "Liberty" is also the work of Mill and such writers as William Graham Sumner. "Procedural" and "restorative" justice and justice as "retribution" go back as far as the Old and New Testaments (in the Western tradition).

[151] Philosopher John Rawls refers to this hypothetical situation as being behind a "veil of ignorance." See Rawls (2001).

[152] http://www.enn.com/ecosystems/article/42699/print (January 27, 2015)

[153] http://www.bbc.com/news/world-us-canada-28203923 (January 27, 2015)

[154] http://www.forbes.com/sites/gregorymcneal/2014/07/12/faa-approves-limited-use-of-drones-for-san-diego-utility-company/ (January 27, 2015)

[155] http://www.federaltimes.com/article/20140804/MGMT/308040014/DoD-hashing-out-new-civilian-performance-appraisal-system (January 27, 2015)

[156] "A pioneer in addressing the line between pollution and public health," August 12, 2014, *The Washington Post*,

http://www.washingtonpost.com/politics/federal_government/a-pioneer-in-addressing-the-link-between-the-pollution-and-public-health/2014/08/12/968f7254-2260-11e4-86ca-6f03cbd15c1a_story.html (January 27, 2015)

[157] "Higher social class predicts increased unethical behavior," Paul Piff, Daniel Stancato, Stephanie Cole, Rodolofo Mendoza-Denter, and Dacher Keltner, Proceedings of the National Academy of Sciences, *PNAS* 2012 109 (11) 4086-4091; published ahead of print February 27, 2012, http://www.pnas.org/content/109/11/4086.full.pdf+html?sid=323dae81-e67e-4209-8b64-7c4eb1773834 (January 27, 2015)

158 "Nameless + Harmless = Blameless: When Seemingly Irrelevant Factors Influence Judgment of (Un)ethical Behavior," Francesa Gino, Lisa Shu, and Max Bazerman, Working Paper, 2008.

159 "You See, the Ends Don't Justify the Means: Visual Imagery and Moral Judgment," Elinor Amit and Joshua Greene, Psychological Science, June 28, 2012, http://www.wjh.harvard.edu/~jgreene/GreeneWJH/Amit-Greene-Imagery-MJ-PsychSci12.pdf (January 27, 2015)

160 "A Different Kind of Training: What New Agents Learn from the Holocaust," March 30, 2010, http://www.fbi.gov/news/stories/2010/march/leas_033010/a-different-kind-of-training-what-new-agents-learn-from-the-holocaust (January 27, 2015)

161 "Missouri Highway Patrol takes over policing of Ferguson," August 14, 2014,by Alan Scher Zagier, http://www.aol.com/article/2014/08/14/Missouri-Highway-Patrol-takes-over-policing-Ferguson-after-St-Louis-County-police-removed-following-protests/20947044/?icid=maing-grid7%7Cmain5%7Cdl1%7Csec1_lnk2%26pLid%3D515785 (January 27, 2015)

162 "Even before Michael Brown's slaying in Ferguson, racial questions hung over police," by Wesley Lowery, Carol D. Leonnig and Mark Berman, The Washington Post, August 13, 2014, http://www.washingtonpost.com/politics/even-before-teen-michael-browns-slaying-in-mo-racial-questions-have-hung-over-police/2014/08/13/78b3c5c6-2307-11e4-86ca-6f03cbd15c1a_story.html (January 27, 2015)

163 "A Study of the Long-Term Effects of the Federal Workforce Reduction in the 1990s," Coalition of Effective Change, March 2013, http://www.federalnewsradio.com/pdfs/Cuts_in_the_1990s_and_Effects_Today_3-2013.pdf (January 27, 2015)

164 "Sense of Fairness Affects Outlook, Decisions," by Shankar Vedantum, The Washington Post, June 9, 2008, p. A8 and "Beware of the Unintended Consequences of Favoritism," Issues of Merit, June 2013, p. 5, Merit Systems Protection Board.

165 "Preserving the Integrity of the Federal Merit Systems: Understanding and Addressing Perceptions of Favoritism," U.S. Merit Systems Protection Board, December 2013, pp. 9-10. http://www.mspb.gov/netsearch/viewdocs.aspx?docnumber=945850&version=949626&application=ACROBAT (January 27, 2015)

Postscript

[166] Mosher (1968) gives an excellent treatment of these changes in the public service.

[167] See Appiah (2010).

[168] See Bowman (2006).

[169] Pops (2009), p. 127.

[170] Frederickson (1997), pp. 4-5.

[171] Ibid., p. 48.

[172] Frederickson, H. George and Hart, David K., "The Public Service and the Patriotism of Benevolence," *Public Administration Review*, September/October 1985, p. 551.

[173] Gawthrop, Louis, "Civics, Civitas, and Civilitas: A New Focus for the Tear 2000," *Public Administration Review*, March 1984, pp. 106.

[174] See "Conclusion" in Newell, Reeher, and Ronayne (2011), p. 409. The excerpt in Box 1 can be found on pages 409-411.

[175] Speech At Princeton, February 22, 1947.

[176] The account of Ed McGaffgian, Jr. is taken from: "A Public Servant to the Last," by Elizabeth Williamson, *The Washington Post*, December 6, 2006, p. A23 and "Edward McGaffigan Jr., Longest-Serving NRC Commissioner, Dies," NRC News, No. 08-112, September 2, 2007, Office of Public Affairs.

[177] "A Review of the FBI's Involvement in and Observations of Detainee Interrogations in Guantanamo Bay, Afghanistan, and Iraq," May 2008, https://www.aclu.org/files/pdfs/safefree/OIG_052008_i_7.pdf (January 28, 2015). See also:"The Torture Scandal's Heroes," Washingtonpost.com, May 25, 2008, http://www.washingtonpost.com/wp-dyn/content/article/2008/05/24/AR2008052401609 (January 28, 2015)

[178] Cicero, written in 44 B.C. (1913 translation), Book I, paragraph 83.

[179] Executive Order 12731 of October 17, 1990 sets forth 14 principles of ethical conduct for federal employees. The first of these is: Public service is a public trust, requiring employees to place loyalty to the Constitution, the laws, and ethical principles above private gain." See: http://oge.gov/Laws-and-Regulations/Executive-Orders/Executive-Order-12731-(Oct--17,-1990)---Principles-of-Ethical-Conduct-for-Government-Officers-and-Employees/(January 28, 2015)

180 This estimate comes from data supplied from two sources: the U.S. Office of Personnel Management and the Bureau of Labor Statistics. See, for example: http://www.bls.gov/news.release/cfoi.t02.htm (January 28, 2015)

181 See: http://www.npr.org/2012/11/21/165663154/moral-injury-the-psychological-wounds-of-war (January 28, 2015). The term "moral injury" was first coined by Department of Veterans Affairs physician and psychiatrist, Jonathan Shay. See also: http://en.wikipedia.org/wiki/Moral_injury (January 28, 2015)

182 Marcus Aurelius (1964), p 4.

INDEX

CPSIA information can be obtained at www.ICGtesting.com
Printed in the USA
LVOW03s2322130415

434481LV00003B/9/P